"TO SNORT COCAINE IS TO MAKE A STATEMENT. IT'S LIKE FLYING TO PARIS FOR BREAKFAST."

Zachary Swan

"ONE OF THE MOST SPECTACULAR AND DAZZLING PIECES OF REPORTING I HAVE EVER READ."

Nora Ephron, *The Village Voice*

"A CLASSIC . . . ROBERT SABBAG WILL BE TO COCAINE WHAT DR. SPOCK WAS TO CRADLE CAP. . . . THIS KID HAS GOT THE DRIVE OF SOMETHING OFF AN INTERNATIONAL HARVESTER LOT. I HEAR FOOTSTEPS BEHIND ME. GOTTA MOVE FASTER. SABBAG IS COMING."

National Review

"AFTER READING *SNOWBLIND* ONE IS OVERCOME WITH A SENSE OF HAVING FINALLY UNDERSTOOD AMERICA. . . . DESTINED TO BECOME AN AMERICAN CLASSIC."

Claude Brown
author of *MANCHILD IN THE PROMISED LAND*

"MR. SABBAG IS A FIRST-RATE WRITER. . . . HIS BOOK IS A TRIUMPHANT PIECE OF REPORTING."

The New Yorker

SNOW BLIND

A BRIEF CAREER IN THE COCAINE TRADE

ROBERT SABBAG

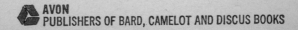

AVON
PUBLISHERS OF BARD, CAMELOT AND DISCUS BOOKS

For Thomas J. Butler
Forsan et haec olim meminisse iuvabit . . .

All of the events reported in this book took place as they are described. The names of certain characters have necessarily been changed. All prices quoted in Chapter V are Smuggler's Prime Rate, current in the spring of 1975.

Grateful acknowledgement is made to the following for portions of lyrics quoted in this book:

The Reverend Gary Davis, for "Cocaine Blues." Hampshire House Publishing Corporation, for lyrics from "Eclipse," as performed in Pink Floyd's *Dark Side of the Moon*. "Eclipse" words and music by Roger Waters. TRO—© Copyright 1973 Hampshire House Publishing Corporation, New York, New York. Reprinted by permission. Ice Nine Publishing Company, Inc., for lyrics from "Casey Jones," as performed by The Grateful Dead. "Casey Jones" © Copyright 1970 Ice Nine Publishing Company. Words by Robert Hunter. Reprinted by permission. Deposit Music, Ltd., for lyrics from the Isis song "Cocaine Elaine," by Carol MacDonald and Ginger Bianco. © Copyright Deposit Music, Ltd., affiliation ASCAP. Reprinted by permission. MCA Music, for lyrics from "Nobody Knows You When You're Down and Out." Words and music by Jimmie Cox. © Copyright 1923, 1929 by MCA Music, a division of MCA Inc., 445 Park Avenue, New York, New York 10022. Copyright renewed 1950 and assigned to MCA Music, a division of MCA Inc. © 1954 by MCA Music, a division of MCA Inc. Used by permission. All rights reserved. Ice Nine Publishing Company, Inc., for lyrics from "Truckin'," as performed by The Grateful Dead. © Copyright 1970 Ice Nine Publishing Company. Words by Robert Hunter. Recorded by The Grateful Dead. Reprinted by permission.

AVON BOOKS
A division of
The Hearst Corporation
959 Eighth Avenue
New York, New York 10019

First Avon Printing, March, 1978

AVON TRADEMARK REG. U.S. PAT. OFF. AND IN
OTHER COUNTRIES, MARCA REGISTRADA,
HECHO EN U.S.A.

Printed in the U.S.A.

Contents

APPENDICES

Breakaway

1

Indian Summer

ZACHARY SWAN is not a superstitious man, but he is a very careful one. Like any professional gambler, he has survived by taking only calculated risks. So, in October of 1972, when he decided to throw a party to celebrate his most recent return to New York, he decided to throw a small one, and his caution was inspired less by the fact that it was Friday the thirteenth than by the compelling reality that on the mantelpiece above his suitcase there were three and a half kilograms of 89-percent-pure cocaine.

The cocaine had entered the United States that morning in the hollows of three Colombian souvenirs fashioned out of Madeira wood. They included a long, colorfully painted rolling pin, the symbol of marital bliss in Colombia; one rough-hewn statue, twenty inches high, of the Blessed Virgin; and a hand-wrought effigy of an obscure tribal head, about the size of a coconut. The fill had been made a week earlier in Bogotá. The load had passed U.S. Customs at Kennedy Airport, New York. It was carried through and declared: "Souvenirs."

The arrival of these artifacts at Zachary Swan's beach house in East Hampton, Long Island, launched a celebration which would not end until the following morning. It began at eight P.M. when the Madeira head was cleaved top dead center across the parietal lobe with the cold end of a chisel. Within minutes of this exotic lobotomy—a procedure reminiscent in equal measure of desperation combat surgery and a second-

3

rate burglary attempt—the skull yielded up 500 grams of high-grade uncut cocaine, double-wrapped in clear plastic.

By the time the skull, which looked like that of a shrapnel victim, was reduced to ashes around the andirons of the fireplace, the celebration had assumed ceremony and the coke was performing fabulous and outlawed miracles in the heads for which it had been ultimately intended. They belonged to Swan himself; his girl friend Alice Haskell, twenty-four, a children's fashion designer; Charles Kendricks, thirty, an Australian national and sometime employee of Swan; and Kendricks's girl friend Lillian Giles, twenty-three, also an Australian. The Bolivian brain food they had ingested was only one course in a sublime international feast which featured French wine, English gin, Lebanese hashish, Colombian cannabis, and a popular American synthetic known pharmacologically as methaqualone.

It is difficult to verify at exactly what point in the proceedings (possibly over dessert) Swan's originally calculated risk became a long shot. The party went out of control somewhere in the early hours before dawn, and the steps he had taken in the beginning to minimize his losses were eventually undermined by the immutable laws of chemistry—his mind, simply, had turned to soup. He was up against the law of averages with a head full of coke. The smart money pulled out, and the odds mounted steadily. By sunrise, Swan was beaten by the spread.

Amagansett, New York, is situated 120 miles due east of Manhattan on the coastal underbelly of Long Island. One of several oceanfront resorts on the fringes of Long Island's potato belt, it owes its maritime climate to the temperate waters in the leeward drift of the Gulf Stream. The region was abandoned by Algonquins in the wake of colonial sprawl, a mounting overture to Manifest Destiny which brought New England to the outer reaches of the Empire State, and Amagansett, a tribute to the Indians in name only, is the custodian of a Puritan heritage. The whales are gone but the weathervanes remain. An occasional widow's walk acknowledges the debt to the sea. Anchors and eagles abound. George Washington would have been proud to sleep here.

In the off-season, order prevails. Time struggles to stand still. But when the weather breaks and the trade winds come in, the elders of Amagansett, like their colonial predecessors and the Algonquins before them, find themselves volunteers in a counterassault on cultural blight—minutemen knee-deep in the onslaught of souvenirs, fast-food and ersatz antiques. A kind of thug capitalism asserts itself. The tourists who come screeching down upon the town and the local retail sharks who surface to feed on them provoke an embarrassing display of provincial paranoia; and every summer, the town fathers, helpless, unhinged, watch their community move one irreversible step closer to the dark maw of the twentieth century, visibly shaken by what they consider to be a pronounced threat to Amagansett's Puritan soul.

Their dread has taken an inevitable turn. Amagansett has become a working model for an aggression/response approach to municipal government. Symptomatic of such an approach is a curious brand of frontier law enforcement, characterized by an allegiance to the principle that ". . . we got a nice quiet community here, son . . . ," dialogue resonant of hanging judges, pistol whippings, and the application of rifle butts to the dental work. You've got until sundown, as it were. In Amagansett the Wyatt Earp spirit runs especially high between the months of May and September, but a residual strain lingers through late autumn, tapering off appropriately around Thanksgiving, after which only the locals have an opportunity to break the law.

This is what Zachary Swan, forty-six, a pioneer

whose embrace of the Puritan ethic had never been an all-encompassing one, would come up against on the morning of October 14. He and his friends would be arrested on the beach at sunrise and charged with public intoxication. And out of this circumstantial confrontation between the energetic bounty hunters of Amagansett, still juiced on adrenalin generated in the summer tourist-hunts, and a man who in six months had spent more money on cocaine alone than he had paid in state and local income taxes in twenty years— out of this head-on collision would grow a Federal investigation spanning at least two continents, twice as many international boundaries, and criminal jurisdictions as diverse as those covered by the United States Department of the Treasury and the traffic division of the East Hampton, Long Island, Police Department.

At five A.M. Zachary Swan, surrounded by $100,000 worth of cocaine, was smiling. He was smiling at the Madonna over his fireplace and dreaming of an island off the coast of Ceylon. Sprawled on the floor athwart three sleeping dogs, struggling to stay conscious, he looked like a besotted country squire out of the pages of an eighteenth-century novel.

Dawn was approaching. The room was quiet. The party had downshifted dramatically. All motor activity not essential to life had been suspended in the interest of the cardiac muscles. The body, in the grip of the downs, was making sacrifices.

Somebody had an idea (remarkable under the circumstances).

"Let's go to the beach and watch the sunrise."

A response, identifiable only in the deepest methaqualone funk, struggled to solitary life somewhere across the room. It contained many vowels. It was affirmative. Call it a sentence. A phrase. Someone had answered.

(We are on the threshold of human interchange here, speech, verbal commerce along the barren avenues of

Quaalude City. Communication at this level, although
sophisticated in its own way, can best be described as
haphazard. It is a kind of space-age remodeling of
traditional counterintelligence techniques—scrambled
messages, predistorted transmissions, sympathetically
programmed transceivers—a kind of mojo cryptog-
raphy which contains no universal cipher and is efficient only when two people are doing the same kind
of dope.)*

Out of the chance marriage between this one re-
markably conceived idea and the crypto-response
which followed, there blossomed, like a flower in time-
lapse motion, what was soon to be a legitimate conversation. It was force-bloomed according to the principle
governing the first law of psychogravitational dynamics:
The quickest way to come off downs *is to do some*
ups. Follow the Quaaludes with two or three lines
of coke and you can throw even the most desultory
dialogue into high gear. There is order in the Universe.

Monosyllables became murmurs:

"The . . . sun."

An odds-on favorite to rise.

Murmurs became phrases:

"See . . . the . . . sun."

But nothing was taken for granted.

That the sun would not rise was a remote possibility,
but one which nevertheless marshalled a certain amount
of attention. Unnecessary risks, such as standing up,
were postponed while an analysis of the odds for and
against the sun's coming up at all was made. This
delay was characteristic of severe psychochemical
shock, but surprisingly it provided the first hard evidence of progress. (It marked the appearance of key
polysyllabic words—participles, certain adjectives, an
occasional predicate nominative—and diphthongs. A
subordinate clause was pending.) The Quaaludes were
still throwing their weight around, but it was a futile

---

* See Appendix I.

display of power; their defeat was imminent, and signaled moments later:

"We haven't got much time," someone said.

A clear, audible statement. The cocaine was closing in. A decision, the final factor in the psychogravitational equation, was inevitable now. It would lead to activity and thus certify the successful application of Newton's first law to the infinite possibilities of drug abuse. In fact the decision came almost immediately, a tribute to the quality of this particular blow of coke:

"Let's go," someone decided.

And so, at the zenith of the cocaine ecliptic, activity was resumed. Status quo. What goes up must come down; what goes down must come up. Q.E.D. Physics, man. But now, with four people behind some heavy coke (one of them a certified Frank Sinatra fan), anything was possible.

Phase II . . . Overdrive. Out-and-out mobilization. Tide tables were checked. Weather information from around the world gathered. Analyzed. Data was collated and patterns were charted. An expeditionary force was provisioned.

"We'll need plenty of drugs."

Yes. Of course. Consider the possibilities. Imagine the appropriateness of it. Standing in the Atlantic tide, welcoming the sun back to the United States of America. We, the people, bent, holding enough dope to fix three Kentucky Derbies. Enough to capture the imagination of . . . yes . . . even the Miami Dolphins. How fitting. How just. (How dangerous.)

They chose the Volkswagen because it was aimed at the beach, not unanimously unaware, certainly, that they were also choosing the only car in the driveway that could float. With their ranks bolstered, and their oxygen supply severely depleted, by the added company of three hyperventilating Labrador retrievers, a total, then, of twenty legs, each jockeying for position, any two feet at the ends of which might have been operating the accelerator and the clutch (the brake, reportedly, was used rarely, if at all), Swan and his friends reached the ocean through the combined application of dead reckoning and the gratuitous hand of God. (It is whispered in the cloakrooms of America's drug underground that *He* looks out for the heavy user.)

A joint, eighty-dollar Colombian, passing clockwise around the cockpit, outlined their efforts in a surreal, purple haze, and acting as a sort of gyroscope it provided slight, but presumably adequate, stabilization. It also pushed everyone's carboxyhemoglobin level to the red line, bringing on that shameful and subversive Reefer Madness (manifest only in the Labradors, however) hinted at in arcane government manuscripts. It was quality dope, and its sharers were suffused with the magnificence and intergalactic splendor of star travelers. But at their energy/output ratio, given the specific gravity of their load and the negligible horsepower of the Volkswagen, they looked more like the Joads leaving Oklahoma.

> Hark, hark,
> The dogs do bark,
> The beggars are coming to town;
> Some in rags,
> And some in jags,
> And one in a velvet gown.
>
> "Hark, Hark,"
> from *Mother Goose*

They erupted like circus clowns out of the overstuffed automobile and onto the beach, a tumbling agglomeration of weird, multicolored ragamuffins. For a moment it was hard to tell the humans from the quadrupeds. And then the dogs hit the water. It was not long before the idea caught on, and within minutes they were all stripped down, ready to celebrate the Rites of Spring—late.

* * *

The sun was on the horizon and all seven were bobbing in the surf when in the distance an intruder appeared. A jogger. He approached, moving at an even pace along the waterline, his face flushed, his breathing steady, his body drenched with sweat and glory, radiating that all-American, infinite faith in the cardiovascular benefits of discomfort. He was about fifty-five and well-fed. Swan recognized him as the owner of a local nursery. It looked as if he were going to pass by, until he saw the strange variety of clothing, like a forbidden invitation, leading to the water. He stopped. And then he looked. When his eyes met Swan's, chivalry was dead. He did not return the smile—admittedly a bizarre one, glassy at best, but everything Swan could muster—he simply stared, squinting against the sun, saying nothing. He was still, and he remained that way, in mute confrontation.

And now Swan, forsaking the smile, staring back in mute defiance, returning the look . . . *yes, we're out here swimming . . . stoned . . . Immaculate . . . spawning on the current . . . all of us . . . breeding tiny and rebellious monsters . . . the Enemy . . . us . . . go on, . . . lock up your daughters . . . scream . . . you sad and friendless man . . . you'll dream of us tonight . . . I know you're going to turn us in, you son of a bitch.*

Without a word, the man left. He continued along the beach and out of sight.

"He's going to turn us in," Swan said.

And he was right.

Somewhere in the accumulated misspending of what was someday to become known as his youth, Zachary Swan was taken aside by a man much older than himself and confronted with what, at the time, was quaintly referred to as the cold truth about life. "Son," he was told, "there's no free lunch." He did not believe it then, and now, for the first time in forty-six years, Zachary Swan had hard evidence to show in support of his opinion.

"Mine was rare without the pickles," he said, "and give me a side of fries with that . . ."

The chow wagon moved rapidly along the cell block, and Swan was left with Suffolk County's answer to winning the hearts and minds of the people.

". . . hold the ketchup," he mumbled.

Three days in Riverhead and he was as close as he had ever come in his life to an overdose . . . *another jailbird, DOA/HAMBURGERS, poor bastard didn't even get the tourniquet off, cover him up, nurse . . .* the mayor must be from Texas, Swan thought, cow country; a Hindu would starve here . . . *Hare Krishna, pardner.*

Swan washed the dry lump down with a calculated intake of jail coffee, a 70-percent solution of refined sugar, viscous, the consistency of syrup. A diabetic would not last an hour in the slammer—one shot of this coffee in the right place and you could throw an eight-cylinder Chevy onto the scrap heap forever. Swan swallowed the slush and felt the soft embolus of the hamburger suzette skidding down his esophagus into that vast wasteland once remembered as his stomach.

On Saturday afternoon, just prior to its second ration of ground beef, that same stomach had taken the punch that was to slow it down for the next two years. It was delivered by a police officer in plain clothes. He was looking at Swan:

"We found drugs in your house," he said.

Swan's established digestive patterns changed radically and forever at that moment. It was the beginning of a progress report. One that would grow tedious. He would become indignant at what the same detective delivered in the way of an uppercut:

"The word is out that you carry a gun."

The word is out? This cop either watches a lot of television or he reads *The Daily News*. I'm an executive, for Christ's sake. I belong to the Westchester Country Club. Charlie, I own stock in some of the largest corporations in the world. My wife was on the Dick Cavett Show. What is this guy talking about? The air duct, Charlie, drop it down the fucking air duct.

While Zachary Swan was parting with his stomach, Charles Kendricks, code name the Hungarian, was parting with a sterling silver coke spoon of great sentimental value. He dropped it through the grill of the air shaft that ventilated his cell on the second floor of the Suffolk County courthouse. His nose twitched goodbye. Where had he gone wrong, he wondered.

They had been busted on the beach. Two patrol cars. That was understandable. It was a slow night and the thought of two young women swimming in the nude must have appealed to the boys on the night shift. Kendricks tried to imagine them spilling their coffee when the carburetors kicked in. They got there fast, but not before the Volkswagen was under way . . . *the Volkswagen, the latest reincarnation of the Dachau boxcar, the unimpeachable symbol of the Fatherland's relentless effort to demonstrate that the Devil himself prefers canned food*. Lillian, at the wheel, had just lost the game of musical laps that began when the four shivering getaways paused in their escape to fight over the three warm-blooded dogs, a regrettable delay under the circumstances, he thought, but then, too, it had taken them a while to get into their clothes. At the time Kendricks blamed it on the earth—spinning so fast, while at the same time . . . *if you can believe it, revolving around the bloody sun*. He remembered Swan trying to get both feet into his pants at once—cutting corners this way, he supposed . . . *but not standing up, man!* He recalled that Swan mumbled a lot . . . *yes, officer, the Kendrickses here, our friends from down under, are members of the Australian Olympic Team, swimmers, you see, and*

*they have just crawled in from Sydney . . . my wife
and I were not expecting them until tomorrow, of
course . . . but then the Gulf Stream and what not
. . . Gibraltar tomorrow, isn't it, Charles . . .* then, "Follow us . . . public intoxication . . . stick around . . ."
and now the gun . . . all that dope . . . it all came
back to Kendricks, whose nose had started running.
The spoon disappeared with a forlorn rattle.

Fingerprints and photographs. More hamburgers.
Then the handcuffs. At one A.M. the four prisoners
were reunited before a judge and arraigned. The
men and women were then driven separately to Riverhead, home of the Suffolk County Jail. They were
disinfected and wardrobed. And then they were confined. The Ides of October. Sunday mornin', comin'
down.

On the night of the party, Swan had loaned Kendricks some clothes, clearly a mistake, for when they
were discovered to be wearing matching briefs, the
processing officer ordered the guard on duty to "put
these guys on different floors." They saw each other
only once in the four days that Swan was there. On
that occasion Swan learned his first lesson in prison
discipline. Kendricks was standing four places ahead
of him in the physical examination lineup, and Swan,
who had been out of boot camp for at least thirty
years, started forward to talk to him. He was rescued
by his fellow inmates . . . *where you goin', man,
they're gonna smack you* . . . who were obliged to
demonstrate the series of casual pirouettes by which
forward and backward progress along a supervised
line is correctly achieved . . . *see, man, you're just
talkin' to me for a minute here, and we're just shufflin' our feet, right? and then just like magic you're
lookin' that way and I'm lookin' this way, and there
you are, and your friend's comin' this way, see that.*
And you've both got all your teeth. It took them about
three minutes to get together.

"How are you holding up, Charlie?"

"The coffee sucks."

"What did they tell you about phone calls?"

"I reckon they're going to let me make one after lunch. Jesus, if it's another bloody hamburger I'll shit."

"Call Seymour," Swan said.

"Where's your beard gone?" Charlie asked him.

"They made me shave it."

"The bastards."

"There's something wrong with these people, Charlie. They take a mug shot of me with a full beard. And then they shave it off. Can you figure that out? I can't figure it out."

"You're near fifty. You've brought the average age in here up to approximately twenty-two. You tell me why they have to play Frank Sinatra and Tony Bennett on the fucking Muzak."

"You call Seymour. Give him Sandy's name. I'll get us a lawyer."

Kendricks yawned. He nodded and turned around.

"Charlie, watch out for this guy, I hear he goes for fellas your age. Keep an eye on him. Don't let the stethoscope fool you; if he smiles, you're in trouble. I'll write soon."

Charlie made the call. Sandy never came through.

Swan opened his eyes. Another bad night. The man in the cell next to his had been masturbating again. Late. Their beds were each part of the same bunk, one elongated bedspring built into and passing through the concrete wall that separated them— the man had been at it again, and with every stroke Swan's bed shook. Jail, he decided, was miserable.

The library boys came around. They preceded the hamburger by about an hour.

"Bookmobile."

"What are you in for?" they wanted to know.

Swan told them. They looked at one another.

"Don't stand trial here," was all they could say.

A black prisoner who occupied the cell opposite

Swan's overheard the conversation with the library boys and felt obliged to say something to Swan. It amounted to:

"Hey, man, you didn't happen to get any of that stuff in here, did you?"

The hamburger came.

While Zachary Swan was washing his hamburger suzette down in the Riverhead Jail, a young Canadian man with blond hair and a horse-latitudes tan was stepping from a jet onto the runway at Kennedy Airport. He was traveling alone and traveling light. And he was traveling on a false passport. And in addition to his expense money, the young man was carrying $5,000 in cold American cash. Within an hour, Swan, by way of his Constitutional rights, would have a lawyer and have his bail reduced. Within two hours, by way of a noble gesture, Swan would have $1,000 in cash in his hand, and the young Canadian, who had come from nowhere, would be booking a flight south.

"Who was that?" his lawyer asked when the four prisoners were released and eating their first lunch together in five days.

"A friend of mine," Swan said.

"He must be a very good friend."

"He is. We're in the same business. We've known each other for about two years now."

"What's his name?"

"Canadian Jack."

"What's his real name?"

"Your guess is as good as mine. I've known him pretty well for about two years, and for two years I've known him only as Canadian Jack. In my business you don't ask your friends a lot of questions. And you especially don't ask them, 'What's your real name?'"

Swan's lawyer smiled.

Ernie Peace, of Peace, Lehrman & Gullo, Min-
eola, Long Island, had been recommended to Swan
by a personal friend. It was only a coincidence, according to Swan, that the friend was, by profession,
a narcotics detective. Swan had had to assume that
there was no one better qualified to rate a lawyer
than a cop, and he was right. Ernie Peace was one of
the best. A lot of narcotics detectives thought so, and
many of them had found out the hard way. Peace
sat across from Swan dressed in an unimpressive
double-knit suit, a white shirt and a blue tie. He was
a shorter man than Swan, about the same age. His
build was average, his hair was short, and all in all
he was a very unprepossessing fellow. He was one of
those people who seemed always to be thinking about
anything but what you were saying, looking here, looking there, taking it easy, preoccupied with everything
else but you—he was also one of those people who
five minutes later would quote verbatim what you had
just said. He was smiling now, a kind of smile Swan
had seen many times. Swan was pleased. It was a
gambler's smile, pleasant, shy, and not a few parts
lethal. Ernie Peace was measuring his man.

What Ernie Peace had on his hands was a middle-
aged cloak-and-dagger freak, a man who betrayed a
wealth of information on bugging devices, police technique, international drug traffic, Customs procedure,
organized crime, pseudo-tribal FBI newspeak, and every other contingency covering his work; Zachary
Swan was a man who possessed an encyclopedic knowledge of every conceivable high-level money transaction in the world. He even knew how to beat the
phone company out of a dime.

Zachary Swan was tall and trim. His posture would
have embarrassed his father. He had a strong hand-
shake, an engaging smile, and a gentle voice an octave below middle C. He had liar's eyes. They were
bright blue, cool, and very hard to ignore. He had a
small birthmark on his left cheekbone. His hair was

short—prison-length—and thick, going from brown to gray. He looked his age. It was because he did not act his age that he was here today. He was wearing about $600 worth of clothes; he was drinking a Martini and chain-smoking Kools. He handled himself well for a man under the gun.

"O.K.," Peace said, "the way it's going to work is like this. I can get the rest of you off. The DA's not really concerned about you anyway. But I want the whole truth. Everything. And then," he said to Swan, "we'll see what we can do about getting *you* out of this mess. Now, they are going to get cooperation from the Federal authorities, so I want you to tell me what the Feds know."

"I don't think they can make a smuggling charge stick. I covered myself pretty well."

"How?"

"Well," he said, "smuggling's easy." He lit a cigarette. "Anybody can do it, and a lot of people do, believe me. They do it a million ways. Some are smart, some are very stupid—for instance there are people who still get busted with false-bottom suitcases, which I want to say right now is something I never used. It is absolutely the worst way to smuggle anything. It's a sucker move. It's the first thing a Customs agent looks for—before he even takes anything out. He puts one finger inside and one finger outside, and if his fingers don't find each other you're in trouble. He's got a ruler and he measures. If the math goes against you, forget it.

"If you've got any brains at all, smuggling is easy. It's covering yourself every step of the way that's tough. If one of my carriers gets busted, he walks away. He's got excuses down the line. No way they can break his story. And that's the trick. You've got to prop up your carriers, because if they talk, you're both finished. My people stand up because they know they are going to walk. Is the smoke bothering you?"

"No, go ahead."

"Most smugglers use mules, usually a girl, and she gets paid one thousand dollars a kilo to walk the load through Customs. Now, tell me, how are you going to say it's not yours if it's strapped to your back? And when the mule gets busted, nothing she can say is going to help her. She's finished, because her man's disappeared. It's really sad, but it happens all the time. And that's the way most smugglers operate. Say you're carrying. He's paid a thousand and given you an airline ticket. You're broke, you want to get home. One of his lieutenants follows the load through Customs—if you get tossed, it's you and the lions. He's gone. I don't operate that way. If you carry for me, you're guaranteed to walk away."

Peace sat back in his chair and looked around the table. It was apparent that the others had heard the sales pitch before. He did not pursue the Federal question any further. He simply nodded and leaned forward.

"Now, they found a lot of cocaine in your house. And they found a gun. I'd be interested to know why you told them where the gun was buried. Apparently all they found in the house were the bullets."

"That's right. The gun was buried under the pebbles of the patio."

"And you told them that."

"Right."

"Did they threaten you?"

"No."

"What happened?"

"They said if I didn't tell them, they were going to take the house apart board by board until they found it."

"So?"

Swan looked at his friends. Then he looked back at his lawyer.

"Well, you see, they missed the load."

"What do you mean they missed the load?"

"You said they found a lot of cocaine in the house."

"They did."

"How much?"

"The police say several ounces."

"Yeah, that's what the judge said when he arraigned us. I wasn't sure."

"That's what it is. And that's how the charge reads."

Swan put his fork down. He looked at his attorney:

"Yeah, well, they missed the load, then. You see, on the mantelpiece, in the house, right now, there are three kilos of cocaine that they *didn't* find. And if the police lab is right, it's about eighty-nine percent pure."

2

Talking to Boswell

ZACHARY SWAN was born at the peak of the Jazz Age with a silver spoon in his mouth. That he would spend the middle years of his life with that same spoon in his nose entered the realm of possibility at about the age of sixteen. Up until that time he behaved like any other boy his age forced to deal with servants around the house and a country club around the corner.

"While all the other kids were going to the creek swimming hole, I was at the country club pool, ordering club sandwiches and milk. I was playing golf at the age of nine."

An audience with his father, known to many simply as the Colonel, was a rare event in those days, one which required a visit to the golf course, a visit which Swan made infrequently. The Colonel, by all accounts, was a man with whom Swan had only chromosomes in common. "I loved him . . . but I never liked him," Swan would say.

Swan was closer to his mother, a woman whose struggle with alcoholism ended in 1965 in a fire which destroyed the house in which she slept and in which she had lived alone since her separation from the Colonel two years earlier. "She collected antique stoves . . . painted them red and planted geraniums in them. They were all over the yard. They looked nice, but it was hell if you went home at night drunk. All my life she called me Cookie. She did it once in Grand Central

Station when I was home on leave. 'Mother,' I told her, 'you don't call a Marine Cookie.' "

Swan shares his father's estate with an older sister, who lives now in Florida and whose privacy he is determined to protect. The Colonel died two months after Swan's arrest, at the age of seventy-five.

Swan is reluctant to introduce his family into a discussion of the events which presaged his decision to take that first round-trip excursion on Avianca Airlines in the fall of 1970. The life that led him to the Riverhead Jail shortly after his forty-sixth birthday began, as far as he sees it, when he was sixteen years old and a sophomore at the Iona Preparatory School in New Rochelle (Westchester County), New York. It was there that an inevitable synthesis of wealth and leisure, generated under the catalysis of the Catholic Church, rendered its first volatile by-product.

At Iona Prep, with the help of a classmate, Swan controlled dice games on the academy handball courts —he had a natural aptitude for math—and managed to squander the proceeds before his capture by the Christian Brothers became imminent. His aptitude for geography found an outlet in the occasional daytrips he and his friends made to New York City, where they bluffed their way into the Times Square burlesque houses. Swan discovered Ann Corio at the age of seventeen. He took up cigarette smoking in deference to his newly acquired manhood, and with the War at hand adopted the hard-edged look of an OSS agent, hardly the rage at the university-oriented Iona Prep. His diploma from that institution, awarded reluctantly, came after a sophisticated and diligent application of blackmail to his Latin professor (an unfortunate man whose career with the Christian Brothers was a brief one) and a bribe well placed with that faction of the administration responsible for supplying the graduating class with a commencement speaker. Swan's father was a personal friend of Jim Crowley, the Fordham football coach, formerly one of Notre Dame's Four Horse-

men. When the best-laid plans of the Brothers went
awry, Crowley was called upon at the last minute to
give Iona Prep's 1944 commencement address.

Before pursuing a higher education, Swan served for
three years in the United States Marine Corps, a tour
of duty which took him to Japan at the end of World
War II. (His only other military experience, the Colonel notwithstanding, was an unsuccessful attempt at the
age of fifteen to join the Free French. He and three
classmates set out for Quebec in a stolen car, financing
their journey with the change taken from an unattended March of Dimes receptacle in a Connecticut
movie theatre. They were stopped at the Canadian
border and held until the mother of one of the boys arrived to take them home. Because they were minors,
they were detained in a jail reserved for women, fated
to cool their heels behind a glass partition instead of
behind bars. It was the cruelest blow of all.) If his
military career is significant, it is so in terms of the
opportunity it gave him to measure his patriotism—
after an honorable discharge, he was able to appreciate the fact that opportunity knocks but once.

His university days were not uneventful. That he
chose to spend them in Coral Gables, Florida, was a
tribute to his respect for formal education. On the GI
Bill and more than ample subsidies from home, he
became an accomplished swimmer. In Florida he
learned how to squander his money on women—the
Marine Corps had failed him there—and, in their
company, how to drink his Martinis dry. And it was
from Coral Gables, as a college student, that he made
his first boat trip to Bimini. He did not know it then,
but what he would learn about that island's Customs
procedure, and what he had learned in four years
about the Florida coastline, would someday be worth
the equivalent in American dollars of at least three Ivy
League educations. He earned his degree from the
University of Miami through the same diligence and
sophistication he had applied to the acquisition of his

high school diploma. He printed it himself. His craftsmanship was so refined (his father's was a packaging business, and Swan was no stranger to industrial arts) that he managed to sell the overrun to fellow students.

But as he had been sure they would, Swan's salad days soon came to an end, and he spent the balance of his youth preparing for old age. After college he joined his father's packaging company as a sales executive, and for the next seventeen years he observed, as honestly and conscientiously as he possibly could, the timeworn rituals of New York's business community. As a salesman, he handled the accounts of some of the country's most prestigious cosmetics firms. He earned a good salary, belonged to the finest clubs in New York, and enjoyed the friendship of many prominent people.

"I handled Helena Rubinstein, Revlon, Coty, Arden, Pond's—good accounts. I designed the Heaven Scent package, the Gino Paoli logo, packages for Richard Hudnut, Eileen Ford. Some of my designs are still on the market. I was underpaid for the volume of sales I was doing—my payment was always 'someday, son, you're going to be president of the company.' But it was lucrative. Everybody got a good living out of it, especially my uncles and my father. They were driving Cadillacs and belonged to country clubs in Westchester. I was living in Manhattan. I was taking art directors to the opera, buyers to the football games, I'd go fishing with the fishermen. And I belonged to all the clubs that were necessary and fashionable at the time."

Swan's wedding in 1958 was not at all necessary, but it was more than fashionable. His wife, Yvonne, was Norman Norell's ace model. Norell designed the wedding gown and provided the bridesmaids. It was a lavish affair. The reception went on forever. The marriage lasted four months. In 1960 Swan married a girl from Brooklyn, an Eileen Ford fashion model who was later to become one of the founding members of the New York Radical Feminists; a few years after her separation from Swan, Holly appeared on the Dick Cavett Show, wearing a Superman T-shirt, debating *Playboy* publisher Hugh Hefner on the subject of Women's Rights. Divorced in 1966, Swan and Holly remain close friends.

"Holly and I were out six nights a week, either at a party or for dinner—El Morocco, Orsini's—we belonged to Le Club and we were swinging around with the jet set. We were invited to discotheque openings, parties in Southampton—I had all kinds of energy and drive and didn't sleep. I didn't know it then, but I was hooked on speed. In 1964 I got a prescription for diet pills from a doctor and kept refilling it—for six years. It was that plus a lot of alcohol. Holly was making forty thousand a year, so between the two of us, with my twelve-five, we were going through fifty-two thousand dollars a year, not counting my expense account, less twelve or thirteen thousand for taxes. We never had a nickel and we always had a bank loan. Our bills were astronomical. Our Bloomingdale's bill one year had to be seven thousand dollars. I had twenty suits. I was wearing fifty-dollar shoes. Holly never wore the same thing twice. We were spending fifty dollars a week in *tips*. More. Headwaiter ten dollars, the waiter ten dollars, maybe a hundred a week in tips alone. That's where five thousand dollars went. But you don't know it. You don't even feel it or see it. You're drunk and you're high and you don't know a thing."

> They dined on mince and slices of quince,
> Which they ate with a runcible spoon;
> And hand in hand, on the edge of the sand,
> They danced by the light of the moon.
>
> "The Owl and the Pussycat"
> EDWARD LEAR

Swan's closest friend at the time was, and always had been, Mike Riordan, his partner in the prep school dice games. Riordan, the Irish heir to a Jewish department store (his father, a vice-president of Abraham & Strauss in New York, had taken over the bankrupt Stern's Department Store in 1932, and by 1940 owned a controlling interest), had graduated from Cornell, and after experience as a mutual fund wholesaler on Wall Street established his own company in Los Angeles. Riordan was loaded, and in the habit of carrying large amounts of his money in cash. One night he threw $8,000 on the bar of the Stork Club in answer to a challenge. (It is said he did it to impress a woman.) When he was not spending money, he was giving it away to anyone who needed it. Bums loved him.

Swan and Riordan had never given up gambling—in fact, the only thing they enjoyed more was taking advantage of some other gambler's greed. Whenever they were together and an opportunity presented itself, they engineered a swindle of one kind or another—either on a bookie, on a rich friend, or on another swindler. Past-posting bookies was one of their favorites.

Riordan had access to a Minneapolis wire (he subscribed for thirty dollars a month) which was reporting local track results on a simultaneous feed—it worked on the wig-wag and was running about 95 percent accurate. He knew the name of every bartender in New York who would turn the clock back for a cut, and he and Swan—one on the phone, one buying drinks for the bookie—were running almost as well as the wire. If Riordan, waiting for a bookie, happened to mention that the Professor was coming over, it meant that the bookie was working for *him*, and the flim-flam was on whoever his and Swan's drinking companions happened to be. Swan would man the phone and flash confusing signals . . . *shit, it was my fault, I'm sorry*. The bookie would clean the conspirators out and leave—Riordan, cursing his luck, would hit his friends for a fifty-dollar charge for the wire and collect from the Professor later.

Anything worth doing was worth doing wrong, and anything worth gambling on was worth cheating at. It had become a habit. Since their prep school days they had been cheating at liar's poker. With the signals they had developed, they could communicate their respective serial numbers within two declarations. Whenever a bank note came into view, they would sandwich its owner between them, suggest a game of liar's poker, and collaborate until they had won the price of the drinks at stake. As Riordan's business expanded, so did his bankroll (by the time he was forty-one, he was worth over thirty million dollars), but even while closing a twenty-million-dollar deal with a corporate president, he was not above cheating the man out of twenty dollars in a game of liar's poker. "That's cash," he would say.

At his engagement party, Riordan grabbed Swan by the arm:

"Here's a guy you've got to meet," he said. "We can play some liar's poker with him."

"Who is he?" Swan asked.

"Thomas Dewey. The governor."

He dragged Swan over:

"Governor, this is my friend [Zachary Swan]. You probably know his uncle."

Riordan would say anything to anyone.

Swan and Riordan could beat a bookie in a bar, and they could beat him on the way to the track in the back seat of a limousine. They could beat bookies on football games, and by handing out phony business cards wherever they went they could beat them without beating them. Through Swan and a Bermuda bank account, Riordan could sell his unlisted and lettered stock, and through Riordan and a phony heart condition, Swan could beat any Park Avenue doctor out of twenty or thirty amyl nitrates. (The headwaiter at El Morocco told Swan that after closing every night he would find two or three hundred broken Vaporole capsules on the floor of the dining room, most of them under the better tables.)

"One night we were at Le Club doing poppers, and some friends of ours came in with Mickey Mantle. Mike and I bought him Scotch all night and sent him home with a woman named Fay—a real tiger we knew would keep him up all night. We bet the Red Sox the next day. Mantle hit a double in the eighth and beat us."

But beyond the law of averages, which presumes the accuracy of a Minneapolis wire and the odds against beating a guy like Mantle, there are other inevitabilities to which working the flim-flam is subject. On one occasion, thinking that he and Riordan had lost $5,000 to a bookie, Swan discovered that he had simply lost $2,500 to Riordan. The swindle had just been carried one step further. When confronted, Riordan paid up, but the two men agreed that from then on mutual robbery was part of the game. Swan's first double-reverse was staged at one of Riordan's favorite nightspots, P.J. Clarke's, an East Side saloon with bright Tiffany lamps over the bar.

Leaving Orsini's after dinner one evening—Swan with Holly, Riordan dating a woman he could easily impress—Swan suggested they all go to Clarke's for a drink. Riordan hailed the cab. Inside his coat pocket, Swan was carrying a Tiffany box he had picked up at his office. Inside the box was a ring he had picked up at Woolworth's. Getting into the cab first, he put the box on the floor and his foot on the box. When the cab was under way, Swan tapped his foot. Riordan caught the move.

"Fifty-fifty," he said.

"Shut up," whispered Swan. He pointed in the direction of the driver.

Swan picked up the box, flashed it at Riordan and put it in his pocket. (What Swan was engaged in here, though he did not know it, was a very famous and time-honored flim-flam—in the slang of the Victorian London rampsman, it was affectionately known as the *fawney-drop*.) Under the lights at Clarke's, he opened the box, held up the ring, and said:

"Mike, I think it's a piece of glass."

Riordan was looking over the box with the Tiffany engraving. He looked at his date.

"I'll tell you what I'll do," Swan said. "You give me two thousand. I'll sell it to you for two thousand, but anything it's worth over ten thousand dollars we split."

Riordan threw the cash on the bar.

Three hours later Swan got a phone call:

"You got me, didn't ya?"

"I got ya."

"It was really beautiful."

"Thanks."

"I owe you one."

"I'm waiting."

But Swan waited in vain. In January of 1969, Mike Riordan was buried by a mud slide that crashed into his Mandeville Canyon home in Brentwood, California, a house that had once belonged to Esther Williams ("with a swimming pool as big as the AC").* He was forty-one years old.

Swan attended the funeral.

"He had a funeral so long you couldn't even count the cars. There must have been two or three thousand of them. Everybody loved Mike. Headwaiters loved him. Bartenders loved him. Everybody. You couldn't count the limousines."

Riordan had left his wife, Jackie, with instructions to sell all of his corporate stock—by then the Equity Funding Corporation was trading on the American Stock Exchange, its reported assets approaching $200 million. She sold the stock immediately after his death for $46 million. It was not until after her second

---

* The New York Athletic Club.

husband, George Getty, died that she discovered, along with the rest of the world, that the Equity Funding Corporation of America, of which Mike Riordan was co-founder and chairman of the board, had perpetrated the largest stock swindle in the nation's history. The figures were reported in *The Wall Street Journal*.

"That's cash," Swan said.

To this day, the Securities and Exchange Commission has not recovered.

At about the time of Mike Riordan's death, Swan's life began to change. Up to that time he had been associating with aristocrats and celebrities, and he was known in every nightclub in town. While one of his friends (later to be known as Mean Mickey) was dating a railroad heiress, Swan was almost dating a famous network bonus baby:

"We were going to go to The Latin Quarter for dinner, but after an hour together we could both see it was going to be a rough evening. I said, 'Why don't we just go to Hamburger Heaven and call it a night?' She jumped at the suggestion. 'Excellent idea,' she said."

Swan was being invited to New York high-society parties thrown for visiting dignitaries like the Chicago Panthers and Cesar Chavez. He and Holly were chumming around with Hollywood types, and throwing parties of their own. A lot of society flotsam was collecting at his door. But at about the time of Mike's death—Swan and Holly had been divorced for three years—Swan began to slow down. He had been living with a young woman, a German named Uta, for five years; she was much crazier than he, and he was pretty near burned out by the time she left. He quit his job with his father's company and started his own packaging business: "My relatives didn't have very good business sense. My uncle saw letterpress as the wave of the future. He thought lithography was a fad."

After Uta left, there was Alice, but before meeting Alice, the long-haired, brown-eyed, free spirit of the sixties, Swan had made the acquaintance of a man named Ellery, a relative of one of his upstairs neighbors. And it was Ellery, more than anyone else, who was responsible for Swan's metamorphosis. Ellery gave Swan his first taste of dope. Mexican. Swan was ready for anything, just about now, and between Ellery's dope and Alice's politics he would get everything but what he had been getting for the past forty-two years. And he would like it. A lot.

Honest Ellery was the nearest thing New York City had to a pony express rider; every day, rain or shine, he made his rounds. If he were working a legitimate job during the day, his rounds began late in the afternoon. If he were out of work, for one reason or another, his rounds began as soon as he got out of bed—late in the afternoon. Ellery did not simply move about town, he revolved. He was that consistent. At the same time every day, he stopped at the same health-food restaurant on Broadway and ordered the same thing—carrot juice. Every night he stopped at Victor's Café on Columbus Avenue for coffee. While his customers sped around town, erratic, trying either to catch him at his last stop or head him off at his next, Ellery revolved, slowly, feeding on his own momentum. At peace. He was like a Swiss watch; the last thing in this life he would be guilty of was change.

An honest dealer, Ellery was the one immutable constant in the life of every dope smoker he knew. The eye of many storms. He was safe, reliable, well informed, but above all else he was available. A message would never fail to reach him. The only thing more consistent than Ellery himself was the flow of messages across the length and breadth of Manhattan's upper West Side that either preceded or followed him. If he did not call ahead for his messages, they were waiting for him when he arrived. His customers, if they did not all know one another, knew *of* one another; if they had not met, they would—they were in continual telephone contact. Ellery's customers—as a class, not noted for their firm connection to the world's labyrinth string—had Ellery in common. Ellery was the glue that bound them, the mucilage to which the errant particles of their lives adhered.

At the end of the day, his pockets were littered with scraps of paper, fragments of matchbooks, napkins and corners of the pages of unidentifiable telephone directories and newspapers, a miniature catalogue of the day's events, meaningful only to Ellery. A message here, a number to call there, a requisition or a promise of payment early in the evening, an excuse for not showing at night. As a dealer in dreams, Ellery was often paid in kind. And in the creases of his pockets, pouched in darkness, he carried the official correspondence of his trade.

Ellery was of medium height and medium weight. His hair and eyes were brown. He was neither dark nor fair; not striking and not unattractive. Ellery was not an extrovert, but he was not an introvert either. His temperament was even. In almost every way he was average—right there in the middle, the arithmetic American mean. Even his age was medium. Ellery could have been anywhere from twenty-five to forty— only his mother knew for certain, and eventually the police department. Alice said he was a Gemini. Perhaps. Ellery wore expensive clothes and custom-made shoes. On his left wrist he wore a gold watch and on the third finger of his right hand a gold ring in the image of a snake. He smoked imported cigarettes, whatever brand struck his fancy when he entered the tobacconist's. He always used an antique silver cigarette lighter to light them.

Ellery smoked a lot of cigarettes, and he smoked a

lot more dope. And like every serious dope smoker, he would acknowledge no ill effect in marijuana, asserting that its greatest danger lay in the possibility that it could lead to cigarette smoking. In contradistinction to the abuse he inflicted upon his body in the manner of that which he inhaled was the fact that he was a proselytizing health-food and vitamin freak. Ellery's daily ration of carrot juice represented only a fraction of his involvement in the cause of organically grown vegetables. His efforts in behalf of natural Dietary Fibre were legion. But, ironically, as mindful as Ellery was of the health-promoting properties of Nature, it was generally agreed that fresh air would kill him. It was the one thing he carefully avoided. To no one's recollection had he ever been out of New York City.

Ellery lived in the Bronx and spent all day in Manhattan. However rich he became—and he was making good money selling dope—he would never move from his seventy-five-dollar-a-month, rent-controlled Bronx apartment, not even to move as far as Manhattan where he spent all of his time. Ellery was happy. His needs were few. He owned a color television and an impressive array of stereo equipment, and home at night he was content to watch old TV movies or listen to opera. In support of the unsyncopated rhythm of his life, he took two Valium every night before retiring. There were only two pursuits in his life which could be ascribed to indulgence: he owned thousands of dollars' worth of antiques, the acquisition of which he was passionate about; the only other thing he devoted as much time to was dope.

There was no one in the city of New York who, if he had met Ellery after whatever day it was he smoked his first joint, had ever seen Ellery straight. Ellery only got stoned once in his life, and he stayed that way for years. He is stoned right now. Zachary Swan, a gin drinker, thought Ellery was stupid when he first met him; it took Swan several weeks, and at least as many joints, to realize that Ellery was simply stoned all the time. It was Ellery's tetrahydrocannabinol level that provided him with his unique circadian rhythm, his consistency in the face of chaos; it was his psychochemical symmetry that put him at the axis of revolution of the world's eccentric. Ellery was a successful dream merchant because he was a dreamer himself. And Ellery was loved because his dreams were humble ones: he dreamed of opening a chain of laundromats in the city—and stopping once a day to pick up the quarters.

Ellery was dreaming when he rang Swan's bell. Alice answered the door.

"Hello, Ellery."

"Hi," he said. "What time is it?"

"About eight-thirty."

Ellery looked at his watch. He nodded.

"I have to make a call."

"There are two messages for you on the table," she said.

"Thanks."

Ellery made two calls, Alice went back to the sewing machine, and Swan remained at his desk, where displayed before him was the upcoming week's professional football schedule. Swan had decided, after applying a simple mathematical formula to the point spreads of the previous year's games, that if, with two exceptions, he picked the home team in every game of the current season, he could beat the bookies this fall. He was behind. His simple mathematical formula, very possibly a failure, was the product of hours of research, derived from statistics that filled an entire manila folder which occupied a place of its own in his file cabinet. The folder was filed between Fabergé and Ford. It was labeled Football.

Ellery hung up the phone and reached for the stereo. With a twist of the dial, John Denver was swallowed by *Die Fledermaus*.

"You don't mind, do you?" Ellery asked.

Swan shook his head. No one ever minded, but Ellery always asked.

"Do you have the newspaper?" Ellery wanted to know.

"It's on the kitchen table," Swan told him.

Ellery put *The New York Times* on his lap and poured some dope onto a picture of John Mitchell's face.

"Do you have—"

Before he was able to finish what he was saying, Swan had tossed a packet of rolling papers onto the headline. Ellery never had papers. It had somehow become part of his image not to. People had given up asking why. Ellerylore called for a certain understanding of the procedure which began with his arrival: he picked up his messages, made his phone calls, changed the radio station, asked if you minded, asked for the newspaper, took out his dope, started a question about rolling papers, commented on the size of the brand you gave him, rolled a joint and passed it around. From there it was free-form until he left.

His departure was marked by the marijuana seeds and stems that remained on the daily paper when he left; it was in this way that one knew that Ellery had dropped by. Alice wondered if he carried empty cigarette packs with him—he invariably left one behind with the seeds and the stems (he never left roaches behind, always sticking them in the end of his first post-joint cigarette).

"I've got some good stuff this time."

Ellery always had good stuff. He dealt nothing but the best.

"How much?" Swan asked.

"It's really good."

"Better than last time?"

"What was wrong with what I gave you last time?"

"It wasn't bad."

"That was very good stuff."

"It cost enough."

"This is even better stuff."

"How much?"

"Well, I'm going to give you a price."

"How much?"

"Now, I'm charging everybody else ten dollars more. I want you to know that."

"You're really good to me, Ellery."

"It's the best you can buy."

"It always is."

"I can get a lot more for this than I'm charging you."

"How much?"

"I'm going to let you try it."

He handed Swan the joint. While Swan smoked it, Ellery rolled another.

"Now, tell me, isn't that great stuff?"

"It's always great, Ellery. How much do you want?"

"Well, I'm going to give you a special price."

"How much, Ellery?"

"Forty."

"Ellery, I love you, but you're a thief."

"I can get fifty dollars an ounce for this anywhere in the city."

"That's what you told me about the last batch."

"That was good stuff."

"It was O.K."

"I'm giving you a good price."

"I know. You did last time, too."

"Panama is getting very expensive."

"You said the same thing about Michoacàn a year ago."

"How do you feel?"

"It's good stuff, Ellery."

Swan finished the joint and handed Ellery the roach.

"How long have you been smoking now, a year?" Ellery asked.

"You're the one who turned me on."

"It was good stuff, too. I was dealing Mexican then, but it was good Mexican."

"Yeah, you're like Tiffany's."

"How old were you then?"

"Forty-two. How old were you, Ellery?"

"How many people do you figure you've turned on since then?"

"I have no idea," said Swan.

"That was good Mexican."

"When was the last time you smoked Mexican?" Swan asked.

"I don't know."

"Well, I don't think you'd get off on it now."

"That depends on how good it is," said Ellery.

"Well, just think of how the grass has grown in your head. You went from Michoacàn to Acapulco Gold and then to Panama Red."

"That's right. Straight up the ladder."

"And straight down the continent."

"Is that right?"

"Sounds good."

"Where's Colombia?"

"That's even farther south."

"And it's *higher* up the ladder."

"I'm sure you'll be dealing it real soon."

"Colombian's hard to get."

"I wonder if they grow it at the South Pole . . ."

"But there's still good Mexican around."

". . . maybe Antarctica."

"I've got a friend who's got some great Mexican Good stuff."

"Mexican?"

"Yeah."

"What kind?"

"Acapulco."

"You got a friend who's selling it?"

"Yeah."

"What's he selling it for?"

"I think he wants to sell weight. You want to tal' to him about it?"

"What for?"

"If you buy pounds, you can sell ounces at a profit. Get your own free."

Swan was selling dope to his friends for what he was paying for it.

"You can even make some money," said Ellery.

"Will anybody buy Mexican?"

"They're *your* friends."

"I guess they will."

"It's great stuff."

"I'm sure it is, Ellery."

"Want to meet him?"

"Will I be buying it from you if I don't buy it from him?"

Ellery nodded.

"I'll think about it."

A year after smoking his first joint, Swan bought his first pound. Ellery introduced him to a smuggler named Vinnie Pirata who wanted $1,000 for ten pounds of Acapulco Gold. Swan bought the dope and had no trouble selling it at $25 an ounce. He made $4,000 on the load and immediately put in another order. Within a few months he was moving two pounds a week in ounces. He was taking in eight hundred tax-free dollars a week when Pirata offered him a franchise.

The franchise consisted of a Chevrolet Bel Air station wagon (one of three Pirata owned) from which the rear seat had been removed (the well, into which the seat was designed to fold down, was covered with a sheet-metal plate machine-screwed to the floor and carpeted over), and it included the use of a villa Pirata rented on a yearly basis in Acapulco where the grass was to be delivered. The car would cost $2,000, the dope—two hundred pounds of it—the same. Swan did the math, liked the bottom line, and called his friend Charlie Kendricks, who had been helping him deal ounces. Kendricks, who needed the money, said yes. Swan paid for the car, arranged to meet Pirata in Aca-

pulco, and before the New Year was a month old—
six months short of his forty-fourth birthday—Zachary
Swan, industrial engineer, had designed his first pharmaceutical package.

3

Brownsville Breakdown

ON A RAINY MONDAY morning in the winter of 1970, throwing the freight-modified Bel Air into operation, Swan and Kendricks set out for Mexico. They crossed the Hudson ahead of the mail. A fog rolled in at their backs, Manhattan disappeared into the mist like the detail on a fading negative, and the prospect of the West lay before them, a sinful Kodachrome promise. They moved fast. They picked up the Interstate just south of the Bridge, and as soon as they hit the open road they went for the medicine. Between New York City and the Texas line they dropped enough Biphetamine to influence the output of two defensive tackles and a weak-side linebacker. They made Dallas in thirty hours.

Just east of Dallas, short of the used car lots and the taco stands, they separated. Swan pulled the car over and let Kendricks out:

"Don't forget to get the license number," Swan told him. "If you can get a name and address, that's even better."

Kendricks nodded. He waved Swan on:

"I'll see you in Dallas," he said.

"Call first."

"Right."

Swan pulled out into the afternoon traffic, headed for the city. Kendricks looked at the sky and frowned. "Balls," he said out loud. It rained. The Bel Air was gone, and Kendricks stood alone on the shoulder of

39

the Interstate. It came down hard. He put out his thumb.

Swan drove into Dallas. Big "D," population about 700,000, he guessed, northeast Texas' answer to the Cherry Hill Shopping Mall; a city, he had always claimed, which owed its ass to oil and football . . . *welcome to the biggest little city in the world, son, take off your boots and stay awhile* . . . the home of Braniff Airlines, H. L. Hunt, and Frito-Lay, one overindustrialized office park of concrete and bean dip cooking in the cowboy sun . . . *this here town's got a big heart, boy, we'll get you all a piece of ass before breakfast* . . . America on the threshold of the twenty-first century, the implications of which were staggering and not a little bit frightening to a man who had been doing Black Beauties for thirty hours.

He drove downtown and checked into a Holiday Inn. It was like checking into a hospital—American Antiseptic, pastels and plastic from sea to shining sea—not inappropriate, he figured, given the conditions under which his nervous system had been functioning recently . . . *send up two bottles of glucose and a bucket of ice, please . . . then void where not prohibited by law.* A germ, he supposed, would never make it out of one of these places alive. If the disinfectants didn't get him, the little bastard would croak from boredom. Swan smiled benignly at the desk clerk. He registered under an assumed name.

Waiting for his room key, he heard a call come over the house intercom; they were paging a man named McCann. He made a mental note of the call, picked up his key, then went up to his room and unpacked. He would have to hurry now: the speed was losing its edge. He was coming down fast, and coming down from the shit he was on was like getting hit by the bends. Before he passed out he made one trip to the lobby.

He walked to the bank of public telephones along

the wall, choosing the phone nearest the desk, and he dialed the number of the phone nearest the door, one of the same bank of telephones. When it rang once, he wrote the number down, hung up the phone and went to bed. It was five P.M.

The following morning Swan woke early. He had coffee in his room. He dressed in a gray flannel suit, a white shirt and a blue tie. He slicked his hair down with water, put on dark glasses and went out.

"I'd like to place an ad."

"You could have called it in, sir," said the woman behind the typewriter, looking up, removing the headset she wore.

"I was in the neighborhood."

She nodded. "What kind of ad is it?"

"A classified ad."

"Yes, but where do you want it to appear?"

He frowned. "In the newspaper."

"Yes," she said, "I know that, but where? Are you selling something, buying something, giving something away? Is it a job, a cat, a car? There are all kinds of categories, you see."

What a curious old bat, he thought. She kept throwing her head around from side to side when she talked. What the hell was that all about? Maybe she was not used to the hairnet. And she was nearsighted as hell. Her eyeglasses were attached to a necklace. But she kept taking them off and putting them on, back and forth, up and down. She was making him dizzy, he realized. He liked her.

"Help wanted," he said.

"Help wanted. And when did you want that to appear?"

"As soon as possible."

"As soon as possible." (Now she was repeating him.) "We can have it in by tomorrow morning," she said.

"That's fine."

"That's fine. Now," she said, turning to the typewriter, "how do you want it to read?"

"Driver wanted—"

"You really don't need that."

"Pardon me?" He tried to focus.

She took the glasses off for this. She squinted.

"You really don't need 'wanted,' do you? I mean, it's appearing in the Help Wanted section, isn't it? All you really need to say is 'driver.' You save money that way—you pay by the word."

"Oh."

"So, do you want me to put just 'driver' and leave out the 'wanted'?"

"Please."

"Fine. And the rest?" The glasses were back on now.

"Southwest Freight Company needs a driver to cover the Southwest and Mexico. No special license required. Call Mr. McCann at—"

"I'll leave out things like 'at' and 'a' and 'the,' " she enunciated rapidly, " 'Southwest Freight Company' is too long even if I abbreviate 'Company,' which I will do anyway, so I'm afraid all you get in boldface is 'driver.' " She looked up.

"Terrific. I'll leave it all up to you."

"How do you spell McCann?"

"You can leave that out. Just run the phone number."

"Very good," she said, pleased, it seemed, to know that he was catching on.

He gave her the phone number, paid her in cash, told her how nice it was to deal with someone so efficient and conscientious, and disappeared. She smiled as he left.

Swan spent the day in his room. He took a call from Kendricks in the evening. He watched television until the national anthem came on, smoked some dope, and went to sleep. At eight the next morning the pay phone in the lobby, the telephone nearest the door, rang once. Swan picked it up:

"Good morning," he said.

"Hello, I'm calling about the ad in the paper."

"Your name, please."

"Kendricks. Charles Kendricks."

"Do you have the paper?"

"Yes."

"Cut out the ad and keep it."

"I did."

"Meet me in the coffee shop. Call me Mr. McCann."

"O.K.," Kendricks yawned.

It was ten o'clock when Kendricks arrived. He was wearing bluejeans and a workshirt. The coffee shop was nearly empty. Swan, the newspaper in front of him, was doing Dow Jones calculations on his napkin. He was wearing the gray flannel suit. His second cup of coffee had just arrived. He waved Kendricks over to the table. He stood up and they shook hands.

"I'm Mr. McCann."

"Charles Kendricks. Glad to meet you."

"Sit down, Mr. Kendricks."

"Thank you. What's that, the racing form?"

"The market."

"Who's winning?"

"Them."

Swan called the waitress over. Kendricks smiled. The waitress smiled back. She was young, about eighteen, tall and still growing. Her red hair was long, but pinned up to keep it out of the food. Her eyes were blue and her teeth were perfect. Swan, who was not partial to red hair, found her attractive. Kendricks thought she was beautiful. Her ears were pierced, and the only embellishment to her face, afforded by features with which she was not born, was provided by the shadows of the elaborate opal earrings she wore and a small scar above her right eye that looked like a knife wound.

"This is Julie," Swan said. "Julie, I'd like you to

meet Mr. Charles Kendricks. Julie was born in October."

"Hello, Mr. Kendricks," she said.

"Call me Charlie."

"Are you English?" she asked.

"Australian," he said.

"This young man is going to work for me," Swan said, "so I want you to bring him a lot of food. Anything you want, son."

Kendricks looked at the waitress:

"I was born in—"

When Kendricks decided to turn on the charm, Swan decided to spill the coffee.

"I'm sorry," he said, standing up.

The young woman moved quickly, in time to save Swan's suit and what remained of his coffee. She told him it was quite all right, that she would bring him another cup; she took Kendricks's order and left.

"She'll never forget you," Kendricks said.

"That's the idea," Swan answered. "Where did you stay last night?"

"Same place. The Pepsi Hotel."

"The Pepsi Hotel?"

"That's what it said. No name, just a fucking Pepsi sign. A real fleabag. Five dollars a night. The Pepsi Hotel, Dallas."

"Was there anyone else there?"

"I talked to the night man. He's also the day man, but he sleeps then. I talked to him at night, inquired about jobs."

"Perfect. Who brought you in?"

Kendricks pulled out his wallet, an expensive one, made of kangaroo hide, and from it he took three small pieces of paper. One had written on it, in another man's handwriting, a name and an address in Fort Worth. The second showed an automobile registration number written in Kendricks's hand; the sevens were crossed. The third scrap of paper was the classified ad from *The Dallas Morning News.* Kendricks handed them to Swan, and Swan looked them over.

"Good work, Charlie. Well done. You'd better separate them so it doesn't look like you had any plan in mind when you put them there."

Kendricks stared:

"I have a friend in Queensland," he said, "who bought Poseidon Nickel a year ago."

"Yeah?" Swan looked up.

"He's a millionaire today."

"Sure. Who was his broker?" Swan asked, handing back the scraps of paper.

"I was," Kendricks nodded. He put the wallet away.

Swan smiled. "I'm sorry, Charlie, I know you're not stupid. You're doing fine, real fine. Keep up the good work."

"Right."

"And I'm sorry about the Pepsi Hotel. We'll fix you up real nice in Acapulco."

"Quite all right."

Swan lit a cigarette, Kendricks coughed, and the waitress returned with breakfast.

Because it was difficult to drive a car into Mexico which was registered to anyone other than the driver, it had been decided earlier that the Bel Air be registered in Kendricks's name. (Traffic was heavy across the Mexican border in cars which were rented in the United States on stolen credit cards and subsequently sold in Mexico; authorities on both sides of the border were suspicious of automobiles in general.) Swan and Kendricks discussed this in front of the waitress. When they left the coffee shop, Kendricks took the phony papers that came with the station wagon and the franchise, and he registered the car in his name. That afternoon they drove to San Antonio. In San Antonio, at a second-hand furniture store, they bought a desk, a swivel chair, a hat rack and some assorted junk, and loaded the car. Kendricks drove Swan to the airport. Swan flew to Acapulco that night.

* * *

To Zachary Swan, late of the New York cocktail
circuit and international hobo collective, Acapulco de
Juarez, known to most as Acapulco—Aca if you had
been there—needed no introduction. This sultry port
on the Pacific coast of southern Mexico, the odds-on
favorite of lower-echelon European nobility and mid-
Atlantic-jet-set Riviera flotsam—known now more for
its dope than for anything else, a kind of crypto-
Casablanca without the Casbah—was what that sixteenth face-lift and Vidal Sassoon were all about.

Swan picked up a Carte Blanche travel brochure at
the airport and read it on the way to the villa. As the
cab bumped along he became even better acquainted
with Acapulco's cultural heritage. It was from here,
he learned, one of the finest natural harbors in the
world, 272 mountainous miles from Mexico City and
the halls of Montezuma, that Hernando Cortés, wit,
raconteur and man of letters, after winning the hearts
and minds of the Aztecs and dutifully mailing them
home to Spain, shipped supplies to his pal Francisco
Pizarro while the latter distinguished himself in Peru
disemboweling the Incas into oblivion. All in four-color.

Vinnie Pirata's villa had been described to Swan
accurately. It was an old Spanish fortress, white-
washed and wired, situated high on a hill overlooking
Acapulco Bay. Behind it to the east, bathed now in
moonlight, was a fertile valley stretching three miles
to the mountains. The villa was surrounded by a de-
caying concrete wall eight feet high and inset with cut
glass. Its wrought-iron gate, Swan decided, was over-
wrought. It would become a pet joke of his. Pirata
was home when Swan arrived.

Vinnie Pirata, dressed now in lightweight khaki pants
and a red cotton jersey, had picked up a tan since
Swan had seen him last in New York. His blond hair
was blonder. His forehead was burned. Pirata was
short, about five-five, and slim; he weighed about 140,

he was in good shape, and his posture was excellent. He dressed down, but wore a flashy gold watch. In New York he drove a Maserati. Pirata was about forty years old, uneducated, and had a long criminal record. He did not drink or smoke, and he never used drugs. He had blue eyes, and he was the only man Swan knew who always carried a gun. He shook Swan's hand:

"The grass is going to be late," he said.

"Terrific."

Kendricks arrived in Acapulco two days later with the car. He registered at La Condesa Hotel, under his own name, as a representative of the Southwest Freight Company. He left the car keys with the clerk at the desk, telling the man that his, Kendricks's, employer would be by soon to pick up the vehicle. He made a phone call and went to the beach. Kendricks was conspicuously absent from the hotel when Swan arrived for the station wagon. Swan chatted with the clerk, asked him when Kendricks had arrived, thanked him, overtipped him, and took the car. He parked the car behind the villa, and for the hell of it he took off the plates. He met Kendricks at the beach that afternoon.

"The grass is late."

"What do we do?"

"We wait. They're bringing the shit in from the mountains by donkey. They're supposed to give us a flashlight signal or something. Do you believe that?"

Sure he did. They both believed it, and they thought it was wonderful. Though neither would admit it, they were, if for nothing else, suckers for the cloak-and-dagger aspects of this operation.

"Do you want me to stay at the hotel?"

"Yeah, you'd better."

"Fine."

While they swam, Swan explained that because the wholesalers were not in the habit of leading mule trains into Acapulco, Pirata would pay a cab driver

$100 to drive him to the rendezvous point in the foothills when the signal was given.

"Fancy that," Kendricks said.

And of course Swan did.

In the week that passed, Swan and Kendricks met daily at the beach, Swan growing weary of the wait, Kendricks growing weary of the sun, both of them making the best of each. With one exception—that they were never seen together in the vicinity of Kendricks's hotel—they behaved like tourists. At night they caught the act of the Quebrada Cliff divers; during the day they took the parachute ride, pulled by a power boat one hundred yards into the air over Acapulco Bay. Swan thought the last was a real hoot and made a point of doing it often. He got a special thrill out of the release he was required to sign, before being harnessed in, which relieved the concessionaires of any responsibility in the event of his near-death. He signed his name: *I'll Sue*.

And in that week Swan learned something, a lesson the impact of which was to hold up for the next four years: smuggling is waiting. Sitting in rooms. Waiting. Killing time. No matter how intricate the preparation, no matter how airtight the scam, smuggling is innovating, winging it, changing the operation because your boat left or your carrier ran out. In the ensuing years Swan would watch a lot of television. And when the heat was on, he would drink a lot of gin. On this trip the wait paid off: Kendricks became so sunburned that border officials could take him for nothing more than an ignorant tourist.

A pair of high-powered field glasses, Navy issue, stolen, were mounted on a tripod in one of the east windows of the villa. They faced the mountains. Just after dark Vinnie Pirata had removed the drop cloth that protected them from the sun and the dust; now he sat in a chair by the window and drank coffee.

Zachary Swan sat facing him with an overcoat draped over his arm. It was late on the seventh day.

"That's all bullshit," Pirata was saying.

Swan, who was still holding on to a packaging business in the United States, was waiting for a cab to take him to the airport. He would leave for New York tonight. He was trusting Charlie Kendricks. Kendricks had come to the villa to see him off and was sitting on a stool by the door applying a variety of topical pain killers to the sunburn which had rendered him almost helpless. His face had begun to swell. Swan lit a cigarette and looked at his watch. It was ten o'clock. He did not answer Pirata.

At five past ten, as Swan was crushing his cigarette out in a pre-Columbian ashtray, the signal came. Swan saw it first. Pirata, whose back was to the window, jumped up when Swan pointed.

"Are you sure?"

Swan said nothing. He looked at his watch again. Pirata turned and looked through the binoculars. He waited. Then he whispered:

"It's here."

Pirata picked up a flashlight from the windowsill and signaled back. His signal was acknowledged. Swan watched the light come from out of the mountains; he turned from the window and picked up his luggage. Pirata checked the cartridges in his gun, called his cab driver, and as Swan was leaving for the airport, he and Kendricks left to make the pickup.

"Keep an eye out behind you," Swan told Kendricks as they parted.

Kendricks and Pirata made the pickup that night. They made the fill together. Early the next morning Pirata delivered the car to the hotel. Kendricks picked up the keys at the desk. Within an hour he was on the road.

Zachary Swan was catching up on the national news in New York when Richard Nixon's terrible shit-hammer came down on Charlie Kendricks. It was late on a Sunday night. Swan, relaxing at home, was reading *The New York Times*. He had just turned to a provocative article on drug smuggling, in which Customs Commissioner Myles Ambrose was quoted at length, when Charles Kendricks made the border at Matamoros and from there drove into the biggest trouble of his life. Kendricks was busted by American Customs agents at Brownsville with a ridiculous smile on his badly sunburned face and two hundred pounds of premium dope in the belly of the station wagon he was driving. The smile cost him a moment of physical agony; the rest could cost him about fifteen years in jail.

The employees of Myles Ambrose read Kendricks his rights, took away his alien registration card and told him, very politely, that there was a law in this country—21 USC 176, to be exact. After they did that, they led him into an interrogation room and confronted him with the evidence. Stacked high on a table in the center of the room was the grass, and as he looked at it, it occurred to Kendricks quite painfully that the last time he had seen the shit was when he had helped to load it into the station wagon. Realizing that his fingerprints were all over the bricks, Charles Kendricks, who had bought his client into Poseidon Nickel at forty cents, contrived to bump into the table and knock the bricks onto the floor. He helped the government pick them up.

"Well?" they asked.

"I've never seen it before in my life," he said.

They locked him up and threw away the key.

On Monday morning, shortly after eleven A.M. Eastern Standard Time, Lillian Giles was coveting her neighbor's goods in the living room of Zachary Swan's apartment on West 88th Street in Manhattan—she wanted Swan's throat. Standing thoughtfully between her close friend and the man whose future hinged on the disposition of the property in question, Alice Haskell, a woman of integrity, was considering the merits of the transaction.

". . . you and all your bullshit . . ." Lillian shouted.

"You explain it to her, will you, Allie? Tell her it's going to be all right," Swan was saying.

"Answer the phone," Alice told him.

Swan picked up the phone on the fifth ring. It was Ellery:

"Charlie's standing up," he said.

Swan sighed. He looked at Lillian.

"Jesus Christ, Ellery, that's great news," he said into the phone, "but I'd sure like to know where you got your information."

"Straight from Brownsville," said Ellery. "Billy Bad Breaks passed the word out."

"Billy?"

"Yeah, he talked to Charlie."

"He what?"

"Billy talked to Charlie."

"Wait a minute, Ellery, I don't understand. Billy Bad Breaks talked to Charlie in Brownsville?"

"That's right."

Swan hesitated. He looked at the two women, who were as confused as he was. Then he asked:

"What the fuck's going on, Ellery?"

What the fuck was going on was this: Billy Bad Breaks had tried to drive across the border at Brownsville over a week before, carrying a plump joint in his pocket. Things began to break bad, as they inevitably did for Billy, when he was pulled over and searched. When the Customs inspectors found the joint, they decided to search the car Billy was driving. The car was one of Vinnie Pirata's freight-modified Bel Airs, and Billy, who for all practical purposes was traveling empty (but not empty enough), had forgotten to bolt the plate back into position; cause for a certain amount of embarrassment as well as inconvenience, it turned out, since Billy Bad Breaks was going the other way—he was busted for smuggling marijuana *into* Mexico. What concerned Zachary Swan, however, was the fact that Billy Bad Breaks had been busted at Brownsville before Charlie Kendricks had left Acapulco. Every Customs man from Matamoros to Tijuana had been on to the Bel Air trick before Kendricks picked up the car keys in the Condesa lobby. And Pirata had known it. Swan's reluctance to take revenge on Vinnie Pirata paid off in the short run; it was not until a few years later that he would wish he had at least contracted to have the bastard's legs broken.

That Kendricks was standing up was certainly good news—it meant that so far he had not admitted anything, and more important, that he had not implicated Swan in the mess. But Swan's principal concern when he received news of the arrest, Lillian Giles's accusations to the contrary, was for Charlie. And all Swan's bullshit, that to which Lillian had made particular reference when she confronted him that day, the same bullshit to which Pirata had specifically referred on the night Swan left Acapulco, was the precise bullshit that saved Kendricks's neck. When Kendricks finally convinced the United States government to listen to him, he not only vindicated Swan; he raised the level of this unique and previously unseen brand of bullshit, *en passant,* to that of an elevated, almost rarefied, and characteristically seamy kind of canon in what was to become a smuggler's equivalent of the Revised Standard Version. It happened like this:

The generous Texan from Fort Worth who had picked Kendricks up in the rain and driven him as far as Dallas had given his correct name and address. There was no need to trace the registration number of his car. When called upon, the man corroborated Kendricks's story, even so far as to recall that Kendricks had asked about jobs in the area. The night manager of the Pepsi Hotel, questioned in the painful light of day, recalled a similar conversation. The newspaper

ad held up. Julie, the waitress at the Holiday Inn, remembered the interview. And the overtipped clerk at
La Condesa Hotel told investigators that the car Kendricks had driven had been out of Kendricks's hands
for five days while he was in Acapulco.

The furniture Kendricks had hauled South from
San Antonio was never an issue. (Swan had dumped
it beside an unpaved road on the outskirts of Acapulco; the next day it was gone.) Mr. McCann, who
had been paged at the Holiday Inn, had given a
phony name or address or both (he was probably
cheating on his wife) and was never located. That he
was not the same Mr. McCann who had placed the
classified ad or had interviewed Kendricks over breakfast was never suspected by the investigators; knowing
that there was a McCann registered at the Holiday
Inn was enough for them. That McCann had given a
phony address made sense, they had to figure, given
the fact that he had intended to smuggle two hundred
pounds of dope out of Mexico. (Swan's double-blind
maneuver, registering under one name, itself a phony,
then assuming the name of an individual actually registered at the hotel, was probably unnecessary, but it
appealed to the clinician in him. In this case, McCann,
or whoever he was, had fortuitously tripled the blind
by registering under an assumed name himself. Eventually Swan would refine his technique, so that in
South America, when checking into hotels or traveling,
he could sign his own name, proceeding upon the as-
sumption that innocence, in fact, is the best disguise.)
Kendricks's fingerprints on the dope, the only flaw in
the perfect scam, had been taken care of by Kendricks
himself. And so, reluctantly, less than a week after he
was arrested, Kendricks was released. The Feds wept.

Kendricks took a bus to New York, where he
stayed stoned for about four days. Swan kept him
company. When it was all over, Swan added it up.
His losses were not staggering. In hard cash, $5,000.
He would have made $25,000 if the deal had gone

through. He did lose Charlie Kendricks, who became border-shy after the Brownsville incident, but only temporarily. Charlie would be back. There was nothing Swan could do about Vinnie Pirata; use him if he could, but never trust him. And there was nothing he could do about his own reluctance to do anything about Pirata. If he had gained anything from the experience, it was by way of a test—he now had implicit faith in his ability to beat the government. That was enough. He knew that before long he would get his money back. How soon was up to him.

He worked the flourish on Adrian a month later.

4

After Math

IKE AND FREDDY were two shooters from Brooklyn who were so good they could make dice do tricks. Ike was particularly heavy—it was said that he could take any pair of legit dice, throw them in a bathtub, and get the number. How Adrian the Mogul spotted these two wizards is a mystery. Adrian, a film producer who was not producing, was making his money by cutting a poker game which he ran two or three nights a week at his apartment on Central Park West. Until he met Ike and Freddy, Adrian's was a legitimate game. When he spotted them, he expanded his operation. He went into business with the two young men, and with their help he opened a casino.

Ike and Freddy supplied the dice table, of a foam rubber variety which they sidelined in, renting them to nonprofit organizations in Queens on occasions such as Las Vegas nights (they came with the franchise and inevitably walked away with the lion's share of the contributions). And they supplied the wheel—where they got this no one asked. Swan, known as a man who liked action, was steered to Adrian's by a friend, and up against Ike one night, about six months prior to the Mexican move, he got clipped for over $2,700. When he found out it was a hustle, Swan figured Adrian owed him one. When the Mexican deal went bad, he figured it was time to collect.

Swan knew that when Adrian was not running the casino, he could be found "over by" Roosevelt Raceway in the clubhouse. One March evening Swan bumped into Adrian at the track and offered to buy him a drink. He pulled out a phony bankroll to pay for it—a Michigan, two hundreds on top and fifty ones underneath. In addition to the bankroll, he flashed a few discarded hundred-dollar pari-mutuel tickets he had picked up from the previous races. It looked as if he were loaded and betting heavy. Adrian went for it.

"What are you doing these days?" he asked.

Swan looked around, then smiled at Adrian.

"I'm moving grass out of Mexico and having a ball," he said out of the side of his mouth.

Adrian bought it, and Swan sold it to Adrian just as Pirata had sold it to him. But Swan put a flourish on it.

Swan fixed Adrian up with a Bel Air in Queens that had been retired after the second bust. "Two thousand. The grass will cost you another two thousand. I'll help you get rid of it." And he fixed Adrian up with a driver, a friend of Pirata's named Homer. Swan introduced Homer to Adrian as Billy Bad Breaks.

Adrian hired Homer, and he drove with Homer as far as San Antonio. He did not bother to set up alibis. He flew to the villa, saw the shipment—two hundred pounds that Pirata had been unable to smuggle out— and paid for it. After the fill, he drove as far as Mexico City with Homer. From there he flew to New York. Homer drove from Mexico City directly back to the villa.

Two days later Adrian got a call from Swan.

"Billy Bad Breaks has been busted," Swan told him.

Adrian would not buy it:

"You're fuckin' with me," he said.

Swan told him to call the Brownsville jail, gave Adrian the number, and hung up. Adrian was angry. He made the call. Billy Bad Breaks was in jail— Adrian never thought to ask how long he had been there. He called Swan:

"What do I do now?"

He was desperate.

"It's going to be rough on you if he talks," Swan said.

Adrian came up with another thousand dollars for a lawyer.

Swan paid Pirata $500 for the use of the villa and the grass. He paid Homer $1,000. Working the flourish on Adrian, Swan cleared about $4,000. He sold the scam eventually, and once a month, between March and July, he received $500 in the mail. Pirata made $500 each time for the use of his villa and for use of the grass he had been unable to move since the Bel Airs had gone bad. (Eventually Pirata tried to make a boat move and the captain stole the load.)

Swan made one more Mexican marijuana move using Vinnie Pirata's villa. In May 1970 he bought a second-hand camper, a converted '66 International pickup truck. It was red, with a deep well between the chassis and the living space. He paid $3,500 for it. He rented a small apartment in Chelsea simply to have somewhere to put a telephone, and placed an ad in *The Village Voice:* CAMPER FOR RENT; IDEAL FOR MEXICO. It was two and a half weeks before he got the response he was waiting for. It came from two Long Island schoolteachers.

The young schoolteachers wanted to go to Mexico City, to an artists' colony northwest of there, San Miguel de Allende in Guanajuato, and they especially wanted to go to Acapulco. Swan rented them the camper for a month—$350. (He made sure they were covered by giving them a contract to sign. The *Voice* ad was added proof of their innocence.) And Swan gave them the name of a friend who rented a villa overlooking Acapulco Bay. They could stay there while they were in Acapulco, he told them. They would, they said. They did.

When the schoolteachers arrived at the villa, Vinnie Pirata, who liked having women around, was there to greet them. Nice Mickey was also there. Nice Mickey (whose name had been given to him by Swan for no other reason than to distinguish him from a small-change hustler named Mean Mickey) was first a friend of Ellery's, now a better friend of Pirata's, and happened to be vacationing at the villa in June. An ounce-dealer on occasion, Mickey had given up smuggling Vinnie's dope when Billy Bad Breaks was busted. He was very professional, a good man who watched himself carefully. Swan had not hired him for this move, but paid him $500 to help out when he found that Mickey was going to be around.

Swan flew down from New York to pay for the grass, and he stayed out of sight. He sent Charlie Kendricks to Mexico City. Then he waited.

The schoolteachers had a good time in Acapulco; the only setback they suffered was a temporary one, an oil leak the camper developed while it was parked at Pirata's villa. Nice Mickey, who discovered the leak, offered to take the camper to a garage and have it repaired. The schoolteachers thanked him, Pirata and the two young women went to the beach that day, and when the three returned to the villa the camper was fixed. It was also two hundred pounds heavier.

Swan flew to New York that night. The schoolteachers left for the United States the next day. Mickey drove with them as far as Mexico City, where they stayed in a hotel which Pirata had recommended. Pirata had made their reservations. The schoolteachers spent one night in Mexico City, and the following morning they set out for the border. Charlie Kendricks followed them through Customs at Nogales.

Swan cleared over $20,000 on the grass. He lost $4,000 in one week betting, paid off an Irving Trust loan with $5,000 of the take, and $2,000 he invested in a hash scheme that failed. The rest went more slowly, a lot of it to bartenders in New York. He and Alice, who were living on West 88th Street in New York at the time, had taken a house on Fire Island for the summer. They lived well. By September the money was gone.

What happened next happened fast, and it began by way of an accident—one of the typically fortuitous events which distinguish Zachary Swan's life from that of the average man.

Zachary Swan is not a personally fastidious individual. In fact, if one were not struck by his almost comic absentmindedness, his undisguised failure to acknowledge the presence of his immediate surroundings (a characteristic incongruity intimated by the meticulous nature of his work), one would be tempted to think of him as sloppy. Traveling in his wake on an average day is like following a Panzer division through Europe. Whatever he touches turns to residue. It is not unusual, for example, to find as many as three of his cigarettes burning simultaneously in various ashtrays around his house, forgotten or ignored after the first puff, not because he does not enjoy them, and not always because he is drunk or preoccupied, but more often because he is simply unable, by virtue of temperament, to collate the necessary data to streamline such a task. When he does manage to devote enough attention to a cigarette actually to smoke it, the ashes more often than not end up in his lap or on the carpet (his own or his host's) at gravity's whim. He confronts them as he would an unexpected guest; to the random evidence of his own existence he is no more than a witness.

The most elementary details elude Zachary Swan. With several thousand dollars in smuggling money one year he bought a new Porsche coupe, and before he had had it a month his and Alice's dogs had torn the interior to shreds, an outcome he had not foreseen, but one with which he was not impressed either. He drove it that way for as long as he owned it. Nor is he any more careful with his clothes; rolling around the yard in a three-hundred-dollar suit with a Labrador retriever is not something he remembers until he is confronted with a wardrobe shortage. His material survival, it seems, is purely a function of contingency. His minute-to-minute life he conducts as if it were a raffle. He leaves the caps off felt-tipped pens, mayonnaise jars and toothpaste containers. He loses phone numbers frequently and is rarely in possession of his eyeglasses. He never leaves a hotel room without leaving something behind. He misplaced his girl friend once on the beach in Cartagena (he found her in the same place a year later). When the hard money is on the line, Zachary Swan is devastatingly efficient, but under routine conditions he makes it through the day on idiot's luck.

Only for a few hours each day, the intimate early-morning hours right after he wakes and while everyone else is asleep, does Zachary Swan seem to be in possession of the rudimentary personal discipline required by daily living; only then does he exhibit the fundamental self-awareness normally associated with the higher primates and commonly thought of as critical to a successful participation in any activity which is not the exclusive province of plant life. And it was at such a time on a morning early in August, while imposing his daily ration of order upon the chaos of being alive, that he stumbled upon part of a neglected back-issue of *The New York Times*. Before stacking it with a pile of periodicals destined for recycling, he folded it neatly, exposing what newspapermen refer to as the break page, page one of the second section (*The New York Times* is a broadsheet—you know, like the *Tombstone Epitaph,* impossible to read on horseback; tabloids, like *The New York Daily News* and *Rolling Stone,* have no break page), and it was a mild shock of recognition that sat him down with it amid the unattended clutter of the previous evening. What Swan had recognized on the *Times* break page was the smuggling article he had been reading the night Charlie Kendricks was arrested, the article in which Customs Commissioner Myles Ambrose had been quoted. He read it now for the second time, and when he finished reading it he cut it out of the newspaper.

Alice awoke an hour later and found Swan sitting at his desk over a pad of legal paper and an uncapped felt-tipped pen.

"Hi," she said.

He smiled, turning to look at her. "Good morning, Allie. How'd you sleep?"

"I don't know," she mumbled, "I was asleep."

Swan stood up laughing and put his hands on her shoulders.

"Al-lie!"

He said her name as if it were two, accent on the last syllable, a song. She rubbed her eyes.

"Hey, Allie, is Uta still living with Michel Bernier?" he asked.

"Uta?" she yawned. "You're asking me?"

"I thought you'd get a kick out of it."

"I don't know. Why don't you call her?"

"I want to talk to *him*."

"I think his name's in the book."

"How do you spell it?"

"In French."

"Terrific."

Swan hunted for the phone book.

"What do you want to talk to him for?" Alice asked.

"I think he used to live in Colombia, didn't he?"

"I think he's lived everywhere," she said.

Swan found the number. When he went to the kitchen to make the call, Alice sat down at the desk. She was waking up very slowly. She took a sip of Swan's coffee and did not like it any better than she had the last time she had tried it. Though she persevered, Alice Haskell had been unable, thus far in her life, conscientiously to develop any bad habits. She put out Swan's cigarette and moved the ashtray. Propping her head up with her hand, she made a serious attempt to keep her eyes open. On the legal pad in front of her she saw a series of calculations Swan had made. The numbers looked familiar. She recognized some of them as the quantities and dollar amounts that dealt with the last Mexican move. But written beneath those were figures she did not recognize. In this second set of calculations the dollar amounts remained the same, but the weights were different—proportionately they were smaller. It became obvious that here the pounds and ounces had been converted to metric weights. Continuing down the paper were still further calculations, where the metric units were embellished with alphabetical notations. The letter "k" recurred most often— it showed up in every calculation—kilograms. The letters "m" and "c" occurred on every other line. Marijuana, possibly. And centigrams? Through sleepy eyes she followed the calculations down the page, feeling sorry for anyone with such sloppy handwriting. Numbers were multiplied, totals were divided, and arithmetical proportions were indicated. At the bottom of the page a large circle had been drawn. Across the diameter of the circle lay the felt-tipped pen. She stared at the pen for a while, then pushed it aside lazily with her index finger. Beneath it, in Swan's distinctive scrawl, she read one word. It was written in longhand, capitalized and underscored twice. It was "Cocaine."

Michel Bernier answered the phone on the first ring.

Michel Bernier embodied all those individual characteristics that Americans find distasteful in a man— he was French. Dark, lean and languid, he wore his heritage like a badge. He was heir to the loose mouth, sunken cheeks and puffy lips that enable the French to deal with their language. He had the eyes of a kept woman and the deep, sultry voice of a Boul Mich café singer. He was narrow at the hip, his wrists were limp, and he moved with the fluidity of a worm. Many women and not a few men found him handsome. Of the men, the most recent was an alcoholic artist named Gomez, who had bought Bernier from a Colombian aristocrat for an unfinished landscape he managed to paint in the gaps of a two-day stupor and who had lately been abandoned by Bernier after having burned himself out so badly he could no longer see straight—and thus, as Bernier saw it, could no longer pay the freight. One of the women was Uta Dietrische.

A German national, from Heligoland in the North Sea, Uta had come to the United States as an *au pair* in 1964. She was eighteen years old at the time and had been in the country less than a month when she met Zachary Swan on the beach at Fire Island. She moved into his apartment in New York a week later and stayed for six years. Uta was an authentic blonde with an even tan and eyes as blue as a night in jail. She had good bones, a narrow mouth that turned down at the corners, and a voice that was resonant of post-war Berlin, the kind of voice that filters well through blue cigarette smoke and the sound of a five-against-two piano playing downstairs, husky and haunted, reminiscent of rainy nights, two-dollar Scotch and black-market penicillin. Her shoulders were broad, her back erect, and she carried herself with the frightening dignity of a woman whose looks had been beaten into her. Her hair was long and straight, she stood five-feet-eight in her bare feet, and she was easily one of the most beautiful women who had ever looked north to the land of the midnight sun. Like anything that good to look at, she was fragile, and from the day she was born to the minute of her most recent drink, Uta had run up against some of the hardest luck in the world. Michel Bernier was her latest mistake.

Michel and Uta were the victims of unsynchronized disgust for one another. Mutual passion was something they worked at. Between the two of them they represented every sexual idiosyncracy imaginable—Uta was bisexual, Michel was everything else. If Uta was not a true manic-depressive, she was not far short of it, and, as if to stave off its rapid approach, she had recently turned over all her psycho-motor responsibilities to the trusteeship of modern chemistry. While living with Swan, she had enjoyed six years of relative peace and stability—probably, although neither would admit it, because they loved each other very much. But living with Michel was another thing; it was his job to look out for her now, and he frequently took a belt to her, beating her brains around as if to remind her that she was crazy. On a cool evening in the middle of August these two creatures of God were sitting at Zachary Swan's dinner table eating his food, conversing pleasantly with their host and hostess, and wondering, not without justification, why the hell they had been invited.

The answer to that question was an involved one, and one which had a lot to do with Myles Ambrose, the Commissioner of Customs. Mr. Ambrose had told *The New York Times,* in front of Zachary Swan and the rest of the world, what every drug cop in America had known for a long time about cocaine— which was pretty much nothing at all with a lot of authority behind it. He did know that cocaine was beginning to show up in increasing quantities as contraband at a lot of his ports of entry and he had the statistics to prove it. He should have quit there. It would have made a nice press release. The rest of his news was a sloppy synthesis of legend and office politics. And worse.

In an effort to illuminate his myths, Mr. Ambrose embarrassed himself further by citing a case study. Using one of his recently apprehended suspects as a model, he took the reader on a trip to South America, explained how a buy was made, detailed the trip home, recommended a 50 percent hit with lactose, and offered as an example his own sucker's method of distribution. Zachary Swan did not know anything about cocaine, and he was not likely to learn much from this article, but he did know something about smuggling, and it was the math that took his larcenous soul by storm. He could not resist the numbers. Even if Ambrose had confused dollars with pesos, even if he had confused them with yen, the numbers came up strong—the truth was that a kilo of coke was worth about three station wagons full of grass, two-point-two pounds, and you could fit that into a loaf of bread. Michel Bernier, late of Colombia, was the man to see.

Before the coffee was cold, Michel and Uta had the answer to their question.

"I'm thinking of going to Colombia," Swan said.

"Business or pleasure?" Bernier asked.

"Business."

Uta was staring at Alice. She lit a cigarette.

"The coffee's delicious," she said.

"It's instant," said Alice.

"Investing in coffee?" Bernier asked.

"No." Swan smiled.

"Is Vinnie still in Mexico?" Uta asked.

"He's doing traveler's checks now," Swan answered.*

"In Acapulco?"

"He's in New York," Alice said.

"No, Michel, not coffee," Swan said.

"And not tea?"

"I'm moving up (sniff)."

"I see."

"Have you been there recently?" Swan asked.

"I have a friend in Bogotá."

"A businessman?"

"He is seventy-two. He was born in Cali with a tree outside his window. He has been (sniff) taking medicine since then and has not stopped. We used to go for holidays to Santa Marta. He would put his finger on his nose as he walked along the beach, and the beach boys would know instantly what he wanted to buy.

---

* See Appendix II.

His name is Vincent. You will like him. I will be writing soon, I will give him your name."

Exit Michel Bernier.

Michel and Uta were not to disappear from Swan's life altogether, but it was to be several months before they returned—separately—to the arena of his operation. Swan's next move, before making the final decision, was to see Ellery.

"Ellery," he said, "I'm looking for a connection in South America."

As simple as that. And Ellery produced, like a magician a rabbit, a connection in South America. His name was Tito. Tito, twenty-two, was a Colombian, and he had an uncle who owned a restaurant in Peru. Swan questioned Tito on more than one occasion, corroborating through him what he had been able to learn from other sources. Most significantly, Tito knew about the mail. He corresponded often with his aunt in Lima, who sent him an occasional package. He told Swan that a large package was considered freight and therefore examinable. A package sent first class was considered mail, and legally, at the time, was not supposed to be opened. Customs did, however, try to X-ray them, he said; they had a fluoroscope, but it would take nothing larger than a loaf of bread.

Swan based his first move on this information and what little more he was able to pick up. He knew he would not need a passport. At the time Americans were allowed to travel to South America on tourist cards issued by the airlines upon presentation of a birth certificate. Avianca Airlines was the carrier of choice.

On a rainy day at the end of September, Alice came in late and found Swan at the desk.

"Hi," she said.

"Hi, Allie."

"Did you get my message?"

"I did. Thanks."

"Ellery's been trying to get a hold of you."

"I got him. You haven't heard from Lillian, have you?"

"Lillie Giles?"

"Yeah."

"No, I haven't. Why?"

"I want to talk to Charlie."

"I don't think they're coming back."

"How long have they been gone now?"

"Since June, almost four months."

"He'll be back."

"What did Ellery want?"

"He had some news for me."

"Good or bad?"

"Good news."

"What's up?"

Swan lit a cigarette.

"I'm going South."

5

Aesthetics and Anaesthetics

COCAINE IS THE CAVIAR of the drug market. On the street, where an equivalent amount of premium-import marijuana can be obtained for a mere $40 (anywhere up to $80 for top-of-the-line Colombian), cocaine commands a price in excess of $1,000 an ounce. And, like high-quality caviar, it most frequently embellishes the diet of the avant-garde and the aristocratic, a leisure class—in New York, a *Who's Who* among actors, models, athletes, artists, musicians and modern businessmen, professionals, politicians and diplomats, as well as that sourceless supply of social-ites and celebrities of no certifiable occupation. The common denominator is money. And it is fashionable in the high-profit purlieus of Harlem—with pimps, prostitutes and drug dealers, any neighborhood heavy-weight with influence on the street. Coke is status.

Significantly overshadowed by cult-fidelity to ups, downs, acid, mescaline and hemp during the drug explosion of the late 1960s, cocaine in the mid-seventies has emerged, unequivocally, as the most popular illegal drug in America—the drug of choice. Its popularity and the attractive profit margin it guarantees have accounted for an indicative increase in its traffic on the black market over the last ten years. In 1960 the United States Bureau of Customs seized six pounds of illegal cocaine at American ports of entry. In 1974 the same agency alone seized 907 pounds. In the five-year period between 1969 and 1974, Federal statistics show a 700 percent increase in the government seizure of the drug overall.*

Because cocaine is illegal and because it leaves no lingering traces in the body, it is difficult to count the number of people who use it; because it is not addictive, they rarely turn up at hospitals or drug clinics. As inelegant as snorting anything seems to be, most of the people who can afford cocaine are not the kinds of people one is likely to find in public hospitals or listed on police registers. More likely they are to be found coming out of the Athletic Club or the rear door of a Rolls. To snort cocaine is to make a statement. It is like flying to Paris for breakfast. These are people who raise the pedestrian procedure of inhaling to the formality of a tea ceremony. Chop up the crystals, divide the pile into "lines," one for each nostril—call it a one and one—and with a bank note of impressive denomination rolled into a straw . . . *snort*. To skip the preliminary ritual, take a bejeweled sterling silver coke spoon, about the size of a dental tool, and scooping the coke right out of its container . . . *snort*.

It's what's happenin'. And at a thousand dollars an ounce, it is probably not *happenin'* to you.

What goes on behind the lines, between the nose and the central nervous system, is what every coke user, regardless of his economic background, has in common. Back there, in the higher centers of the brain, something is taking place—he feels good. And that is the name of the game. Psychoactive organic chemicals are Nature's way of saying "high." And this psychoactive organic chemical, which has been saying it for centuries, may very well say it the best.

Cocaine is a white, crystalline alkaloid derived from the leaf of the coca bush, *Erythroxylon coca,* a shrub cultivated in the Andean highlands of South America. The plant grows best on the eastern slopes of the

* See Appendix III.

Andes, in Bolivia and Peru, between 1,500 and 6,000 feet above sea level in a cool, humid, frost-free ever-green zone with a mean annual temperature of be-tween 65 and 68 degrees Fahrenheit that varies very little from day to day. Coca requires little attention and provides three to four harvests a year, attributes that few other crops can offer. Left upruned, the culti-vated plant may grow as tall as twelve feet; South American *campesinos,* peasant farmers, exploiting the botanical principle of apical dominance (it works as well for coleus and cactus as it does for coca), cut the tree back to three or four feet, keeping it within reach, forcing it to branch outward, thicken and produce more leaves. The green leaf, glabrous on one side, dull on the other, varies in size and shape according to the subspecies of *E. coca* to which it belongs, but is gener-ally oval, pointed at its outer end, and marked by a prominent central vein; it grows from one to four inches in length and from half an inch to two inches in width. The leaf of the coca tree is the plant's cash crop.

The leaf's known existence and use dates back at least a thousand years to high-plains Inca reli-gious ceremonies. In the sixteenth century, morality-legislating Spanish conquistadores discouraged its use among the Indians slave-laboring in the King's gold mines—until they discovered its potential as an in-centive to the twenty-four-hour workday. Several mil-lion Altiplano Indians still chew coca leaves today to fight fatigue and to anaesthetize themselves against the high winds and chilling temperatures of altitudes of up to ten thousand feet above sea level. And to get high. The leaves are dried carefully over a fire, or in the sun, then allowed to "sweat" for about three days until the crisp, dry leaf becomes pliable. The *coquero,* the Indian coke-chewer, chews his quid of leaves with an alkaline ash-paste or a bit of lime—these liberate the existing alkaloids, at least fourteen of which have been isolated in the laboratory from the coca leaf, and only one of which is cocaine. The natural plant contains only 0.5 to 1.5 percent cocaine, a bitter alkaloid; the Indians seem to prefer the sweeter leaves, lowest in its content. It was the coca leaf, and not, as commonly thought, cocaine itself, with which Pope Leo XIII's *Vin Coca Mariani* was infused: a tonic for which Parisian pharmacist Angelo Mariani selected only the sweetest leaves and one which was esteemed for its therapeutic value by many leaders of nineteenth-century European society.

In its natural form, coca is rather nourishing. It contains Vitamin C and many B vitamins, and as a non-habit-forming stimulant recommends itself for therapeutic use in modern medicine. It cures altitude sickness, tones the entire digestive tract and promotes the health of the oral cavity and teeth, properties which result from synergy between cocaine and the associate compounds in the leaf. According to Andrew T. Weil, M.D., formerly of the Botanical Museum of Harvard University, "If there is a cocaine problem, its essence is the confusion of the whole leaf with a single component isolated from it. That confusion is a legacy of misinformed science of the last century, which has burdened us with a troublesome white powder and deprived us of the benefits of a useful green medicine."

And that brings one to an investigation of this "troublesome white powder," this motiveless malignity called cocaine, to which is attributed the downfall of more than one poor soul, but one which, by all accounts, is much less malignant than it is maligned.

Coca arrived in Western Europe with the blood and the gold of the Incas, but it was not until 1855 that a German scientist named Gaedcke first isolated from it an alkaloid he called *Erythroxyline* after the genus name of the plant (classified by A. L. DeJussieu and listed in Lamarck's *Encyclopédie Méthodique Botanique* as *Erythroxylon coca* in 1783). The species name, *coca*, is Spanish, derived from the Quechua word *kúka,* then *cuca,* meaning tree, primal tree to

the Incas; and it is from the Spanish that another
German, a chemist named Niemann, who purified
Gaedcke's alkaloid in 1860, derived the name cocaine.

Cocaine is an organic crystalline compound, C_{17}-
$H_{21}NO_4$—benzoylmethylecgonine, an ester of ecgo-
nine, an amino alcohol base, and benzoic acid. In its
pure form it is white. Its crystals are long and prism-
shaped. Its chemistry is that of the hydrocarbons. Its
elements, carbon, hydrogen, nitrogen and oxygen,
bond covalently—they share electrons. As an alkaloid,
cocaine is, by definition, a complex, organic base. Its
pH is greater than seven. In solution it turns litmus
paper blue. It is water soluble, and by giving up an
unshared pair of electrons it will react with an acid
to form a salt. To the taste it is bitter. Loosely, it is
a carbohydrate. It contains no protein. Or fat. A cocaine diet must be supplemented with food in order
to sustain life. This much Niemann knew in 1860.
And little more.

It was not until twenty-four years later, when a
young, twenty-eight-year-old Viennese physician,
never to be distinguished for his medical traditional-
ism, took the first close look at it, that anything new
was learned about this drug. And since Sigmund
Freud's *Über Coca* and five subsequent papers, issued
between 1884 and 1887, were published, no official
study of the drug's impact on human beings has been
made. (In 1974, 114 years after cocaine's discovery,
90 years after Freud, and 60 years after the United
States government in a seething righteousness-frenzy
began funneling massive amounts of money into the
enforcement of its statutes prohibiting the possession
and sale of cocaine, Dr. Robert Byck, a pharmacolo-
gist at the Yale School of Medicine, was awarded a
$200,000 National Institute on Drug Abuse contract
to study the acute effects of cocaine in man.) Freud's
cocaine papers, delivered while various surgeons were
experimenting with cocaine as a local anaesthetic, detail the results of research he performed upon himself

and a colleague, and they remain the only source of empirical data available to modern scientists. What is known today about cocaine is principally hearsay. Freud's firsthand research and the clinical evidence he produced was for years interred—as Marc Antony warned us it might be—with his bones. Only the folk-lore lived after him.

Freud discovered cocaine to be medically beneficial as a general stimulant—toward the enhancement of a sense of well-being and the temporary suppression of lassitude—and saw in it therapeutic possibilities for the treatment of digestive disorders. He recommended it as a treatment for severe malnutrition and as a local anaesthetic. He thought it might cure neurasthenia—the condition he later called neurosis—and tried it on some of his neurasthenic patients with some success. In oral doses of from .05 to .10 grams, liquid solution, Freud announced, cocaine lifted him from depression, steadied his mind, suppressed his appetite, and strengthened his hand; it was beginning to seem to him a wonder drug:

"Long-lasting, intensive mental or physical work can be performed without fatigue," he wrote; "it is as though the need for food and sleep, which otherwise makes itself felt peremptorily at certain times of the day, were completely banished. . . . The psychic effect consists of exhilaration and lasting euphoria, which does not differ in any way from the normal euphoria of a healthy person . . . one senses an increase in self-control and feels more vigorous and more capable of work . . . one is simply normal, and soon finds it difficult to believe that one is under the influence of any drug at all."

Freud was describing the moderate use of small doses of cocaine, and modern clinical research corroborates his findings—Freud was right. Where Freud went wrong, ultimately, was in expecting too much of the drug. He was sure cocaine would cure morphine addiction, and in his enthusiasm for the miracle powder he pressed it on a senior colleague, Dr. Ernst von Fleischl-Marxow, a morphine addict, who took what Freud called "frightful" doses of cocaine in an attempt to relieve his pain and in the hope of curing his addiction. It was cocaine's failure to do either and von Fleischl-Marxow's disastrous reactions to the mega-dosage (among which he claimed hallucinations) that did so much to invalidate Freud's work in the eyes of Viennese doctors and cause Freud's other claims for the drug to be ignored. In one of the later papers Freud found it necessary to defend himself against charges made by a Viennese physician, Emil Erlen-meyer, that he had loosed "the third scourge of the race," worse than the first two, alcohol and morphine, upon the world.

Leaving the further investigation of cocaine to his colleague, Carl Köller, who had found the drug to be an effective local anaesthetic in eye surgery, Freud eventually abandoned his research.

Eye surgeons soon discovered that Köller's anaes-thetic damaged the cornea and excessively dilated the pupil of the eye. (This dilation is known as mydriasis.) They would not discover cocaine's synthetic equiva-lents until early in the twentieth century. (Einhorn synthesized procaine in 1905.) At the same time, how-ever, William Halsted, of Johns Hopkins, who would become known as the father of modern surgery, was developing nerve-block anaesthesia in the United States, using cocaine as a regional anaesthetic. J. Leon-ard Corning, in 1885, produced spinal anaesthesia in dogs, but several years passed before the technique was used in clinical surgery. Hall, with the use of co-caine, introduced local anaesthesia into dentistry in 1884.

Between 1884 and 1906 in the United States, co-caine achieved such popularity that it glutted the mar-ketplace, spawning an era described by some historians as that of the "great cocaine explosion." Cocaine parlors, which catered to a polite clientele, opened in many major cities, the drug was available in saloons, served in whiskey shots, and the hoi-polloi could buy cocaine preparations from any number of door-to-door salesmen. Advertising had brought it into every home in America. Patent medicine companies packaged cocaine, coca extract or coca leaves in syrups, tonics, liqueurs, capsules, tablets, hypodermic syringes, cigars, cigarettes and nasal sprays, everything from Agnew's Powder to Ryno's Hay Fever-n-Catarrh Remedy; until it was made illegal, cocaine was endorsed by the Hay Fever Foundation and touted by American doctors as a cure for everything from alcoholism to the common cold. By 1902, surveys indicated, only 3 to 8 percent of all the cocaine sold in major metropolitan areas was going to doctors and dentists. America was buying the rest off the shelves. (In 1906 it was estimated that some 50,000 patent medicines were being manufactured in the United States. U.S. Treasury Department figures for 1904 show that 4,125 pounds of cocaine, either refined or in the form of coca leaves, were imported into the country; in 1905, 4,060 pounds. In 1906, 2,600,000 pounds of coca leaves, enough to yield approximately 21,000 pounds of cocaine, reached America.)

It was during this era that soda fountains first appeared in America's drug stores (in New England, soft drinks are still called "tonic"). In 1886 an Atlanta, Georgia, company introduced a patent medicine containing coca extract, marketed, amid a lot of fanfare, as a tonic to "cure your headache" and "relieve fatigue." They called this "remarkable therapeutic agent" Coca-Cola, "the pause that refreshes." But by 1903, seventeen years after the drink's debut, a growing body of medical opinion, indicating that cocaine might be hazardous to Americans' health, and the pressure applied by fear-crazed Southern politicians to keep cocaine out of the hands of blacks, was enough to prompt the Coca-Cola Company to remove the cocaine from its soft drink. From then on the drink was flavored with de-alkaloided coca extract and hit with caffeine to give it an edge. In 1906 the Pure Food and Drug Act effectively put an end to the cocaine explosion.

It was not until 1914, however, that the drug was made illegal. In support of its ultimate proscription was that same campaign to legislate morality which led to the Volstead Act six years later; prohibitionists were as passionate about coke as they were about alcohol. But the charge against cocaine which engendered the greatest fury and led to its classification (erroneously) as a hard narcotic—its prohibition never to be repealed—was a racist one, and it was given currency by the medical profession. Writing just before the First World War, a Philadelphia doctor named Christopher Koch warned of the dangers the country faced from cocaine-using blacks of the rural South: "Most of the attacks upon white women of the South," he said, "are the direct result of the cocaine-crazed Negro brain." In *The New York Times,* February 8, 1914, Dr. Edward H. Williams, citing Koch and echoing fears firmly established by 1910, reported "Negro cocaine fiends [as] a new Southern menace." The fear spawned by these and other physicians coincided with a rise in lynchings in the South and helped speed the passage of the legislation reinforcing segregation and voting restrictions which was designed to limit the social and political power of blacks in the early years of this century. (Though there was no concrete evidence of this "cocainomania," some Southern law enforcement agencies converted from .32 to .38 calibre ammunition, convinced as they were by these medical reports that the smaller rounds would never stop a "coke-crazed nigger.")

Soon black crime in particular, and the demented and the violent in general, became so closely associated with cocaine use that most Americans welcomed its prohibition. History suggests that cocaine was condemned by the medical profession not on the basis of any evidence that the drug was dangerous, but in fact because it severely threatened the physician's traditional privilege to grant and withhold medicines. While delivering the final blow to the multi-million-dollar patent-medicine industry, the spectre of the black cocainomaniac—just what the doctor ordered—helped secure the image of the doctor as public benefactor, an image tarnished by a miracle "feel-good" drug, the prescription of which put a doctor on par with a cosmetologist or wine-merchant, who catered to whims rather than needs, and it is in keeping with the tradition of modern medical practice that shortly after the eradication of cocaine, the American medical community began touting a new "feel-good" drug—the amphetamines—synthetic, marketable, and well under the medical thumb—and probably the most dangerous piece of chemistry since Alfred Nobel gave us dynamite.*

Cocaine was finally driven underground by the Harrison Narcotic Act of 1914. (By then forty-six states had already passed legislation restricting its use and sale.) It disappeared briefly, surfacing in the twenties and thirties as the drug of choice among musicians and film people, *à la recherche du temps perdu,* and was effectively absent during World War II, not to emerge again until the rock years, when musicians picked up on it once more. With the passage of the Act and subsequent legislation (specifically the amended Narcotic Drugs Import and Export Act, 1922), cocaine was classified as a narcotic—which by any pharmacological definition it is *not*—surprising to no one today, given the ignorance and moral frenzy that surrounded the drug at the time; what staggers the modern imagination is that in the year of America's Bicentennial, the mistake has not yet been officially acknowledged, let alone corrected. Today, the possession or sale of cocaine carries the same penalties as that for the possession

---

* See Appendix IV.

or sale of heroin—five years under the Federal statutes, fifteen years to life in New York State. The considerable medical evidence that has come to light in defense of the use of cocaine since the drug culture gained establishment status in the late sixties only seems to reinforce a citizen's mistrust of the government wisdom.

Cocaine, externally applied, is a vasoconstrictor—it inhibits bleeding. And it inhibits impulse conduction in the body's nerve fibres; it was in this way that it became the first local anaesthetic in modern surgery. It is still used in operations on the larynx and in certain surgical procedures on the pituitary. Ear, nose and throat specialists sometimes use it, applied in liquid solution, for nose surgery. Its synthetic relatives are benzocaine and procaine, the latter marketed (in quantity to dentists) under the trade name Novocain. The synthetics differ from the original, however, in terms of versatility and application.

Coke taken internally, either in crystalline form or in solution, acts as a peripheral nervous system stimulant. It does so in much the same way that other antidepressants do. Norepinephrine (or noradrenalin), the hormone released by sympathetic nerve endings in the human periphery whenever they are stimulated, and which causes the blood pressure to rise, is normally reabsorbed by the nerve so quickly that the reaction is imperceptible. Cocaine reinforces this stimulation by inhibiting the reabsorption of norepinephrine by the nerve. There is no clinical evidence to support that a similar process occurs in the central nervous system, but the suspicion is that it might. Because there is no evidence that cocaine increases the strength of muscular contraction, one must assume that the ability of the drug to relieve or delay fatigue results from central stimulation, which masks its sensation. While the blood pressure increases, the body temperature, due to greater muscular activity under nerve stimulation and a decrease in heat elimination under vasoconstriction, rises (cocaine is markedly pyrogenic). The heartbeat accelerates, the pupils dilate. You are high.

The body metabolizes cocaine quickly. The high is brief. Cocaine takes effect more rapidly when injected (Sherlock Holmes was fond of a 7 percent solution), slightly less rapidly when snorted (the average dose is 20–30 milligrams) or gummed (rubbed into the gums of the mouth), and least rapidly when swallowed (hydrolized in the gastrointestinal tract). The stomach begins breaking it down immediately. When taken for the suppression of appetite, essentially by way of stomach-lining anaesthetization, cocaine in oral dosage may be the best. Freud often drank his cocaine in an aqueous solution and did not enjoy what users today, most of whom snort the crystals, look for in theirs: the rush that comes when the powder, dissolving in the nose and upper throat, is rapidly assimilated into the bloodstream, and the clear, open breathing that comes when the cocaine shrinks the mucous membranes and clears the sinuses and bronchi. The "freeze" that some coke users cherish is the numbing sensation that follows the drug's anaesthetizing of the mucosa of the nose; if it is an authentic freeze, it comes from a heavy hit of Novocain or Lidocaine—Freud had the advantage of pure; hard to come by on the street.

Cocaine's rush, or flash, is most profound when the drug is taken by way of the intravenous injection of a prepared solution. Call it the mainline. But the intravenous injection of anything, especially an illegal drug, is risky at best. Even doctors muck it up sometimes. And as far as sterile equipment is concerned—well, it is something you have trouble finding even in a lot of major hospitals. Given the state of the art, and the random sampling of cuts available to every dealer through whose hands street-coke passes, shooting up is a sucker move. (Sherlock Holmes was buying pure, and he was cutting it himself, with water. And he was Sherlock Holmes.) Forget it.

The effects of cocaine upon the average individual

are so subtle that many users do not recognize a reaction until one is pointed out to them. Many acid-freaks, most mushroom-types, an addict of any kind, alcoholics and some heavy marijuana smokers think cocaine is a waste of money. Serious dopers hate it. Cocaine has no edge. It is strictly a motor drug. It does not alter your perception; it will not even wire you up like the amphetamines. No pictures, no time/space warping, no danger, no fun, no edge. Any individual serious about his chemicals—a heavy hitter—would sooner take thirty No-Doz. Coke is to acid what jazz is to rock. You have to appreciate it. *It* does not come to *you*.

Street-coke, if you buy it by the gram, may be cut as much as 80 percent; by then all it will do is numb your nose, and that is more likely the work of the cut than of the cocaine. At fifty to a hundred dollars a gram, it *is* a waste of money. High-grade coke (anything 80 percent pure or above) is something obtained only in quantity. And that subtle, seductive *frisson* that pre-ops you for about six hours of root-canal work on the brain is expensive. The greater the number of people who handle coke before it gets home, the more often it is going to be hit. Everybody puts a whack on it before he sells it. Lactose (milk sugar) is a common cut; dextrose is sweeter, easier to spot; various amino acids, which are tasteless, provide a high-grade cut, but are much more expensive and harder to come by than the carbohydrates, and thus are not often used; nor is quinine. The Italian laxative, *Mannite,* is very popular; it is heavier than lactose (coke is sold by weight) and it takes on the coke excellently. Procaine and the other synthetics are used because they enhance the freeze. Amphetamine cuts are popular because they ensure a noticeable high—they also burn the nose.

A good coke dealer will choose his cuts according to his clientele. And what every coke dealer knows is that there are very few people out there who know anything at all about cocaine, and fewer still who have ever snorted pure. Everyone's expectations are different. Every user's standard of quality is a measure of what he snorted the last time. If a user wants speed, a good dealer gives him speed; if he is looking for a freeze, he gets Novocain. Some think lumps are a sign of purity—a dealer will wet the coke down. A dealer dealing in quantity, buying and selling kilos, will hit his product with borax, because it is extremely heavy. He not only doubles his weight, but he doubles it with less than a full hit. If he ounces out a good count to his steady customers, he peddles what is left to the sucker trade, keeping the customer satisfied. The retail sucker market in cocaine thrives on the same buyer mentality that prevails on Madison Avenue—*if he's selling it for seventy-five dollars a gram, it must be cocaine.*

Latin America supplies all of the cocaine sold in the United States, where the demand for the drug has increased so greatly that the price of coca leaves in some South American countries has risen 1,500 percent since 1973, from four dollars to sixty dollars a bale (or *tambor*). Because of the large quantity of leaves required to produce cocaine—in kilos, anywhere from 100/1 to 150/1—the leaves are often processed by the *campesinos* themselves (most of them Indians) in stills close to the growing areas. (The cultivation of coca is carried on in small terraced plantations called *cocales,* usually hillside clearings of two or three acres with an average of seven thousand plants to the acre.) The stills required are no more than oil drums containing a solution of potash (potassium carbonate), water and kerosene in which the leaves can soak. When the alkaloids soak free, the fluid is drained off and the leaves removed, leaving behind a brown paste, which when treated with hydrochloric acid will yield an equivalent amount of cocaine. (Call it cocaine hydrochloride, which is what illegal cocaine actually is. The chemical division of Merck Sharp & Dohme, one of the principal manufacturers of official pharmaceutical cocaine in the United States, markets the alkaloid bonded to the same cation. "Merck," as it is commonly called, is cocaine hydrochloride.)

Cocaine processing does not require sophisticated chemistry; a lab can be set up with about $1,500 worth of equipment. Bolivian traffickers buy the paste from the *campesinos* and either process it themselves or export it at a 300 percent profit to laboratories in Argentina, Paraguay, Brazil and Chile. Until the 1973 Allende overthrow, Bolivia exported most of its paste to Chile, which has always been known for having the best cocaine chemists in South America; it was they who first taught the Bolivian *campesinos* how to turn the coca leaf into paste. Peru (with Bolivia, the only other Latin American country where the cultivation of coca leaves is legal—together they produce approximately 11.5 million kilograms of leaves a year, the world's largest importer being the United States, which buys 200,000 to 250,000 kilograms annually) exports chiefly to Ecuador and Colombia. And Colombia sends more cocaine to the United States than does any other country in South America.

The mathematics of the cocaine trade, from South American soil to New York nose, in the absence of any other contingency which attends it, is enough to keep the traffic alive forever. A South American farmer makes less than $2 a kilo for his coca leaves. A trafficker will pay him around $350 for a kilo of paste. A chemist, if he buys from a paste trafficker instead of directly from the farmer, may pay up to $1,000 a kilo for paste. Delivered in Latin America, a kilo of cocaine, 90 to 98 percent pure (as pure as it gets), costs anywhere from $4,000 in Lima to $8,500 in Buenos Aires. A dealer with a mobile lab can turn a $350 raw-material investment into a $6,000 product. A good lab can process one hundred pounds of cocaine a week.

When the cocaine leaves South America, the mathe-

matics gets heavier. In New York, a kilo of coke sells
for over $30,000. That is what a smuggler charges.
But the kilo which the smuggler pays $6,000 for in
South America is pure. He can put a full hit on it, turn
it into *two* $30,000 kilos, and sell his product 50 per-
cent pure, converting a $6,000 investment into a
$60,000 product. And he can make more if he ounces
it. Most smugglers, however, who will always sell their
product in quantity when they can (like anything else,
especially something as perishable and incriminating as
cocaine, the faster you move it, the longer you stay in
business), will not step on their product that hard.
They will move kilos at no less than 80 percent. They
will sell their ounce-dealers coke that has been stepped
on a little bit more. An ounce-dealer will pay between
$850 and $1,000 an ounce for 70 to 80 percent
pure, then step on his ounces himself and turn them
over for a few hundred more. Grams go for $50 to
$100 in New York; a gram-dealer never sells better
than 50 percent coke. After all, he has to pay for the
tinfoil. Cocaine is a seller's market. A dealer can hit
his product as hard as he wants, and the sucker trade
is large enough for a gram-dealer to unload his goods
fast. The only way to get pure is to buy in quantity,
and even then there is no guarantee. A smuggler who
snorts his own product will usually cut it slightly to
mellow its passage, but what he is cutting is pure, and
he is only cutting it slightly. And he is snorting it right
away. And as any smuggler will tell you: There is
only pure, there is nothing else; if you are not buying
pure, you are not buying cocaine.

"The stuff they blow on the street is shit compared
with what we're doing. That's why they're doing two
and two's and three and three's. We do a one and one
and we're high."

The smuggler is the man out front in the cocaine
traffic. And the traffic is getting heavier. People are
crossing the border every day with coke stashed in

everything from vaginas to live snakes. Drugs are coming into the country in boatloads bypassing those borders. Since the day the doctor stopped making housecalls and we all learned to dose ourselves, and since the day we learned that alcohol was not the only game in town, dope has become a very big business. There manifests itself today in the United States an increasing demand for drugs of all kinds. Alcohol consumption is up, tobacco consumption is up, marijuana consumption is up, pill-popping is as popular as ever; Americans are taking a greater variety of drugs, and taking them in greater quantities, than ever. Uncle Sam calls it drug abuse.

The term *drug abuse,* as employed by the Federal government, enjoys about as much grammatic and syntactic validity as the term *self abuse.* And their own abuse of the English language is not the only thing these two expressions have in common—for example, they both refer to activities that feel good. Where they differ is on much more subtle ground. The former, *drug abuse,* lacks the theological thrust by which the latter excuses itself; that is, in the stale locker rooms of Judaeo-Christian tradition, an individual has the opportunity to abuse a body not theologically his own, a body on loan from a higher Office, say, where interest rates are low. Hence, *self abuse* evolves and is embraced by the language. But in order to participate correctly in *drug abuse,* one would be required to anthropomorphize the drug in question— impart to it human characteristics—or ultimately to abuse the drugs of another (which is done not infrequently, but usually only by agents of the Federal government). Drug *misuse,* on the other hand (also frequently practiced by agents of the Federal government), is what the laws of the United States in fact prohibit. And it is these laws that are at issue here. One is compelled to accept the implications of a medical and legal *misuse* of drugs. It is in an attempt to rationalize the determinants of this misuse that one encounters difficulty. After all, it did not take medical science two thousand years, and this in the shadow of the Church, to prove clinically that masturbation does not lead to blindness. If it takes that long to show that a little dope is just as harmless, it is not because the biochemistry is any more complex—it is because medical science is exerting all its efforts to prove the opposite.

What medical science, under the auspices of the United States government, has been able to uncover in the way of *prima facie* evidence to support the Drug Enforcement Administration's case against chemicals on its list of Controlled Substances parallels the strides made by the Unicorn in its pilgrimage across the minefield of evolution. What at first required a mere exercise of faith on the part of the American taxpayer now, on the threshold of the twenty-first century, calls for the willing suspension of disbelief. The mound of misinformation generated unashamedly by the hulking and etherized beast of government research is dwarfed only by the stack of money it costs to feed the monster, while the bureaucratic campaign to keep the beast incumbent thrives on nothing more substantial than its own propaganda. The rewards of the system are minimal. And the Controlled Substances list is the Domino Theory of the seventies.

Government antidrug literature tells us that cocaine use results in paranoia and organic psychosis. The country's most reliable experts on cocaine have been unable, either through hospital admittance records or through evidence given by clinical psychiatrists, to uncover any case of psychosis directly attributable to the drug. The best one can gather from the data available is that psychotics who use cocaine will be psychotic. The same literature tells us that coke users experience suicidal depression when deprived of the drug. Such depression has not been reported in recent medical history, even among users who consumed coke daily for years. Cocaine is not habit-forming, nor do its users develop a physical tolerance to it. Any "craving" for cocaine will develop along the same lines as the craving for money, sex, apple pie and chewing gum. Nor is cocaine an aphrodisiac—there is nothing in the chemistry of cocaine, beyond its properties as a peripheral-nervous-system stimulant and mood elevator, to indicate that it in any way enhances human sexual response—although inhaling seventy-five dollars into your bloodstream in a matter of seconds, and that at the risk of fifteen years in jail, must do something for your libido. Most of the drug's folklore, including its ability to prolong sexual performance, is anecdotal. Some men believe in applying cocaine to the glans penis to anaesthetize it against premature ejaculation, but doing so is more an act of bravado than one of clinical merit. Solarcaine, available over the counter at a fraction of the cost, works as effectively. In terms of myth, what cocaine has done for fornication it has done ten-fold for formication—the spontaneous abnormal sensation that insects are crawling over your skin. That is one of the things they like to tell you will happen if you get on the wrong side of coke—one of the literature's favorite horror stories. It is as untrue as the rest. What *is* true is as conspicuous by its absence in the literature as is the folklore by its presence. Because the government knows nothing about drugs, it does not know that there are *good* reasons for not doing cocaine.

Long-term snorting of cocaine can irritate and possibly damage the tissue of the nose, especially the septum. The chronic vasoconstriction results in ischemia and subsequent sloughing of the mucosa, by which the avascular septum is protected; and though antihistamines will do the same thing, chronic cocaine use, after tertiary syphilis, is the second most common cause of septal perforation.

". . . *my mucous membranes is just a memory*
Cocaine . . ."

"Cocaine Blues"*
REV. GARY DAVIS

There is abundant proof that the local anaesthetics
are destroyed chiefly by the liver. Because cocaine is
broken down and detoxified there, those with severe
liver damage are advised to stay away from it. A few
people who use cocaine may be allergic to it, as one
might be allergic to bee stings or penicillin; for them
the risk of anaphylactic shock is a serious one. There
are certainly more deaths each year attributable to
aspirin than can be attributed to cocaine throughout
history; like almost anything else, however, there is a
lethal dose. It can be found to vary from individual
to individual, and can be found very easily: fill up a
syringe and shoot a gram of pure; if it does not kill
you, increase the dose until it does. (Do the same
with coffee, Scotch, delta-9 tetrahydrocannabinol or
lighter fluid, and you are playing the same game.) It
has been demonstrated clinically that, since 1914, the
greatest danger connected with the moderate use of
cocaine is legal and not chemical.

Cocaine's popularity in the United States may very
well be a function of the fact that it, more than any
other of the recognized psychoactive drugs, reinforces
all those character qualities that have come to be ad-
mired as truly American: initiative, drive, optimism,
the need for achievement and the embrace of power.
Wherever it comes from, that popularity is clear and
present. (A recent experiment showed that rats,
Pavloved to push a reward lever, did so up to 250
successive times for caffeine, 4,000 times for heroin
and 10,000 times for cocaine.) Cocaine is called "nose-
candy" for a reason. People like it. It makes them feel
good. And it makes them feel good in a way that its

---

* Additional lyrics.

substitutes, procaine and benzocaine, do not. Cocaine has a sweet and subtle second-strike capability. And it was this second-strike capability that appealed to Zachary Swan—the mind-caressing, power-infusing, psychic jolt that carried him beyond the dreams of his childhood and into the kaleidoscopic wonderland of middle age.

Going South

6

A Rainy Day
in Santa Marta

"COLOMBIA. And that's not an Ivy League University"
—Zachary Swan.

Nor is it located in Morningside Heights. Colombia, with an "o," one of the few conspicuous republics in South America, occupies 439,828 square miles of prospective real estate on the northwest coast of the world's fourth largest continent. Embellished by the umbilical Isthmus of Panama, the continent's overland route to the north, it is embraced by both the Atlantic (in the costume of the Caribbean) and the Pacific Oceans, and bordered inland by Venezuela on the east, Brazil on the southeast, and Ecuador and Peru on the southwest. Its population hovers somewhere near twenty million. At Santa Marta in the north, the Sierra Nevada rise out of the Caribbean, a prologue to the Andes which dominate the western half of the country from Venezuela to Peru. At Leticia, in the country's southeasternmost corner, the Amazon, coming out of the Peruvian Andes, begins its two-thousand-mile journey across Brazil to the Atlantic. North of Leticia, delimiting the country's lower quarter, is the Equator.

Colombia's capital and largest city is Bogotá, population three million, located 8,660 feet above sea level in the Cordillera Central range of the Colombian Andes. The country's natural resources include vast tracts of arable land, a favorable climate, abundant mineral deposits and two oceans. Colombia is the world's largest exporter of emeralds—it accounts for

80 percent of the total. It is famous the world over
for its coffee. Its economic and political history is
the subject of more than one course of study at
Georgetown University's School of Foreign Service
(because its economic and political future, like that
of every South American country, is the foster child
of United States business interests and the CIA); its
cultural history, American Indian in origin, is of interest to archaeologists and anthropologists everywhere;
and, because it has the greatest variety of birds of any
single country in the world, one might say it is of interest to a few ornithologists as well. But to a significant majority of the world's under-thirty population,
Colombia, South America—national flower, the orchid
—is best known for its dope. The finest marijuana
in the world grows here. And though Colombia, itself,
is not South America's largest producer of cocaine,
it is, through a combination of geographical, economic and political forces, what amounts to general
headquarters and central bank for worldwide cocaine
traffic.

When Zachary Swan stepped off the plane in Santa
Marta with his finger on his nose, neo-dynamite, high-
altitude, Colombian-loco-weed marijuana had just hit
the headlines back home like a debutante at a cock-
fight. Colombian dope, overnight, had become a
growth industry. Like every fishing village along the
coast, Santa Marta had come alive, and was throwing
all its resources behind the national effort. At least
two nights a week the local power plant would shut
down while the smugglers, by cover of darkness, took
their cash-crop cargoes aboard and shipped out. Police bribes were the savings bonds of the nationwide
drive. Swan had flown first to Peru, but left after two
days, having been advised by Tito's uncle, the restau-
rateur and an avid coke user, that things there were
hot, there was nothing coming down, that the police
in Lima, alas, were honest.

After walking around on the beach in Santa Marta

for three days, coming on to all the acid-heads like a kind of shipwrecked, beat-generation Ronald Colman with a sinus condition . . . as if the sight of a middle-aged packaging executive in cut-off, tie-dyed Levis were not enough for *them* . . . Swan decided to give his index finger a rest. After all, he had charged this trip to American Express. And if Michel Bernier had been wrong about Santa Marta, it was a good bet that he had been wrong about his elderly friend in Bogotá as well; and if in the end every lead was going to dead-end on him like this, Swan figured, at least in Santa Marta he could pay some serious attention to working on his tan. On the evening of the third day, after dinner alone at his hotel, Swan spotted a campfire on the beach about a hundred yards from the hotel grounds and strolled down toward it (with his hands in his pockets) to take a look.

Here, silhouetted in the firelight, he saw many of the same faces he had been passing on the beach during the daylight hours, the faces of young people, camped out, dug in for the night about thirty yards from the tide line, waiting for the sun, the Apocalypse, Godot or the local police to move them on, killing time and themselves in the process. It was what Swan would see very much of throughout Colombia before he left the country for good, and having never seen it before in his life he was unprepared to see it now for the nightmare it would be. Here he met a young man named Blackie, whom he had not seen previously. Blackie, who spoke English and was determined someday to live where it was spoken by everyone, was pleased to have found an American to talk to. Blackie was about twenty years old, half-Indian and half-Negro. Raised as part of a tribe near Leticia, he saw Santa Marta beach life as a kind of upward mobility. His African genes governed his skin color and hair. He was lean and strong. Dressed in a bathing suit and wearing a silver Aztec medallion around his neck, he was something extraordinary to behold. He gave Swan his first hit of Santa Marta Gold, and before long the two of them were old friends.

From Blackie, Swan learned of an American in Santa Marta, a Texan named Paul who was rumored to have a cocaine connection. Blackie himself had a friend in Barranquilla with a definite link, but advised Swan to see the American first because he was local. Swan was staying at the Hotel Tamaca in Santa Marta's Rodadero district. The next morning he and Blackie walked along the beach to Tahiti Estates, a tract of low-income oceanfront housing where Paul lived. The Texan wanted $8,000 a kilo and $1,000 down, a price Swan knew was way out of line. (In questioning people around town, Swan subsequently learned that the Texan was actually supporting himself by taking advances and then disappearing on his customers, hanging out in Tobago until the heat was off.) Swan would have to go to Barranquilla.

Before he left Tahiti Estates, Swan was introduced to two American women, in their early twenties, who all of a sudden began to tax his understanding. He could not tag them. *Two American girls . . . not on the track . . . in their early twenties . . .* was all he was able to put together. They had been making lunch when he met them, a kind of fish stew, and there were bones and fish parts on the floor all around them. In the air around them there was an aura of dope and mushrooms.

The older of the two was Jane, tall and big boned, whose dark brown hair took on the appearance of a hat. It covered her ears and almost met her eyebrows. It was thick and curly, fluffed up into an Orphan Annie Afro, but she looked more like Sluggo's girl friend than Punjab's. She looked Jewish, and Swan was sure she had spent more than an afternoon in Brooklyn. Her friend, April, was short. Her hair was blond and straight. She was rather plain. She played the guitar. Both of them were dressed in long, loose blouses and nothing else.

Jane and April had fish stew and psilocybin for lunch. Swan asked them how they liked the stew. A half hour later, April said:

"We like it, we're stuffed."

They removed their blouses and ran out into the ocean. Swan asked Paul who they were.

Paul explained that a rich, middle-aged lunatic from San Francisco, appropriately named Mad Walter, in 1968 had chartered a plane and given fifty Haight-Ashbury street people round-trip tickets on it to Tobago. About twenty of them had made it back to the States. The rest, having sold their tickets—for dope or to extend their stay—or having been robbed of them, were now strung out all over Colombia and Venezuela, camping, backpacking, hitchhiking, getting beaten, robbed and raped and periodically jailed, some of them trying to get home, some trying simply to get by, and others, like Jane and April, just not trying at all anymore.

Swan would meet Jane and April again, in Cartagena, and, as he had done today, he would refer to Jane as June and ask questions like, "April? May June?" But beneath it all, he knew that the joke was on him. The nightmare had begun. Because these two women (and he thought back to the campfire of the night before) were just two of the many such people he would run across (and over, and around, by and sometimes with) on this and subsequent trips to Colombia, people of no certifiable age, background, job description, socio-economic class, outlook or future, people who were just . . . *there* . . . young men and women with the likes of whom Swan had had absolutely no previous experience, and for whom he would be able to do little but occasionally draw bail. These people were on the edge, their presence sometimes no more than physical, anchored to a place in time only by an accident of physics, the children of Einstein, their existence relative . . . *the only Universal constant known to man is the speed of light* . . .

each in his own accelerated frame of reference . . .
here they were, right out of the pages of the *Mutability
Cantos,* Spenser's doubts confirmed . . . all is flux . . .
*pass the mescaline . . . what's that, an aspirin, I'll
have one of those* . . . anything . . . up is down, day
is night, communication is dead.

> "All that you touch
> All that you see . . .
> All that you do
> All that you say . . .
> . . . everything under the sun is in tune
> but the sun is eclipsed by the moon."

> "Eclipse," from *Dark Side of the Moon,*
>   PINK FLOYD

That evening Blackie's sidekick and dope curator,
Fernando, rolled one of his special joints—an entire
issue of *Time* Magazine rolled around almost half an
ounce of Colombian chiba-chiba; it took three matches
and a Zippo to torch it—and Swan spent the night in
Never Never Land with all his new friends. He left for
Barranquilla the next day.

Santa Marta is the oldest European-founded city on
the South American mainland. Established in 1524,
still devoted chiefly to agriculture and fishing, it stands
surrounded by a string of nine bays backed by the
Sierra Nevada, the highest peaks in Colombia and the
present-day home of the Arhuaco Indians. Snow-
capped year round, the mountains provide an awe-
inspiring contrast to the tropical Caribbean—if Balboa
had come this way he would never have discovered
the Pacific. El Rodadero Beach, where Swan stayed
when he was in Santa Marta, lies between the airport
and the city itself and is rapidly becoming the country's
most important resort.

Barranquilla, the second-largest city in Colombia, is located about a hundred miles southwest of Santa Marta at the mouth of the Magdalena River, eight miles upstream from the Caribbean Sea. A combination port city and industrial sewer, Barranquilla displays all the drawbacks of South American coastal life and none of its advantages. An embarrassment to most Colombians, it is a city choked and teeming with disease, a south-of-the-border Dickensian cesspool, decidedly urban but in no way cosmopolitan, a kind of backwater Bogotá without the mountains that everyone wishes would disappear. They do not mention it much in the travelogues. What it amounts to, in the minds of Colombian tourists, is one vast and uncomfortable waiting room to be tolerated as briefly as possible while making international flight connections at its airport. Americans never hear about it until they get there.

Swan and Blackie, with Fernando in tow, took an express bus from Santa Marta to Barranquilla, a four-hour ride through the countryside and Swan's first exposure to the rural realities of South American Indian life. The trip also afforded Swan his first look at the Colombian Army, by way of the soldiers who manned the numerous checkpoints along the road. More of a Federal police force than an actual army, these men provided the government with a kind of internal Customs, a grass-roots privacy-invasion force designed to intimidate long-hairs and indigents in transit, enforcing the dress code, as it were, and taking advantage of young women on the lam . . . *Uncle Simón Wants YOU . . . good pay plus all the contraband and ass you can get.*

In Barranquilla, Swan met Blackie's friend, whose name was José. José was short and round, a lower-middle-class Colombian with an apartment of his own, who spoke a little English, and, though Swan did not know it yet, was a rank amateur. But José was trying. He went out to score a sample and was gone six hours.

He was trying hard. The room was hot (as they always are ten degrees north of the Equator), and by the time José returned, Swan needed the lift he had expected cocaine would give him. But Swan was something of an amateur too, at least as far as cocaine was concerned, and when he failed to get an immediate reaction, looking for a rush more on the order of that which speed is famous for, he was disappointed. He gave José $100 and took ten grams. He had come with $4,000; he would look somewhere else. Swan said thanks, Blackie said goodbye, Fernando said nothing, and they left. They missed the last bus to Santa Marta, so they took a cab.

The next morning Swan was back on Rodadero Beach. This time he met four Americans. Bill was a bookie from New Orleans. His girl friend's name was Elaine. Mike was a bartender and was traveling with a woman named Terry. Both of the women were cocktail waitresses. All had just come from San Andrés, a Colombian island off the coast of Nicaragua. They were on vacation. They had grass and mescaline and invited Swan back to their hotel to get wrecked. Swan accepted the invitation and brought along his cocaine.

From the Americans, Swan learned that his cocaine was, in fact, excellent. They explained the subtlety of the cocaine high, and they told Swan his connection had done well by him. Swan then decided that if he did not find anything better in Santa Marta, he would go back to Barranquilla and invest the balance of his grubstake in José's product. If he did go back, however, he would not go back alone—the next morning on the beach he met René Day.

René Day was a Canadian, tall and quiet, broadshouldered and lean in the face. He had short, curly dirty-blond hair, and eyes the color of smoke. He was twenty-eight years old, more intelligent than anyone Swan would run across in Colombia, and he was careful, or at least appeared to be. He and Swan would become close friends. Swan would learn later that

René had been born into money in Quebec and did what he did for the hell of it.

What René Day did before he started smuggling cocaine was pretty much whatever he felt like doing. When Swan met him he was carrying at least three passports. He had been making money cashing his traveler's checks in at banks and casinos in cities throughout Colombia and the next day going somewhere else to report them stolen. He was a very casual fellow, a good con. He loved Colombia and had backpacked throughout South America. He would hit a city in the morning looking like a vagrant and at ten in the evening would show up at the nearest casino wearing a white linen jacket, sipping Scotch and breaking the hearts of elegant women at the blackjack tables. He was well educated, confident and mature. His father was English, his mother Québecoise. He spoke fluent French. He loved women as a class, they loved him, and René was never out of their company for long.

The woman he was traveling with when Swan met him on the beach at Santa Marta was twenty-three years old, a Canadian law student René had known for two years and who had come back to Colombia with him after his most recent trip home. Her name was Debbie. She was tall and fair, as attractive as one would expect a law student to be, with long brown hair and dark brown eyes. She was nearsighted and wore wire-rimmed glasses which she never adjusted once they were on. She was a vegetarian by inclination (which made staying alive in Colombia difficult) and a Chapstick addict by virtue of her need for at least one identifying vice. She had a mind of her own, and Swan thought she talked like a lawyer. Debbie and René had just hit town and were off to visit friends. Swan went along.

Over the next three days, as Swan and René got to know each other, they pooled their efforts in the search for a coke connection. It became a two-man operation. Swan was seeing René and Debbie every night at dinner, and he was hanging out with them on the beach during the day. Blackie was always around, though he was not allowed near the hotel, and Fernando was always somewhere nearby. Mike, Terry, Bill and Elaine had left town. One evening after dinner, Swan was sharing his coke with Debbie and René, snorting through a hundred-peso note, when René suggested that the three of them try the casino.

"Can I get in like this?" Debbie asked. She was wearing jeans.

"I doubt it," said Swan.

"No problem," said René.

René reached for his knapsack, pulled it over to the bed on which he was sitting, dug his hands into it and pulled out a cellophane bag. He handed the bag to Debbie.

"Try this," he said.

In the bag was a cocktail dress.

"Rennie!"

"My little bag of tricks," said René.

"Perfect," said Swan.

"This is a survival kit." René heaved the knapsack onto the bed. "Man does not live by bread alone. Casinos are very important to me."

René reached into the sack again and pulled out a pair of trousers to match his linen jacket.

"Do you believe this guy?" said Debbie.

"You call him Rennie?" asked Swan.

"That's his name."

"Yeah, I guess it would be," Swan said. "Rennie."

Swan loved it. He called him Rainy. The name stuck.

When Swan and his pal Rainy Day failed to come up with anything in the way of a cocaine connection in Santa Marta, they decided to see José in Barranquilla.

Swan had been advised to stay at the Del Prado Hotel when he got to Barranquilla: "Everybody stays there. Every deal that happens, happens at the Del

Prado. There's no second-level hotel in Barranquilla. It's a hot, sweaty town. Spread out all over. If you tell somebody you're in Barranquilla, they just go right to the Del Prado to find you. You're either there or at the discotheque across the street. You just don't go any farther."

Swan had sent a message to José via Blackie and was waiting at the Del Prado when he bumped into Mike and Terry and their friends having dinner by the pool. (They had been asked to leave their hotel in Santa Marta when it was discovered that they had been smoking dope in their rooms. They were heading west.) Swan was planning to meet José that evening and set up a score for both himself and René. He sat down with the Americans and ordered coffee. His back was to the door. By the time his coffee arrived it was dark out. Swan was lifting his second cup of coffee to his lips when Terry said:

"There's your connection."

Swan, a bit confused, put down his cup and looked over his shoulder. He let out an audible groan, ducked his head and said:

"Uh huh."

Mike, who had decided to make a buy after talking to Swan, said:

"I've changed my mind."

José had come through the door, stopped, shifted his eyes from side to side without moving his head, pulled at his sleeve cuffs, twitched his shoulders and begun to stroll nonchalantly around the pool. He was wearing wrap-around sunglasses. He passed Swan's table without looking, paused, moved away very casually and sat down a few tables away. He took in the scenery, looking everywhere but in the direction of Swan and his companions. If one did not know him, one would think he was a cocaine dealer making a connection with five Americans . . . *at that table over there*. Swan and his friends all stood up and left the place.

Five minutes later, looking from the window of his room, Swan saw José standing below him in front of the hotel talking to a young, well-dressed Colombian with blond hair. When the stranger left, Blackie walked up. He and José talked for a minute, until Blackie was run off the grounds by a hotel employee. Blackie called Swan at the Del Prado later that evening from José's apartment.

"What happened?" he asked.

"Meet me in an hour across the street," Swan said.

An hour later, Swan was feeding Blackie at a hamburger stand around the corner. He ordered him a milk shake and said:

"I want to jump José."

Blackie stopped chewing.

"I want to get to his supplier. I want to meet with the blond kid."

Blackie took the milk shake.

"José's my friend," Blackie said.

Swan pulled out his money.

The blond kid's name was Emilio. His father, a Frenchman, was a money changer, one of Barranquilla's chief currency dealers. During the day, Emilio worked in his father's office. At night he handled about 80 percent of the cocaine sales to Americans out of Barranquilla. Swan met him that night at the discotheque across the street from the Del Prado. Emilio wanted seven dollars a gram. He could deliver in 24 hours. Swan and René scored the following night at the hotel.

Before leaving New York, Swan had been introduced to a very heavy individual named Anthony. Anthony was a man involved in crime in a rather professional way. He was organized—from above. He was not at all what Swan had expected. He was young, literate, and among thieves honest, but he was at the same time very dangerous, and Swan was not above showing him the proper respect. Swan had been introduced to him by Ellery, who had explained to Anthony that Swan was reliable, had stood up when Charlie Kendricks was busted, and was a very good investment if he, Anthony, were looking for one. "He's going South," Ellery had said. Anthony, as it happened, was looking for a sound Southern investment, and Swan was looking for financial backing. But between the time Anthony was able to change the unmarked tens into currency streamlined for travel ("Maybe you could give me hundreds, instead, something I can carry without the briefcase") and the time Swan was ready to pick it up, Anthony had talked to Nice Mickey, Pirata's friend, who suggested that a man with techniques as Byzantine as Swan's might be a bad risk. So Swan left New York with a polite excuse from Anthony (instead of the money) a "maybe next time," and what he had been able to pick up in the way of an education. Anthony had shown him how to run cocaine purity tests.

The deal went down in a room two floors above Swan's at the Del Prado, a room near the stairway, reserved exclusively for the transaction. Swan was carrying $3,000, and under his arm he had a satchel in which to carry the coke back to his room. He was nervous. Emilio came in with a young man named Ricardo, a partner. Emilio, a professional, knew better than to walk into a room with cocaine and no backup man. René was behind Swan. The cocaine was triple-wrapped in clear polyethylene to protect it from the moisture. Swan ran two tests on it before snorting it.

A water test is done with a clear glass tumbler and cold water. Crystals of pure cocaine dropped into the water will dissolve before they reach the bottom of the glass. Impurities will slick out on the way down. A smart buyer will fill the glass himself, because a smart dealer will fill it with warm water if given the chance (which is exactly what Ricardo did when Swan let him fill this one). Swan had never seen the test done, and because he did not know exactly what he was looking for, he gave the coke a passing grade. It looked good enough to him. The second test he ran was a burn test. He placed the crystals on a piece of cigarette foil and heated them from beneath with a match. If the coke were pure it would bubble and leave a light brown film. A mix would turn black and leave lumps. In this case the film was dark brown and there was some scum, but the residue was not dark enough or lumpy enough to key Swan. Before he snorted the coke there was a knock at the door. He froze.

Emilio reached into his shirt and pulled out a revolver, pearl-handled, beautiful. Swan was impressed. Emilio stood behind the door while Ricardo opened it. Swan reached into his satchel as if he were carrying a gun, which reciprocally impressed Emilio, and he discovered then that René always traveled with a knife in his boot. It was like television. Ricardo opened the door to find a hotel maid standing outside the room. She apologized for the disturbance, handed him four towels and left. Now everyone became that much more professional. They had shown off their hardware.

Ricardo reached into the overnight bag he was carrying and pulled out a three-posted gram scale, folding model. It was worth a lot of money and of a kind rarely seen outside a pharmaceutical lab. It was very impressive. While Ricardo was setting the scale up, Swan sampled the coke. He experienced a distinct rush. He was pleased. He paid for three hundred grams, and René bought half a kilo. They said goodbye, and Swan was out of the hotel in thirty minutes, wondering what to do next. He checked into a nondescript, pay-as-you-go tourist inn, and that night, alone in his room, he made the fill.

The package Swan mailed to New York was the product of painstaking preparation, much more elaborate than necessary. The load, 300 grams, was the smallest he would ever send, and the package in which he sent it was the largest. He had spent several days in New York preparing the necessary materials and over six hours in Barranquilla making the fill.

The package measured 30 x 20 x 20 inches, too big for the fluoroscope, according to what Tito had told him. But that was not enough for Swan. In the event it *was* somehow X-rayed, he wanted the package to be deceptive. In New York he and Alice had taken a corrugated cardboard box, ripped it open, and measured the distance between the corrugations. Alice did a piece of artwork, black on white, which simulated striped wrapping paper, the distance between the stripes corresponding to the distance between the flutes in the corrugated cardboard. Swan went to a printer he knew and had gift wrapping printed to match the artwork. The stripes he had printed in metallic ink.

In Barranquilla he took a large, corrugated box he had come up with down there, and with a coat hanger broken at both ends he enlarged the flutes along its edges. He funneled the coke into the flutes with a piece of stiff plastic he had carried from New York, not sure he would be able to find any in Colombia. He spent six hours funneling the coke into the flutes. Inside the corrugated box he placed another box, filled with infants' gifts—a large doll, various stuffed animals, rattles and the like, and two of the largest containers of Johnson's Baby Powder he could find. He punctured one of the containers with the coat hanger and spread the powder around the inner box, figuring that if the outer box broke, there was a chance that the cocaine would be taken for baby powder when the package was opened. The inner package, the package of infants' paraphernalia, was gift wrapped with the metallic-stripe paper. If the box was X-rayed, the stripes of the inner package would be picked up, and they would convincingly account for the inordinate density along the corrugations caused by the presence of coke. Only Zachary Swan could have invented this puzzle. Ultimately confronted with the package, a Customs agent who was more than curious would have come down with a stroke. Swan double-wrapped the whole thing in supermarket gauge, plain brown paper, addressed it, tied it with heavy string, and waited for the Post Office to open.

Swan checked out of his room a few hours later, pounced on one of the tourist-hungry cab drivers hanging around the front entrance of the establishment before the cab driver had a chance to pounce on him, and said:

"*Oficina de Correo.*"

Colombia has two mail systems. One is run by the government for in-city mail as well as domestic and international surface mail, called *Correo Urbano* and *Correo Nacional* respectively. The other, air mail, or *Correo Aereo,* is run by Avianca Airlines with both a domestic and an international service. Swan used the latter. He had the cab driver mail the package for him. He said he wanted it sent first class, gave him some money, and waited by the door for his receipt, ready to run if the package were nailed. The cab driver asked what was in the package—he had to make a Customs declaration—and Swan said, "*zapatas,*" leather sandals, a favorite with American tourists in Colombia. The cab driver mailed the package, handed Swan the receipt, and drove him from the Post Office to the airport. Within an hour Swan was on a plane to Cartagena.

Swan spent three days in Cartagena, working on his tan, and took a direct flight from there to New York. (Pan American was flying via Miami once a week.) He arrived home at about midnight. Alice, who had been doing everything but offering Masses in her anxiety over his absence, gave him a desperate kiss at the door and said:

"The package is at Davis's."

Swan felt like Eisenhower entering Europe.

Davis, an old college friend of Swan, owned a small wholesale cosmetics business on Broadway near 48th Street. The loaded package had been addressed, in care of Davis's offices, to Jorge Enrique Ramos, a former company stock boy who had quit the previous year and gone back to Puerto Rico. Davis had been told to expect the package. Ramos was a part of his corporate records, so in the event of a bust, Davis was covered. On each trip to Colombia, no matter how much coke he was moving, Swan would send a package to Davis as a matter of course. He quit doing so, however, the day Davis called to tell him his latest package had arrived with a new mailman. (On that occasion the pickup was never made.)

Waiting for his flight in Cartagena, Swan, from his hotel window, had spotted René and Debbie walking on the beach, and on his way down to catch up with them found Blackie being chased around the hotel pool by a groundskeeper with a machete. Blackie was captured and carted off to jail by tourist police.

(Being black or Indian—Blackie was both—or an indigent white in Colombia is bad karma, especially in a resort town. On the weekends it is particularly rough, because middle-class Colombian tourists converge on the Caribbean beaches then, and on Friday afternoons, in preparation for their arrival, the local police begin cleaning the place up. The overall effect on people like Blackie and his friends is that of a harvest, and by Friday night everybody is hiding, either in the woods or on the outer beaches like the one at Tahiti Estates. The rap—just being caught off limits—is usually worth a weekend in jail and a few beatings; for a young woman, that and the chance of rape by either the cops or the jailers or both, although she can buy her way out of a stretch with what amounts to the same thing performed with the arresting officer; and if there is a dope charge on top of the vagrancy rap, particularly if the kid is an American, there is often a four-figure release fee set by the arresting officer's immediate superior, or whoever is in a position to collect the money when the check arrives from the folks back home.

When the blackmail is not applied directly by the cops, it is handled by the defendant's lawyer, who takes his blood money off the top and *then* cuts in the superior police official. The American consulates and Embassy are very good at recommending the right lawyer for the job. It is not without reason, therefore, that the cop making the collar negotiates on the scene —if he follows through with the arrest he ends up with nothing, or, at best, the smallest slice of the pie.) *

That afternoon Swan and René, who finally caught up with each other, put some money together and bailed Blackie out. Later, Swan, René and Debbie were sitting by the pool having dinner, not talking about cocaine, but not unaware of the danger represented by doing business in the company of the likes of Blackie. (Swan had not asked René if he had yet moved his coke. René would tell him later that he had simply stuffed it into a couple of souvenirs and mailed it from Barranquilla, addressed to himself in care of his father's business in Montreal. Maybe.) Swan said, with reference to Blackie:

"Rainy, that guy is heat."

René nodded. He thought for a minute, then turned to Debbie and said:

"We gotta shake him."

Debbie frowned, looked at René and shook her head.

"Blackie is trouble, every place you go," Swan told her.

"Do what you want," she said. She turned again to René. "I'm staying with Blackie."

The next day she and Blackie took off. Down the coast. Swan, who had not seen it coming, tried to apologize to René.

"If it's all right with her, it's all right with me," René

---

* See Appendix V.

said. "She's old enough to take care of herself and as long as she's O.K., I'm not going to worry about it."

Swan and René said goodbye. René flew to Canada to distribute his coke. He showed up in New York, three weeks later, with another woman.

7

A Way With
the Spoon

ZACHARY SWAN'S FIRST CAPITAL investment upon his
return to the United States was a laboratory gram
scale. It was the one precision instrument, with the
possible exception of a good automatic weapon, that
was demanded by the cocaine trade. Swan selected an
Ohaus, three-posted, equal-arm pharmaceutical balance with stainless steel trays—it appealed to the professional in him. It cost $150. And it was metric. It
did not know an ounce or a pound from a counterfeit
Deutsche Mark. He was impressed.

For almost two hundred years Americans have been
trying to come to grips with the metric system; refusal
to adopt it, from black market conversion tables in
the elementary school arithmetic classroom to bisys-
tematic mileposts on the nation's interstate highways,
has come to be regarded as one of the unimpeachable
insignias of citizenship. There is pride to be found in
the embrace of a system of measurement that is
unique in the world, truly one's own—different even
from the British Imperial System, though few are certain exactly how it is different—and an even further
glory, it seems, in not actually knowing what that system of measurement is called. The U.S. Customary
System, as it *is* called, officially and everywhere, is as
American as shoo-fly pie: Olympic swimming pools
have confounded us for years; displacement in liters
we have acknowledged as having something to do with
foreign automobiles and French wine; and kilometers,

whatever they are, we know had something to do with extraterrestrial real estate in "The Day the Earth Stood Still"—it might as well have been cubits our alien visitor was asking for. The International System of Units—for that is what *theirs*, the one the rest of the universe uses, is called—is un-American; if it is not furlongs or fathoms it is foreign, it is something we grant chemistry teachers for their amusement. Or so one would have thought. Until recently. Only recently—and seemingly overnight—did an entire postwar generation of schoolchildren learn that the metric system was a postgraduate course.

Whatever Congress decides, and no matter how long it takes a box of Spoon Size Shredded Wheat to go from twelve ounces to 340 grams, the truth is this: the United States of America effectively converted to the metric system in, or around, 1965—by 1970 there was not a college sophomore worth his government grant who did not know how much a gram of hash weighed. That little piece of empirical data had become a matter of pride. And, on many occasions, a matter of survival. Here was some dude, not even a chemistry major, coming on to you with mikes, grams, bricks, kilos and hundredweights; off the top of his head he could go from grams to ounces and he could tell you how many ounces he got to the kilo. He hit you with lids, caps, keys, tabs, nickel bags, blotters, buttons, spoons and everything from milligrams to boatloads. You had to protect yourself. You had to have your weights and measures down, and the metric system was where you began. Anything that came out of a pharmaceutical house or across a border . . . well, man, they just did not *know* avoirdupois weight . . . *avoir do what*? The time had come to get it together. And so today everyone over the age of twelve *knows* that there are 28.3 grams to the ounce and 35.2 ounces or 2.2 pounds to the kilogram. He may not know how many swimming pools to the standard football field, but he knows how to buy dope:

Q: *And so, Johnny, if you had a pound of apples and a pound of oranges and a fifth of a pound of cherries to sell, and you needed 600 Colombian pesos to buy a second-hand bicycle, how much would you have to sell the fruit for?*

A: *Twenty dollars a key, teach—more, of course, if I ounced it.*

There is nobody in the world, let alone at MIT or Lowell Tech, who is faster at math than a dope dealer.

When he returned to the United States, the only thing Zachary Swan knew for sure about the mathematics of the New York cocaine market was that coke was sold by weight. What he was able to learn before the distribution of his first 300 grams was minimal; what ultimately accounted for his success in distributing the load was a complementary ignorance on the part of the consumers he reached. What he began with was a guaranteed marijuana market—a broad-based, middle-class clientele that was ready for cocaine—and a small network of professional ounce-dealers who were ready to open it up.

Ellery. For all his humility, kindness, honesty and seeming sloth, and beneath the ingenuous, childlike manner which made him everyone's candidate for least-likely-to-survive given the unsavory nature of the business he was in, Ellery was a professional—no flash, no jive, nothing romantic about Ellery: he was simply one of the best dealers on the street. He had been going for years, untouched, dealing quality dope in consistently high volume, and he commanded a large slice of the market. (It is interesting to note that, apart from dealing, Ellery did nothing illegal, nor had he ever done so, in his life—he did not fool around. He did not do traveler's checks, a scam that was popular among many of Swan's friends; he did not handle credit cards or counterfeit money; he did not steal or handle stolen merchandise, and he never cheated anyone. He would drive a hard bargain with drugs and that was all. To this day he has never done anything but be an honest and dependable dealer. And, as with all of Swan's acquaintances—with the exception of Pirata, "who didn't give a fuck about anyone"—he never dealt in heroin.) Something of a joke, or maybe a curiosity, to those who did not know him well, Ellery was a man who never failed to deliver the goods; and it was to him that Swan owed every connection he had ever made in New York.

Charlie Kendricks. Swan's lieutenant, the man Swan relied on more than anyone else, Kendricks rarely worked exclusively independent of Swan as did the other ounce-dealers. The least professional of Swan's men, he was valued more for his wits and courage than for his ability to read people, and Swan missed him when he was not around. Shaken by his arrest in Brownsville, he had given up handling Swan's dope and had taken a long vacation with Lillian Giles on the money he had earned shadowing the schoolteachers through Customs at Nogales; it was not until Swan had made his third trip to Colombia that Kendricks came back to work for him. As an ounce-dealer in cocaine, Kendricks would ultimately fail—he had no street sense and was repeatedly robbed of ounces Swan had fronted him—but he would remain an invaluable right-hand man in the smuggling operation; he was a close friend as well as a professional asset. He carried a knife on occasion, which he never opened, used everything but heroin and cigarettes, and was so obviously Australian that Swan felt obliged to refer to him as the Hungarian. A former stockbroker, Kendricks was born in West Africa of British parents and had lived in Australia for more than ten years. He and Lillian Giles had come to New York via London, where they had met, and they were living on Long Island when Swan and Alice were introduced to them. The introduction was made by Roger Livingston.

Roger Livingston. Code name, Seymour; it was he whom Charlie Kendricks had been instructed to call from the Riverhead Jail. Nearly bald at thirty, bearded, nearsighted, five-ten, fair and husky, Livingston was a meticulous man, a well-organized and intelligent dealer through whom Swan moved a lot of ounces. When he and Swan met—through Ellery—Livingston had been shooting heroin, a habit he kicked shortly thereafter and one he never went back to. He had dealt a good share of Swan's Mexican marijuana load, and he was the only dealer of Swan's cocaine who mainlined the product—he still carries the scar on his right leg of a third-degree burn he received after an overdose knocked him down and unconscious against a bathroom radiator pipe in his apartment. Livingston was an excellent mechanic, a man fascinated with the world's physical equipment; he drove a jeep and owned enough tools and expensive gadgetry to open a repair shop; he knew his way around a darkroom, was comfortable in a chemistry lab, and his acquisitive mind was open to information of any kind. He wore a scuba diver's watch, and could put an elaborate pocket knife to good use. He carried a lot of keys. He had an attention span far greater than that of most of his friends, and unlike many of them, he was never idle. A biology teacher in the New York City school system, he lived with a children's clothing designer, a close friend of Alice's named Angela De Santis. He shared his apartment with her, a hundred houseplants, a vast aquarium of fish and a number of amphibians and reptiles, many of the last being snakes who often escaped their cages and had the run of the house for days. Livingston was honest, trustworthy and a good man to have around when there was trouble. He kept a cool head, knew how to take care of himself, and remained a consistent, dependable dealer on the retail end of Swan's network.

Nice Mickey. Irish, tall, thin, with blond hair, blue eyes, a deep, mellow voice and the face of a choir boy, Nice Mickey was cautious, intelligent and extremely professional, the only complete, all-around pro moving

Swan's ounces on a regular basis. Though he dealt in everything from credit cards to cocaine, he had never been busted, and for as long as Swan would know him he would not be. He had the finest street sense of any man Swan had ever encountered; quick and alert, his instincts uncanny, he seemed to possess interior antennae preternaturally sensitive to danger. He could read a street in a second, and never stepped onto one without knowing right away whether or not he was being followed. He was not particularly dangerous, but he was as elusive as the wind; his timing was superb, and he could appear or disappear in an instant. Well coordinated and sharp of eye, Nice Mickey could read an opponent like a Bertillon poster —it was a mistake to gamble with him. An expert gamesman, he consistently scored 700 in Scrabble, was lethal at cards, darts, backgammon and golf, and was a nationally ranked three-cushion billiards player. As a con artist he was unsurpassed. In the summer he worked carnivals and resort city beachfront concessions. He was self-assured, well mannered and elegant; he wore expensive clothes and owned thirty pairs of seventy-five-dollar shoes. At thirty-four he lived with his mother, who had worked most of her life as a professional cook; it was in the homes of her wealthy employers that Nice Mickey had lived as a child and in addition to everything else, he was an excellent chef. He was one of Pirata's closest friends and a good friend of Ellery. Of all Swan's ounce-dealers, Nice Mickey was the most self-reliant. His life was his own, he shared very little, and he was not as heavy a user of the product as the others. The reaction of most to Mickey was one of respect, casual trust and a certain amount of awe. He was strictly professional, and unlike the others, in the dark no-man's land where cocaine was traded, he never got beat.

Moses Wellfleet. Dr. W, six-four, 220, thirty-five year old, black and married to a white woman. Moses counted among his "friends" Sly Stone, Miles Davis

and Flip Wilson. Moses did not work for Swan, nor
was he part of the inner circle, but he handled enough
ounces to affect significantly the distribution of Swan's
cocaine. He had been handling coke for several years
before Swan met him, and his was the initial indication
that Swan's first load was "shit"; there was no way he
could move it, he said, his customers were too sophisticated. It was not until the second load came in pure
that he began dealing Swan's ounces. Moses was the
quintessential black dealer—weight meant nothing to
him. Dealing from car windows and the back rooms
of bars, a man did not tote a gram scale—he carried
spoons. A "spoon," sometimes called a "quarter," is
the equivalent of a level tablespoon. There are four
"spoons" to a "piece," which is just over an ounce.
(Sometimes the words "eighth," "quarter" and "half"
are used to refer to those fractions of a kilogram.)
When Moses scored from Swan, he spent hours over
the deal—blowing coke, talking trash, taking a break
from the street. He always came with his spoons, like
a pastry chef, and because Moses was buying by volume instead of by weight, Swan had made a small
investment in the interest of preserving the edge—a
Waring Blender, in which he fluffed up the coke just
before Moses's visits. It is significant to an understanding of Swan's position in the cocaine trade to realize
that, in all the years he was smuggling, he never
learned what, in the way of business, went down on the
street. Nor did he want to know. He dealt in weight
only and stayed as far away from the gram-dealers
and the street traffic as he could. Moses, buying
spoons, was probably dealing in lower quantities than
those to whom Swan was ouncing, if not as a rule then
at least more often, but he was turning it over fast
enough to keep Swan busy with the blender. He was
the manager of two bars in Manhattan, and it was probably through the clientele that he was moving a lot of
it. As little as he and Swan had in common, they
seemed to enjoy each other's company, and because

Moses was a responsible dealer they got along well. Dr. W was a pro; there was no nonsense about him.

Anthony. Young, younger than one would expect a man with so awesome a reputation to be, what this man was *not* was an ounce-dealer. In Swan's words, he was a very good friend and a very bad enemy —to Swan he was Mr. Big. Introduced to Ellery, Swan had gone to Anthony for investment money, cash to finance the first Colombian trip. It was Anthony who had shown Swan how to conduct the purity tests. Initially Swan had regretted not taking the money when he had had the chance, when it was offered to him in denominations of ten—he would have turned the thousand into ten thousand—but he soon had reason to be thankful for Nice Mickey's having warned Anthony off: Swan was spared the embarrassment of offering Anthony a share of the first load—Anthony, indeed, would have had first call on it—a product which, in the end, was shown to be more cut than cocaine. It was Anthony, however, who ultimately had cause for the greater regret—when Swan began showing up regularly with pure, Anthony found himself paying top dollar for a product that would have been his own by dint of a partnership. And after the third trip he never bought less than a kilo. Anthony did not keep a scale in his house, and he did not hold on to cocaine; his was a completely different way of doing business. He simply asked, "Is it a key?" If the answer was yes, it damn well *had* to be a key. He kept his buyers waiting in one room and Swan waiting in another, and the cocaine was out of the house as fast as it was in. Anthony owned at least three guns and a radio which was always tuned to police calls. He had bodyguards who were always on duty. He subscribed to a service that laundered his money and legitimized his income. He was obviously paying his dues. Aside from Swan he had another six or seven contacts, he never smuggled himself, and he was never in the vicinity of incriminating evidence for more than a minute. Swan stood to make more money ouncing a kilo to his dealers than he did selling it outright to Anthony, and at times, when the cocaine was moving as fast as he could supply it, Swan held back; but under routine circumstances, his policy was to unload in as large a quantity as possible —it did not pay to have the product hanging around —and on those occasions Anthony was the man to do business with. Cash immediately, no questions, no heat, and a 500 percent return on the investment.

Only rarely did Zachary Swan entertain the notion that, smuggling cocaine, he might be some brand of counterculture hero; and only a little less rarely did he amuse himself with the thought that being a smuggler made him a bold and rather dashing sort of figure. From the beginning, he saw himself principally as a businessman—a rather shrewd one. And as a businessman he was able to divine early many of the unwritten rules of the game.

A cocaine smuggler, once he has beaten the border, is a wholesaler dealing in a very marketable commodity. His success, like that of any wholesaler, depends on the *volume* of business he does, obviously, and on the speed of his *turnover*. But where turnover, for the average wholesaler, is the fundamental, commercial reality upon which volume is based—you cannot have one without the other—for a cocaine smuggler turnover is a manipulable variable, and its implications are a bit more complex.

For a cocaine smuggler, turnover seems not only to work significantly independent of volume, but it would seem, on the surface, to work in one's favor at whatever speed it is generated. A coke smuggler, for example, being his own supplier, stands to make *more* money dealing his product in ounces than he does dealing it by the kilo (he could make more, still, dealing it in grams, but unless he hit a few Miles Davis sellouts he would not be South again for a year).

Though ouncing cocaine is slower than turning over a kilogram, ounce-dealing yields a better bottom line —it may take a week or two to unload the ounces, but the difference, over three kilos, say, may amount to better than $50,000, which is not bad for a few weeks' work. (Kilo price does not vary significantly with volume. While gram prices are cut in half with the purchase of an ounce, and ounce prices go down respectably with the purchase of a kilo, two or three or five kilos are likely to cost exactly two, three or fives times the price of one.)

Ounce money is better than kilo money. But the fact is that a smuggler will almost never pass up the opportunity to move his product at the kilo level. He not only welcomes a rapid turnover, he depends upon it. And he depends upon it to a far greater degree than the average wholesaler. Why? In the first place, but by no means the foremost—Swan, in fact, did not learn this until later—coke is perishable. The potency of cocaine diminishes rapidly with age. The product goes bad. If the product is cut, it goes bad faster—a good cut will eat up cocaine as fast as the weather will.* For this reason alone, a cocaine smuggler cannot afford to have his inventory lying around. But there are other reasons. And to Zachary Swan these became obvious almost immediately:

If a smuggler's inventory, his stash, amounts to an ounce of cocaine, it is worth about $1,000. He can afford to lose it. If his stash is hit, he can afford the take-off; $1,000, at the level on which he is dealing, is small change. He can kiss it goodbye and forget about it. If, on the other hand, a take-off man comes

---

* There is a respectable body of opinion which holds that the potency of cocaine, a very stable alkaloid, is affected neither by time nor by any of the known cuts. Perhaps borax (sodium borate) provides an exception. Most agree that pharmaceutical cocaine, when protected from the air, has a very long shelf life. Zachary Swan knew as much about pharmaceutical cocaine as he did about nuclear physics—his was the smuggler's opinion.

at him and there are three kilos at stake—call it $150,-
000—the take-off man is going to come in on the tail
end of an M-16. And he is going to come in with that
kind of hardware because he knows, with that kind of
money at stake, that coming up against a professional,
he is going to be coming up against a shotgun at least.
The value of life, where dope is involved, fluctuates in
inverse proportion to the value of the dope; it gets
cheap fast when the dope is cocaine. If the smuggler
is lucky, and instead of a take-off man he greets the
Feds at the door, the difference between a one-ounce
stash and a three-kilo stash is the difference between
some serious heat and some life imprisonment. And
that is why the Feds carry hardware. It doesn't take
a genius to figure out that a man facing that kind of
time has nothing to lose.

Zachary Swan was not a coward, but he was not
stupid either. And it did not require any on-the-job
training for him to see that bloodshed, specifically his
own, or a stretch at Leavenworth, however long, would
be bad for business. He could guess immediately
how either eventuality would be counterproductive
—in terms of public relations alone the implications were catastrophic. Though he was by no means
shy, and though (as he would discover later) there
was an untapped reservoir of courage stagnating somewhere inside of him, Swan, by nature, had a very low
threshold of discomfort. He would give the cocaine
business a try, but only on his own terms; as soon as
the going appeared to be getting rough, for him or
anyone for whose safety he was responsible, he would
get out.

Swan was of the opinion that there was an intelligent way to do almost anything. And a justifiable way.
In addition to an adverse adrenalin reaction, he suffered a philosophical flu in the company of guns. He
had been a lousy Marine. He generally took his virility substitutes on the rocks, or lately, by way of his
mucous membranes—firearms he found perverse.

Drug running would change that eventually, and unfortunately, at least for a while, but in the beginning he was determined to play it safe. And turnover, to Swan, was where safety began. Turning over in quantity, he would deal with people who were that much more responsible. And he would deal with *fewer* people. The higher the level at which he dealt, the fewer would be the people he dealt with, and the more substantial would be that distance between himself and the street. And the street, as any smuggler knows, is where carelessness, stupidity, violence and, subsequently, risk are the greatest. Swan would deal in weight. And he would deal honestly.

After distributing the first load, Swan rarely moved cocaine out of his apartment. Out of necessity he would break it down at home, but immediately thereafter would check into a hotel—very often the St. Regis, New York's most exclusive, where security was the best—and from there he would ounce it. Swan would generally begin with a twenty-two-and-six cut. Six grams of dextrose or lactose to an ounce. If the coke was good, it could take a twenty and eight. Swan never cut it more than eighteen and ten. When he discovered borax, Swan could afford to hit the coke less. Borax was heavier, and though it made his ounces look smaller, it did not hurt the trade—there was always a gram scale nearby. Borax's other advantage was that it took the coke on well. Dextrose was a bad cut—if the coke was too sweet, the price had to come down. Lactose, not nearly so sweet, did not take the coke on nearly so well—sophisticated buyers could get a percentage by pointing out the granular differences and the change in consistency. (Also, in New York, because of the heroin problem, lactose and dextrose were unavailable—they had to be bought either on the black market or out of town.) Borax added weight without volume. Swan would stay with it until he discovered *Mannite,* and he would go back to it because of its availability vis-à-vis the Italian laxative, regarded by many as the more sophisticated cut. Though he touched the ounces, Swan never stepped on the kilos he dealt Anthony.

Swan's standard procedure, once the cocaine was in town, varied little: he broke down the packages that the coke arrived in, unloaded as many kilos as he could immediately to Anthony, then moved into a hotel and cut and packaged the remaining ounces. He always had a supply of cut on hand at home—borax required a significant amount of preparation. It first had to be boiled, then the liquid placed in a baking pan to dry. After the borax crystallized, white and shiny but less flaky than before, the crystals had to be ground down with a rolling pin, pulverized until they could pass through a tea strainer, the larger chunks being discarded. The strained crystals were then ground again and run through the mesh of a nylon stocking, stretched over a bowl, and worked back and forth with a spatula until the process was complete. It was tedious work, and Swan had better things to do, but the one time he paid someone else to do it, he had trouble—customers complained about their cocaine.

When the cocaine was cut, Swan weighed it again, then wrapped each ounce in a polyethylene sandwich bag, rolled it tightly, and placed it into another bag which he then rolled and secured with three rubber bands. He cut some ounces differently from others, and color-coded them by way of the rubber bands. He knew that Roger and Ellery would take a gram or two out and put in some of their own powder, stepping on the product before they passed it on to their customers. He knew that Nice Mickey, being the pro, would not even open the package, but go directly to the customer, deliver the goods, and pick up the money. Consequently, Swan made Mickey's ounces a little short.

In the beginning, Swan sold to his dealers at $700 an ounce. Later the price went up to $850. By the time Swan returned from his third trip (after the first, he was rarely in New York for more than a month at a time), his deals were each moving an average of three ounces a day. And it got better later on. Very often Swan fronted the ounces to Roger, Ellery and Mickey. He always fronted them to Charlie. Moses did not need the credit. There were other people, casual friends of Swan's, who occasionally handled ounces, but none who did so on the order that these men did. It was not uncommon, for example, over coffee at Victor's Café, for Ellery, Roger or Mickey, or any combination thereof, to slip Swan a couple of thousand dollars under the table. The working relationship was a good one—in the end, Swan was meeting no one new and dealing only with this select group of people. He soon moved permanently to the Hamptons, where once every two or three weeks he would call in the ounce-dealers and throw a party. On New Year's Eve, 1972, fewer than ten people went through over a thousand dollars' worth of cocaine, an entire ounce of pure which had been placed on the coffee table in a tobacco humidor.

If there were fewer women than men in the inner circle of Swan's New York network (there were none in Bogotá when that end of the operation was established), it was not something that anyone noticed; if their impact upon the business was secondary, it was ordained as such by tradition.

By smuggling standards prevalent at the time—and unchanged now—Zachary Swan's approach to women was an enlightened one; if his attitude on occasion seemed a bit Pleistocene, his behavior, more often than not, was applaudable. In dope-trading circles, as reflected in the lore, women are generally distinguished only insofar as are the men with whom they are associated. Mules, the carriers, most of them women, who when busted are often abandoned, are the hallmark of industry prejudice—a smuggler, on most occasions, laments their arrest less than he does the loss of the load. The fact that Swan never used mules—every one of his smuggles was designed with a loophole through which the carrier could walk away— is probably more a reflection of his attitude toward people in general than of his attitude toward women. And, in the end, maybe the best one can say for Swan is that he exploited women no more than he exploited most men. But if he was guilty of discrimination on the basis of sex, he was no more guilty than any man of his generation, and if his metamorphosis was slow, it was because he had that much more to learn and unlearn when he began hanging around with women of the likes of Alice Haskell.

Alice, of that newly and somewhat reluctantly emancipated breed of young woman that emerged fast in the 1970s, was by every measure a feminist; though she may not have been so successful as someone like Angela De Santis in asserting her rights—Alice was the victim of an even temperament—her politics were in the right place. She, more than anyone, taxed Swan's archaic sense of justice. Coming and going with no apparent regard for his ego, it was she, more than any counterculture contact he may have achieved by way of the dope he was smoking, who was responsible for the bearded, beaded, unbleached-cotton look he began to sport at the age of forty-two. In 1969, as she set out for Washington to march in protest against the war in Indochina, Swan, a lifelong champion of Wall Street, found himself saying, "Holler at 'em for me," and it was not long before he himself was walking down Broadway with candles in his hands, chanting. From there it was only a small step to an appreciation of the fact that, as a woman, Alice possessed more than "an important set of jugs."

Of the women who significantly affected Swan's business, there were only three in New York: Angela De Santis, by way of the constant pressure she applied on everyone to get out of the business; Alice, who in the end helped provide Swan with the courage to do so; and Lillian Giles, the only one of the three who actu-

ally participated in the operation—who herself probably had more courage at the bottom line than any of
the men involved—and who parlayed that participation
into the ultimate removal of herself and Charlie
Kendricks from the business altogether.

None of the women was ever involved in ounce-
dealing, although Alice was always on hand while
Swan was breaking down the coke and did involve
herself in occasional pickups and deliveries by way of
her unique, part-time self-employment in the neighborhood: ALICE'S HOUNDS *Professional Dog Walking Service; East Side Care, West Side Cost, Bonded,
Insured, Loving.* Alice, when her aid was enlisted, was
principally employed in the transaction of money—she
rarely handled the cocaine. On one occasion, going
directly home with the cash and the dogs—Swan was
hosting a poker game—Alice lingered, and because it
had been raining and the dogs were dry, she and Swan
had to soak them down in the bathtub before they were
returned to their owners. Swan took great delight in
the charade.

But the first masquerade in which Swan participated
as a cocaine smuggler was one that was engineered at
his expense. His first time out he had been suckered.
And he did not have to take Moses's word for it. He
was in town only two weeks when René Day showed
up. René had flown from Canada, and he had brought
his cocaine.

"I can't sell it," he told Swan.

"Your customers are obviously more sophisticated
than mine. I'm selling it with a 25 percent hit."

"Yeah, well from what I've been told that brings
it down to about 15 percent coke."

Swan and René would later discover—through
Ricardo, Emilio's lieutenant—that what they had paid
for in Barranquilla was borax, speed, aspirin, and
maybe 40 percent cocaine. The sample Swan had
initially taken from José was pure, but Emilio, know-

ing Swan had not liked the sample, had hit what he finally sold to the two smugglers with a lot of speed, a drug with an edge and one on which they were sure to get high. The heavy speed cut would have been obvious to any experienced coke user, especially in view of the purity test results. It was because Swan's customers had had no more experience with coke than he that he was able to sell it as easily as he did.

When René showed up in New York, Swan was preparing to go South. He arranged to meet René in Santa Marta within a week, took two of René's ounces and moved them before he left—he had no trouble unloading the dope. When Swan finally arrived at the Tamaca Hotel, René, who had waited over a week, was on his way to Bogotá in search of a connection— Ricardo had given him a name. René was moving fast. If René had gotten a connection through Ricardo, Swan had to assume he had already been to Barranquilla. He had. And not only that. Rainy Day had smuggled his *cocaine* back into Colombia—having crossed two borders with it on the way—and he had returned it to Emilio. He got his money back. That is how cool *he* was.

8

Snowbound in Carthage

THERE WAS NOBODY in the Western Hemisphere who was better for public relations than Uta Dietrische. No matter how you stretched it, there was never anything within eyeshot that was better to look at. She was a knockout—grown men wept when she walked by. The fact that she was absolutely crazy did not detract from her appearance; in fact, the supposition that she was in no control of her destiny whatsoever was somewhat provocative. She was a hymn to inconsonance, a bouquet of wounds.

On their first date together, Swan and Uta had gone to a cocktail party thrown by Mike Riordan. After the party, they went with Mike and his date to Orsini's for dinner. They were all drunk when they arrived and ordered more drinks before dinner, soon reaching the unanimous opinion that they needed some amyl nitrates. Swan rushed home and hit his stash. When he returned to Orsini's, Riordan was outside, in front of the restaurant, talking to two policemen in a squad car.

"What happened?" Swan asked.

"You won't believe it," Riordan said.

"Where's Uta?"

"They took her to Roosevelt Hospital."

"Mike?"

"You won't believe it."

"Tell me."

They had ordered dinner without Swan. Uta was hungry. She was so hungry, in fact, and so drunk, that she had started eating her fettucini with her hands. The captain came over to the table and told her to stop. Uta stood up and threw the fettucini at the captain. Mike took everybody outside. When they got outside, Uta threw a small fit—she was very excited. A woman walked over and said to Riordan, "I know how to handle her." The woman slapped Uta across the face—the sure cure—whereupon Uta reached back and threw a right cross, knocking the woman to the sidewalk. The police arrived three minutes ahead of Swan.

A week after their first date, Uta moved in with Swan. They lived together for six years. She was living with Michel Bernier when Swan made his first trip to Colombia. She was leaving him when Swan returned. For two or three years she had been the chief love interest of a young woman who worked on the desk at Lufthansa, and it was into the young woman's apartment that Uta moved when she split with Bernier.

When Swan decided to take Uta to Colombia with him on his second trip, he made his decision with three things in mind. First, there was the knowledge that it would be easier to look like a tourist if he were traveling with a woman—he and Uta would spend two weeks on San Andrés, an island off the beaten track recommended to Swan by the Americans in Santa Marta, and come home with scuba equipment and a suntan. And cocaine. Second, and more tantalizing, was the scam itself. Gabrielle, the Lufthansa clerk who was in love with Uta and who had done it before, would meet the plane and escort Uta through Customs reserved for airline personnel. A shoo-in. Uta would carry the coke. The third factor in Swan's decision was Uta herself. She was Uta. Only a fool would say no.

Swan met René Day in Santa Marta. René was on his way to Bogotá to meet Ricardo's connection. They arranged to hook up on San Andrés. If René scored,

Swan would buy in; if he did not, they would both go back to Bogotá and look up Bernier's friend Vincent. They said goodbye, and Swan and Uta, changing planes in Barranquilla, flew to San Andrés.

San Andrés, as a resort, was just emerging at the time. It was unspoiled. A beautiful, tropical island with small hotels that were clean and comfortable, but not deluxe, it had excellent restaurants, beaches of crushed coral, no hot water, no crowds, and one casino. Swan and Uta stayed at the Hanser Club. Their cabin was on the water. Over dinner, their first night on the island, they were approached by a well-dressed American who asked Swan if he were a photographer—he thought Uta was a model. He had sent drinks to their table by way of introduction. Swan said no, but invited the well-dressed gentleman and the suntanned man he was seated with, another American, to join him and Uta for coffee.

The gentleman who had asked the question worked for Avianca Airlines. His name was Arnold Noel. (Uta would refer to him as Mr. Christmas.) His friend was an underwater photographer. They were making a publicity film for Avianca, a skin-diving movie to be shown at American scuba clubs, which they hoped would lure tourists to Colombia and its islands. Their itinerary included all the major coastal resorts, and they had been granted the use of local boats to make the movie. They asked Swan and Uta to join the tour as models (Uta could lure a hydrophobe to the islands). It was offers like this one that suggested to Zachary Swan that God supported the legalization of cocaine. He and Uta accepted the invitation.

The next day they boarded the boat and began the filming. Uta and Swan were both excellent swimmers, and they both loved the water. Making the movie was a piece of cake. Aboard the boat that day, they met *El Commandante No Barco*, exercising his official privilege as the commanding officer of the Colombian naval station on San Andrés. *El Commandante* had a name of his own, but Swan and Uta preferred to call him *No Barco* because he had no boat. The naval station was supposed to have one, but the boat had been in for repairs for a long time now. *El Commandante* spent his time drilling his troops and going to the beach. He had command of two hundred Marines who marched a lot. He used any boat he could borrow to fool around with. It was *El Commandante* who, after the first day's shooting, introduced Swan to *aguardiente*, the Colombian anisette. After one belt, Swan went immediately for a Gelusil (probably his favorite drug of all).

With *El Commandante* aboard the next day, the crew sailed to Jonny Kay, an islet about a mile out on the coral reef, where they filmed a barbecue and shot some coral-diving footage. Uta brought back an exquisite piece of driftwood. That day René showed up. He had scored a little over half a kilo in Bogotá. He was carrying it in his golf clubs, hidden in the shafts. There were no golf courses on San Andrés. He looked funny getting off the plane . . . *And what in heaven's name brought you to Casablanca? . . . My health. I came to Casablanca for the waters . . . What waters? We're in the desert . . . I was misinformed.* Swan wanted to stay with the tour. He told René the plan he had for getting the coke into New York via the Lufthansa desk and offered to let René in on the scam if René would go back and score for him in Bogotá. René liked the idea—he did not want to risk the confiscation of his irons—and agreed. He told Swan the coke was running $7 a gram (which meant it was running anywhere from six to six and a half). Swan gave him $5,000 and held onto the golf clubs.

A few days later, René called from Bogotá:

"I'm on the girl," he said.*

René had scored the coke, and he gave Swan his

* See Appendix VI.

flight number and the time of his arrival. He told Swan he was worried about coming in.

"The girl's a little fat," he said.

"Don't worry about it," Swan told him, "Uta and I will meet you at the airport."

Swan and Uta met René at the airport in *El Commandante's* car. They drove right onto the field and parked thirty feet from the plane. They were accompanied by two armed Marines. René did not even go through the terminal. He went from the plane to the car, and he and the cocaine left the airport through the back gate. René joined the tour, and after two more days filming on San Andrés, they all set out for Cartagena. *El Commandante* stayed behind.

The tour was scheduled to go from San Andrés to Santa Marta. At Swan's suggestion the itinerary was changed. Santa Marta was out. Cartagena was just a nicer place. Cartagena is without question the most beautiful city in Colombia, possibly the most beautiful in the Hemisphere. It is the only walled city in South America, fortified with seventeenth-century stone battlements thirty feet wide and five miles long, behind which run narrow cobblestone streets with overhanging balconies. Known as the Heroic City for having resisted a 106-day siege by the Spaniards in the days of Simón Bolívar, it was where treasure was stored in the days of the Spanish Main. It suffered continual pirate attacks then, and eventually was sacked by Sir Francis Drake. Beyond the walls of the old city, out on the peninsula, are the hotels and the lush beaches. It was there that the tour took up residence.

In Cartagena the film company was afforded the use of a fleet of boats at the Hotel Caribe marina. And just as they had met *El Commandante* aboard one of the boats at the Hanser Club, Swan and Uta met Ramón Greco aboard one of the boats at the Caribe. Ramón Greco, about twenty-one years old, educated in the United States, was one of the wealthiest young men in Colombia. His father was "in emeralds." Ramón, in addition to everything else he had going for him, was a very handsome fellow.

At about this time, Uta was beginning to show the coke, the grass, and the Johnny Walker Black. She was putting a lot of Scotch away, and she was getting a little shaky. She was doing dope before she got out of bed in the morning. Swan and René were saying, "This ain't gonna work"—Uta was losing her grip. René finally gave up. He was not going to trust her. He disappeared one day with his golf clubs and left Swan a note saying he would call from Montreal. That same night Uta disappeared with Ramón Greco and did not show up until breakfast. Swan, his ego shot, figured that was it. He made plans to go home alone.

Uta moved to Greco's ranch—she would end up on the beach at Cartagena again a year later. Swan took the 600 grams of coke, bought some twine, a chisel, glue, sandpaper and lacquer and drew a bead on the driftwood. It was all he had. He opened it up with the chisel, hollowed it out and fit it with the coke, gluing it back together using the twine as a clamp. He sanded down one end of the driftwood just to get some sawdust, and sprinkled it over the glue at the seam. He ended up lacquering it—the exquisite piece of driftage was going to be hatcheted at home anyway.

He took an El Condor flight to Barranquilla, changed there to Avianca and headed north. Wearing a white Pierre Cardin jacket, navy blue slacks and a necktie, his hair short, his temples gray and his gold-rimmed glasses fitted tightly in place, he did something he would never in his life do again. He carried the cocaine through Customs. The driftwood was over his shoulder and his scuba gear was out front. He looked legitimate. He felt like hell—like the respectable forty-three-year-old gentleman he was, he crossed the border in a daze, his body full of Bloody Marys and his head full of coke. His pulse rate was abnormal, his adrenalin was high, and he learned what it was like to face some very serious trouble. From then on he would know how to prop up his carriers. He would know their thoughts, he would know their doubts, and he would know just how much dope to give them before they went across. It was a front-line lesson in drug running. He passed the exam.

Swan hit the 600 grams right away with 200 grams of borax. (René had recommended it.) He met Anthony at Clarke's and offered him half a key at $10,-500. Anthony took the sample Swan gave him and put it in his pocket. He would look at it later. They ate hamburgers, drank Vodka, and got to know each other better, and after an hour they left. Later that day, Anthony called Swan at the St. Regis.

"It's not like I thought it was," he said.

They agreed on $9,000 and Anthony met Swan in his hotel room. Swan had the scale. They blew some coke and discussed the future.

"We can make more money if you don't hit it," Anthony told him.

"I touched it a little," said Swan.

"We can do much better on the pure."

Swan thought for a minute. Then he nodded his head:

"O.K.," he said. "When the next shipment comes in, I'll make sure you see it in the original container."

Anthony pulled off $8,000 in hundreds and handed them to Swan; he gave Swan the balance in fifties. Swan reminded Anthony of the time he tried to give him a thousand dollars in tens. They laughed, shook hands, wished each other luck and said goodbye. Swan moved the remaining ten ounces through Ellery, Mickey and Roger in three days. He made $7,000 on the ounces, bringing his total to $16,000. He went back to Colombia with $10,000.

The enforcement of the laws that Zachary Swan was breaking in the late 1960s and early 1970s in the

United States was the responsibility of more than one Federal bureaucracy. Smuggling cocaine, Swan was in violation of the criminal statutes listed in Title 21 of the United States Code Annotated—21 USC(A)—dealing with the possession, sale, transportation and importation of what the Federal government had designated Controlled Substances (by way of the Comprehensive Drug Abuse Prevention and Control Act of 1970). The power to enforce those statutes, when Swan was smuggling, was mandated to the Federal Bureau of Narcotics and Dangerous Drugs (BNDD), then an agency of the Justice Department, and to the Bureau of Customs, an agency in the Department of the Treasury. The BNDD's duties were principally domestic. Customs handled smuggling. As with all bureaucracies, the duties and responsibilities of these two agencies became less clear in time and began to overlap. When the bureaucratic rivalry came to a showdown, the Treasury Department lost. Since July 1, 1973, under Richard Nixon's Presidential Reorganization Plan Number One, all Controlled Substances investigative work has been handled by the Justice Department in the form of the Drug Enforcement Administration (DEA).

The DEA, already showing signs of decay, is the latest in a long line of White House attempts to come down on international drug traffic. In 1914 the United States Customs Bureau was assigned responsibility for enforcement of the smuggling laws. Between 1932 and 1967, however, the Treasury Department saw fit to let another of its agencies, the Federal Bureau of Narcotics (FBN), carry out the Customs Bureau assignment where drugs were involved. Bureaucratically it made sense. They were all Treasury men. It was not until 1967, when the FBN went over to the Justice Department (to become BNDD), that Customs began to emphasize its mandate to enforce the drug-smuggling statutes. And that is when the infighting began. The drug traffic was now the bureaucratic baby of two

Cabinet members—the Secretary of the Treasury and the Attorney General. BNDD agents and Customs agents, not to mention the local police, were all showing up at the same grass buys, stepping on each other's joints.

While all this was going on, Richard Nixon was paying off political debts and handing out favors on Pennsylvania Avenue. In 1970 he created the Special Action Office for Drug Abuse Prevention. It was charged with duties like "development," "treatment," and "study," and put forty friends, or friends of friends, to work pushing paper for Dr. Jerome H. Jaffee. They went to a lot of cocktail parties in Washington. Then Nixon brought his Republican crony Myles Ambrose (Commissioner of Customs, 1962–1972) over from the Treasury Department and made him the Director of a new agency called the Office of Drug Abuse Law Enforcement (ODALE). Under Ambrose were gathered BNDD men, Customs agents and local police narcotics people, a true bureaucratic *mélange* and ultimately the perfect Ambrosia from which to culture the DEA.

The DEA, established in 1973, consisted of all former BNDD agents (about 1,200) and 500 former Customs agents, a staff which was beefed up to 2,200 during the first year of its operation. Into it were absorbed the functions of ODALE and Jaffee's boys. On the Justice Department's Table of Organization, the DEA is an agency administratively equivalent to the FBI. It is headed by a Director who is answerable to the Attorney General. Myles Ambrose, who would have been a natural for the job of Director when the agency was formed, was booted out of the running when he got himself into an embarrassing situation soliciting funds—apparently on Nixon's behalf—from a Texas Republican, a previous campaign contributor, the source of whose income, it turned out, happened to be under investigation at the time by Ambrose's former employees over at the Customs Bureau. Nixon's "top narc" went back to private practice.

With the formation of the DEA, the Customs Bureau's drug powers were limited to interdiction at the border; Customs inspectors have the authority to make arrests, but prisoners must be turned over to DEA agents for processing, prosecution and follow-up investigation. The DEA has between 200 and 250 agents abroad. They work under the authority of the American Ambassador to the country in which they are posted, but report directly through their own chain of command to the DEA Director in Washington. DEA agents overseas serve in an advisory and intelligence-gathering capacity and are not supposed to be operational, though some countries have invited them to be. (There are twelve DEA offices in South America.) Overseas, the DEA works with the cooperation of various other American agencies under the supervision of the President's Cabinet Committee for International Narcotics Control (CCINC), which is chaired in Washington by the Secretary of State and has among its members the Secretaries of Agriculture and Defense. Established in 1972, the CCINC has no manpower of its own, but designates a State Department official in every target country to act as its narcotics control officer, coordinating the efforts of agencies such as the CIA, AID and the DEA in coming to grips with the drug traffic. Predictably, Henry Kissinger has very little interest in his job as chairman of CCINC, and the Central Intelligence Agency insists that its agents have more important things to do than hang around with DEA types. CCINC, as well as being the coordinating force behind the nation's international drug effort, is also a funding agency. The State Department's Foreign Aid Budget for fiscal 1974 contained a $43 million budget line for CCINC, spent mostly on the equipment and education of foreign personnel. In Latin America, for example, training classes were held for local narcotics and Customs police, and communications equipment, weapons and vehicles—such as helicopters for the Mexicans—were purchased. It was CCINC to which Egil Krogh was White House rep when the Nixon Administration started feeling the heat.

The 800 series of 21 USC(A) is a list of Federal violations governing the domestic possession, sale and transportation of Controlled Substances. The 900 series pertains to the illegal importation of same. To *conspire* to indulge in any or all of the activities suggested by the foregoing is also a Federal crime— under 21 USC 846 and 963—and is dealt with separately in the Code under the General Federal Conspiracy Laws (18 USC 371). The fifty States have their own laws against possession, use, sale and transportation of Controlled Substances as well as the conspiracy to break the laws that prohibit doing so, and their laws are enforced by the narcotics divisions of local police departments (Zachary Swan was arrested in Amagansett on a State charge.) The States, however, have nothing in their statutes equivalent to series 900. Smuggling is a violation only of the Federal law. An individual charged with smuggling is tried in Federal court. An individual charged with any other drug violation may be tried in either State or Federal court or both—it usually depends on who makes the arrest and how serious the charge is. Penalties for State violations vary widely, and in many cases are more severe than those of the Federal government. In New York, for example, since what is known as the Rockefeller law went into effect (September 1973), conviction on a charge of trafficking or the attempt to traffic in any amount of heroin, morphine or cocaine carries a life sentence. Mandatory. The maximum under Federal law is fifteen years for a first offense.

As a smuggler by profession rather than by inclination, it behooved Zachary Swan to keep the area of his operation clean. He did so for his own protection. The more American college students who were killed,

robbed or arrested smuggling cocaine, the greater became the heat applied in South America to professional
smugglers by United States drug-enforcement agents.
The amateurs were easy enough to spot—they were
begging to be killed or ripped off—and Swan and his
friends, unsuccessful in their attempts to discourage
them, shuttled them to safe hotels and small, safe connections, and when possible they showed them the
safe way out with their loads. They put the strung-out
ones on planes for home, or notified their parents in
the States—they were, in essence, a second U.S. drug
agency, helping young people who were going to smuggle anyway, saving them from winding up dead or
possibly behind bars in a foreign jail.

Federal agents, those subsidized by the American
taxpayer, will customarily wait for a bust before talking to such people. Rather than walk up to someone
obviously headed for trouble—where they might flash
a badge and say, "Get smart, kid, it's not going to
work"—they will, as a matter of policy, allow him to
risk his life with the local heavies, get a few snorts of
pure, and walk into jail at the airport back home.
*Why prevent smuggling when you can punish it—isn't
that what jails are for?* (Federal drug-enforcement
agencies, like police department narcotics divisions,
work on what is called the "body count" system, where
promotion is based on the number of arrests made
rather than the quality of the arrest. Under the system, two junkies with glassine bags or three college
kids with a joint apiece are worth two and three times
more, respectively, than the diplomatic attaché with
six kilos of cocaine.) When the coke traffic began to
get heavy—before it was monopolized by Organized
Crime—Colombia began shipping a lot of bodies back
home to the States. The kids that survived the heavy
trade they threw in jail.*

The jails in Colombia are exactly what one would

* See Appendix VII.

expect them to be. If you survive the rats, the lice and the dysentery, you still have to go up against the guards. Fernando, Blackie's friend, who came from a wealthy Colombian family, just barely survived his fellow inmates. Asleep in his cell, doing a weekend in Santa Marta after a Friday night roundup, he had his leg slashed with a razor blade by an inmate who was going after the money in his pockets. Swan put him on a train to Bogotá, hoping to get him home before the gangrene killed him. Blackie was on hand, without his medallion and without René's girl. Debbie had gone back to Canada with the jewelry. Blackie had done some hard time in jail himself—his head had been shaved.

"He looked like a chick in the French resistance," Swan said.

In Cartagena, with the film crew, Swan and René had looked up *El Medico,* a local doctor who Blackie had told them was moving cocaine. *El Medico* presented his coke in a cardboard container sealed with masking tape. Written on the tape, in what looked like the doctor's handwriting, were the words "factory sealed." One snort of the merchandise and Swan's nose went up like a balloon—*El Medico's* coke was hit hard with procaine. Swan and René paid him for an office visit and split.

It was *El Medico* who told Swan that Blackie turned in smugglers for *"plata"* (silver), which was all Swan needed to know to stay clear of the Indian for good. But on his third trip South, Swan would meet so many new people, and make so many new friends, that Blackie, Fernando, the doctor and the entire population of Barranquilla would fade into history. After his first trip to Bogotá, smuggling cocaine would be like running at Churchill Downs in May—nothing small-time about it.

9

The Carpenter Said
Nothing But . . .

ZACHARY SWAN, his confidence and his bankroll
boosted by the events which had followed his last
move, returned to Colombia on the crest of two decisions. He had decided that wood held the key to
his future as a smuggler; it was adaptable, it was
available, but even more than that it was what had
worked for him once already, and he was determined
to exploit it further. He had decided also that, if
again, under any circumstances, he even considered
carrying the cocaine through Customs himself, his days
were numbered.

He arrived in Bogotá with $10,000 and four weeks
of preparation behind him. His plan was sound. Having covered the delivery of at least two packages in
New York, he would mail the coke. He would use
René's connection, and he would package the shipment in wood, probably in one or two of the many
different souvenirs he had seen in the airport gift shop
on his last trip. If there was going to be a problem,
it would come on the New York end. There he had
two addresses, but only one of them had been previously tested and could be considered reliable. That
was Davis's. The second address belonged to a
stranger. And its reliability would be determined by a
man code-named the Lothario.

The Lothario was one of Swan's more conventional
friends. Though an intelligent fellow, rather shrewd,
and, in his own way, pretty high-powered, he was not
the kind of man who would have made it in the thick

of the cocaine trade. Probably spoiled as a child, he was not accustomed to long-range gratification, and coming from privilege he was somewhat above the hucksterism required by the street. He took what he wanted as it came—he lived well and he got his kicks in a way that required as little risk as possible. He liked to gamble and he was pretty good at it. But when he lost, he lost big. When he was deep in the hole he would shill at Adrian's casino on the park, earning a hundred a night to mingle and make the place look full. He was also paid to bet on the crooked shooters and turn his winnings over to the house. Swan and the Lothario gambled a lot together. Swan met him over a dice table.

It was hard to say whether the Lothario ever worked for a living. His family owned a well-established and lucrative, but hardly posh, Jewish bakery in Manhattan and the Lothario, a young man who fancied himself something of a swinger, was rather embarrassed about it. He did, however, like the money. When the Lothario's father died, a few years after his association with Swan, he was obliged to take over the corporation, but at a cocktail party he would say no more than, "I have a business here in New York."

The Lothario, a likeable man, worthwhile to many, was a man very much impressed with names. He measured himself by way of his friends and his worth by that of the people he knew. Very few of the shooters at Adrian's knew anything about the Lothario, but they all knew everything about the people whose names he dropped. He had some fringe-Hollywood connections—as Swan put it, he had a lot of secondary-lead friends. He liked to advertise that he had been out with Joey Heatherton, and he claimed a popular film star as one of his closest pals. It was not that the Lothario ever lied about these things; he just let the truth get the better of him. On a gambling junket to St. Martin with Swan, the Lothario brought a friend who had a supporting role in *The Lawyers* on television. The prevailing opinion was "so what."

It was pointed out as meaningful by those who knew him that the Lothario smoked brown cigarettes, Nat Sherman's Cigarettellos, manufactured in New York and a mark of distinction especially on the East Side. But the infinite complexities of the Lothario's thinking were ultimately synthesized in an offhand observation made by Alice, a woman blessed with insight and a gift for clarity:

"He drives an MG with the steering wheel on the right-hand side," she said.

Yet, as attenuated as it was, the Lothario's was not an exclusively vicarious life. The Lothario did one thing well. And it was something everyone knew he did well without his telling them: the Lothario was one of the world's most accomplished assmen. Yes. The Lothario had a way about him. He was in his thirties, tall and pretty, and he flashed a kind of backstairs elegance. He dated high-priced fashion models three-at-a-time, and this was his idea of class. It impressed his New York friends. And it impressed Swan, who knew that the Lothario had a lot of poker debts and could use some easy money. It was not long before the two talked business:

"What's in it for me?" the Lothario wanted to know.

"You get five hundred a package."

"I don't want to touch it, now. I don't want to be anywhere near the shit."

"You have the keys to their apartments?"

"Some of them."

"Just open the door for me. I'll make the switch."

"You'll have to come when they're at work."

"No shit."

"Look, I don't want any trouble."

"Have you ever been to Colombia?"

"No."

"Then how are they going to put you with the package? No fingerprints. No return address. You don't know anything. You're clean. I'm clean. Everybody's clean."

"What about her?"

"What *about* her? Her picture's been in every magazine in the world. She must get love letters every day. What does she know? She walks away."

"What if she doesn't want it? What if she throws it away?"

"Don't take out the trash. Look, if you tell her to keep it, she'll keep it."

"And you'll do the switch."

"When she's at work. Just stay close to her at package time. Remember that. And call me when it comes in."

"How much do I get?"

"Five hundred."

Bogotá, the political, industrial, commercial, economic and cultural capital of Colombia, is located on the 74th meridian just north of the Equator, 2,984 miles due south of New York and just over an ocean due west of the Liberian coast. It lies beneath Orion on a high savanna 8,660 feet above sea level in the Cordillera Central range of the Colombian Andes—a grassy plateau officially stolen from the Chibcha Indians on August 6, 1538. In the more than four hundred years since the city's founding, its population has risen to near three million—the majority of which is Spanish in origin—and the quality of life within its boundaries has sunk immeasurably.

Bogotá is an unclean city, crawling with street urchins and unfed dogs; 1,180 square miles of polluted, deoxygenated mountain air, cooler year round than the coastal resorts farther north—Colombia's climate is vertical—its average daytime temperature 57 degrees Fahrenheit with no significant variation from season to season. The Colombian businessman here wears a *ruana*—the traditional Colombian poncho—over his business suit to keep him warm during the day. At night he stays home. Any Colombian, a Bogotano first, will warn you that the streets of the city are *muy peligroso*—very dangerous—at night. A cursory acquaintance with the history of the civil strife Colombia has known over the years would be enough to impress a member of the Weather Underground—the body count is a figure to behold. In Bogotá, life is cheap.

The streets of Bogotá, in their layout, reflect the population's regard for the terrain out of which the city grew—*carreras* run parallel to the mountains, *calles* run perpendicular (east-west)—and maps of the city reflect a consonant disregard for the cartographic traditions of the rest of the world—polar north is to the left. Eldorado International Airport is located on the western edge of the city (at the bottom of the map), about twenty minutes by cab from downtown. *El centro,* the city's core, or downtown area, is where the principal hotels are located and where most tourists get their first taste of the city's night life. Outside any hotel, one can find a number of touts offering emeralds, hookers, currency and cocaine—in fact, these sinister characters, confronted immediately upon arrival at one's hotel, serve as a kind of chamber of commerce to welcome tourists to Bogotá. Alighting from his airport cab, Zachary Swan saw the promise of an adventure begin to unfold—arriving in Bogotá spawned the preliminary excitement and base-line fear experienced only upon entering a whorehouse.

Swan checked into the Hotel Tequendama. Owned by the Colombian government and overstaffed, the Tequendama would remain the most exclusive hotel in the city until the Bogotá Hilton opened six months later, and with eight hundred rooms it was the city's largest. The Tequendama was infested with amateur dealers and narcotics agents, but it had a twenty-four-hour coffee shop, and if a man were careful enough never to do business anywhere near the hotel, it was a good place to pick up information. On his second day in town, Swan met René Day at the coffee shop.

"What have we got?" he asked.

"We've got two new agents now," René said. "We've got the one with the beard over there. And we've got one with a gold earring—he's around here somewhere, you can't miss him—if you don't make the earring, you'll notice him because he wears jeans and talks like a acid freak. Very transparent."

"It makes sense. Only the smugglers wear suits," Swan said. "Is your connection still good?"

"He was busted last week. I'm dry. I was hoping you'd have something."

"All I've got is this name, Vincent van Klee."

René leaned back in his chair: "Call him," he said.

"Why not?" Swan made the call, and returned to the table five minutes later.

"I'm having lunch with him tomorrow at noon. Hotel Continental. He has a suite there."

"Does he know who you are?"

"Only by way of Michel. All he knows is my name and that he'd like to meet me. Very polite."

"What do you know about him?"

"I know he grew up with a coca tree outside his window. I know he likes coke and I know he buys it. I'll play it by ear."

"Why don't you take enough for a few lines. I've got that much."

"Good," Swan said. "It'll make things easier."

The next morning Swan took a cab to the Hotel Continental, located downtown on Avenida Jimenez, about fifteen blocks from the Tequendama and not far from the Gold Museum. He gave his name to the desk clerk and was told to go up. He was greeted by his host at the door.

Vincent van Klee was lean and wealthy. His clothes and his manner fit him well. He was neither tall nor young but he carried himself as if he were both, and like many Colombian aristocrats he was unashamedly European. His hair was white and his irises were brown, and if Swan were to abstract the essence of the man's bearing in one well-chosen word, it would be distinguished. Vincent van Klee had presence. He was alert and erect, and he moved with the grace of a fencing instructor. He was soft-spoken. He was courteous. His smile was easy, his English fluent, and his voice was that of a man who enjoyed listening. He had emerald smuggler's eyes. Swan knew that he was a man who could be trusted.

Vincent van Klee was seventy-two years old. In his youth he had dabbled in black market emerald traffic, but he was now content to indulge himself along more discreet avenues. Insulated by old money, he confined his pleasures to the moderate use of cocaine, fine wine and liqueurs; the company of close friends, those Bogotá socialites who determined Colombia's economic and political destiny; the acquisition of pre-Columbian art and choice real estate; and the sexual companionship of handsome young men and boys. A well-educated and intelligent man, he was a gentleman always, had traveled extensively, and was fluent in at least five languages. He and Swan were to become good friends.

"I have heard so much about you," he said.

"And I you," Swan replied.

As they came to know each other better they would lie less frequently.

Vincent served filet of sole for lunch. Swan served the coke René had given him. It was a pleasant afternoon all around. Over *aguardiente* Vincent demonstrated a flair for storytelling. He talked about Aztecs and Incas, cocaine and pre-Columbian jewelry, then broke down and admitted he had been an emerald smuggler.

"I will take you to the black market some day and show you how to buy emeralds," he told Swan.

(Swan bought an emerald on a subsequent trip to

Bogotá. He carried it through Customs in his mouth up to the point at which it became evident he was going to be searched. Then, in terror, but calmly, he swallowed it. To retrieve the emerald he had to employ an elaborate sling fashioned out of toilet paper, a process which ran contrary to the romantic illusions he harbored with regard to smuggling; and because he made only $150 on the ultimate transaction, he gave up smuggling emeralds after one try.)

René's coke lasted no more than an hour and a half; old Vincent's pupils peaked at about f/4, held steady for a while, and began stopping down from there. Before they hit 5.6, Swan made his move:

"I would like to buy some more *coco* for us," he said.

Vincent invited Swan to stay for dinner, informed his cook, and called his connection.

Vincent van Klee's connection was a small-time street hustler named Lallo. In the presence of Vincent he cut quite a figure. About twenty-eight, black, sporting a close-cropped Afro and an elegant goatee, Lallo was rather shady looking. He moved very slowly, said very little, and it was a good guess that he had a knife somewhere. Swan wondered how he had made it through the lobby—that he was black, in itself, was enough to get him poleaxed at the elevator. In addition to an air of the street, Lallo had brought in with him ten grams of coke. Swan paid him the sidewalk price, $100, and invited Lallo, to the dealer's surprise, to stay for a sniff. Lallo, with Vincent's tacit approval, accepted the invitation.

The coke was wrapped in a scrap of white, lined looseleaf paper, the customary package, almost a trademark in itself, for a *muestra,* or sample, of coke on the Bogotá streets. Swan cut out six lines, did his last, and after an appropriate silence, addressed Lallo:

"I have a friend," he said.

Of course. One always has a friend. Lallo nodded.

"He might be interested in some quantity," Swan added.

Yes. Lallo nodded again. He could handle it.

Then politely, and very carefully, Swan pointed out that his friend might like to buy directly—from the Man.

"And, of course, there would be a bonus in it for you," he concluded.

Lallo nodded, made arrangements to meet Swan the next day, bid Vincent a silent good night and left. Swan and Vincent got stoned and waited for dinner. Vincent played Roberta Flack records and poured *aguardiente,* impressing Swan with his wit and his stamina—it was very likely that after dinner, Vincent would head for the nearest discotheque. Dinner was served late, Swan left after coffee, and as Vincent dressed for the evening Swan returned to his hotel with the profound feeling that good things were beginning to happen.

The next day in the Tequendama coffee shop Swan laid out $200 and Lallo took him from there to meet the Man. The Man's name was Armando. Armando was a Cuban, about fifty years old, six-two, 225, and hard all around. His complexion was fair and his dark curly hair was on its way out. He had a potbelly and the wrists of a .400 hitter. Swan would learn later that Armando had played Triple-A baseball in the United States, had kicked around for a while with Philadelphia's farm team, and very possibly had pitched for a year or two with the Cubs. He had played against Charlie Keller. But now Armando was strictly a cocaine dealer, and Swan was immediately impressed with the fact that their meeting took place in his home. If they got together, it would mean an end to dealing in second-rate hotel rooms and ill-lighted bars.

Swan wanted quantity, and Armando offered it to him at six dollars a gram. It was the best price Swan had ever been quoted, but, being Zachary Swan, he figured what the hell, and said that he heard he could get it for five. Armando said five and a half, they settled on that, and Swan was sure he had now found his first honest connection—a former used car salesman from pre-Castro Cuba who had played major league ball against Charlie Keller. They shook hands and Armando said, "Next week." As a demonstration of good faith he gave Swan what Swan would later find out was a handful of the finest grass in Colombia. Swan returned to the Tequendama and gave René the news.

"Splendid," said René. "Did you get us a good price?"

Swan nodded. "Six dollars a gram."

Connections in the cocaine trade are made very much as they are made in the legitimate business world. The difference is one of direction rather than of degree. Where a legitimate businessman makes money selling his customers to a wholesaler—by way of a mailing list, for example—a cocaine smuggler makes money selling the wholesaler to the potential customer. A smuggler's connections are worth money to him—he almost never gives them away. Observing the same tradition under which René had connected for Swan—charging Swan seven dollars a gram for cocaine that might have been going for six—Swan introduced René to Armando, who, under instructions from Swan, charged René six dollars for coke offered at five and a half. The $500 overage per kilo went to Swan, and until Armando and René became friends or mutually trusted business associates, and the price was altered, Swan would collect $500 on every kilo Armando sold to René. It was an understood and accepted business practice—René *knew* he was paying more—and it was never questioned by any of the principals involved. It was a tacit agreement among professionals, one that prevailed throughout the world.

In Bogotá, waiting for Armando's cocaine, Swan and René entertained themselves independently of each other. René had friends of his own there, and

Swan was chumming around with Vincent van Klee. After meeting Armando, Swan called Vincent and invited him to dinner. Vincent recommended *El Zaguán de Las Aguas* on Calle 19 when Swan suggested they go native. Prompt service was rare throughout Colombia, and *Las Aguas* was one of the few restaurants Vincent endorsed. Swan, at Vincent's suggestion, ordered *ajiaco con pollo*, a thick soup which consisted of chicken, avocado, several kinds of potatoes, corn on the cob and other heavy vegetables, embellished with capers over a dollop of sour cream. *"Muy tipico,"* the waiter said. Swan smiled. The restaurant and the dish would become a favorite of Swan's, and two years later he would be eating the same thing, by the same fireplace and to the same music, while he propped up a new carrier, Lillian Giles.

Also *muy tipico* of Bogotá at the time was the after-hours club Vincent led Swan to later that night. Swan had heard stories of places thus named. In the midnight travel brochure of his mind, indexed somewhere under America, South, the copy scanned something like this . . . *hookers everywhere . . . for men and for women . . . a coca leaf floating at the top of your drink . . . getting it up your nose, taking it through your mouth and getting laid between highs . . . you're smoking dope and drinking* aguardiente *and thinking about going home around ten in the morning . . . by then everybody is falling down . . . everybody is getting robbed . . . the pickpockets and bandits are working overtime . . .* The tourists love it. It is so very *tipico*.

The place was dark and crowded. The music was preponderantly brass. And, in the smoke-drenched atmosphere, there was the dominant aroma of sin. While Vincent sipped *aguardiente* and talked to young men, Swan disappeared with a woman. Together they relived their most boring liaisons. Swan found it nostalgic. When he returned, Vincent was still talking, but clearly growing bored. It had been a very pleasant evening—Vincent's watch had been stolen—but now

it was about six A.M.—time to go home. As they
headed for the door they were presented with a bill.

"Your whore," Vincent said.

Swan's glasses, which were gold-rimmed, had been
stolen earlier. He handed the bill to Vincent, whose
eyes were no better, in fact, but who managed to
read the numbers in transit as they passed three feet
from his face. The bill read 600 pesos. They were
hitting Swan with a 500-peso room charge for the
hooker.

"This is ridiculous," Vincent said. "We won't pay
it."

Swan looked at Vincent. We won't? We won't.
Vincent sat down. The police were called in to deal
with this recalcitrant old faggot. They were on the
payroll. They stood with the bouncers. Swan gave
them a Delta-9 grin. Vincent refused to move. Swan
was nervous.

"Let's just pay it and get out of here," Swan said.

Vincent said no. He threw the bill at the waiter.
(Oh, Jesus, thought Swan.) The policeman in charge,
experienced at this kind of work, conferred with the
manager and came back with an offer.

"Two hundred and fifty," he said.

Vincent remained seated. And Swan finally became
caught up in it all. He was stoned and he started to
get funny.

"Dos cientos cincuenta pesos! No es Brigitte
Bardot!"

They had to agree. They settled for a hundred and
twenty. Swan paid, and he and Vincent left.

It was at about this point in his career that Swan
had occasion to regret having let lapse his prescription
for diet pills. That evening, having slept the day away
in his hotel room, Swan attended a cocktail party.
Vincent was throwing it at his suite in the Continental.
Swan staggered in late. Vincent was flying.

"How nice of you to come."

"You continue to impress me, Vincent."

"Oh, don't tell me."

"You look dashing."

"I have had only my first *aguardiente*."

"Vincent, I can't wait."

"You will stay late. Many people have yet to come."

"I thought I *was* late."

"The night is just beginning."

"Perhaps I had better clear my head."

"Help yourself."

Swan, after removing his coat, made a wrong turn and ended up in the kitchen. He found a carpenter working there, a young man building cabinets, who smiled politely at Swan and wished him a good evening. In his late twenties, with a pleasant face and a cheerful smile—an ingenuous-looking lad—the carpenter was working later, it appeared, than he had planned. Swan smiled knowingly, returned the greeting, and righted his course in the direction of the living room. He spotted the cocaine on the coffee table and availed himself of a blow. Interesting, he thought. He spread himself around, let his mind wander, and after a half hour had passed, he casually drifted back into the kitchen. The carpenter was still there.

Swan said hello. The carpenter said hello. By way of a strange blend of English and Spanish, Swan complimented the young man on the excellence of his work. Bilateral communication was established when the carpenter, by way of the same linguistic blend, thanked Swan for the compliment. Swan smiled. The carpenter smiled. Progress was made. They said other pleasant things and smiled some more. Swan was pleased. The carpenter was pleased. Eventually Swan managed to point out:

"I have a friend."

The carpenter, as it turned out, had a friend too. His name was Rudolpho. Swan had met him in the living room. Rudolpho had been doing cocaine.

Rudolpho, Angel the Carpenter's good friend, had been Vincent van Klee's lover as a boy. As a handsome young man he had traveled with Vincent to France and to Italy, and now, in his thirties, he was a a constant companion. He was married to a young woman, a seamstress named Evelyn, and he and Evelyn had two small children, but because Evelyn made very little money and because Rudolpho was such a poor businessman, it was Vincent who supported the family. It was done in a very oblique way, of course, and typically, as it turned out, with as little efficiency as possible. Vincent would invest in a business of one kind or another, and Rudolpho would run it into the ground. Their latest venture was a ranch outside of Bogotá.

Swan did not know any of this yet, nor did he know for a fact that Rudolpho was not particularly fond of his dependence on Vincent. What he did know was that Rudolpho was a friend of Michel Bernier, another of Vincent's lovers, and it was with mention of him, their mutual acquaintance, that Swan engaged Rudolpho in conversation when he left the kitchen. Rudolpho spoke English well, he dressed like a gentleman, and Swan could see that he liked cocaine. But nothing pleased Swan more than the discovery that Rudolpho, the carpenter's friend, was passing counterfeit fifties for Michel.

"Angel, the carpenter, tells me he is also a friend of yours," Swan said.

"Yes," said Rudolpho.

"How nice," said Swan.

The impact of a carpenter upon the scope of Swan's business would be, to say the least, a profound one, especially in light of his decision to exploit the properties of wood in its behalf. But things began to break so fast that before he was able to address himself seriously to the possibilities suggested by the talents of Angel and Rudolpho, talents that would ultimately provide the core for a far-reaching Colombian operation, he was to find himself sowing the seeds of fraternity among a broad network of cocaine smugglers working out of Bogotá. And again it was Vincent who opened the door.

On his fourth day in Bogotá, waiting for Armando to come through with the cocaine, Swan, at Vincent's suggestion, checked out of the Tequendama and took a room at the Hotel Continental. Vincent was quite eloquent in explaining his reasons for recommending the move—he said he thought the Tequendama was a "dump." Swan moved out—what could he say—and was not at the Continental more than twelve hours before Michel Bernier paid him a visit. Bernier, not one of Swan's closest friends, stumbled around the room for a while, stoned, making incoherent conversation—he asked Swan about Uta, talked about his friend Vincent van Klee, and after hearing that Uta was in Cartagena and that, yes, Vincent was indeed *un homme formidable*, he came to the point. He wanted $1,000. Swan explained that he, Swan, was a little short of cash. Michel smiled and explained that he, Swan, did not understand. Oh? It was not a loan. It was extortion. Oh. Swan understood perfectly. After looking around the room and satisfying himself that there was nowhere he could reasonably stash the body without forcing a showdown with the chambermaid, Swan made a deal with Michel. He gave Michel $100 and told him to come back the next day for the rest. Michel took the hundred and said he would be back. Swan said he did not doubt it and showed Michel out. An hour later Swan checked out of the Continental. He moved across town to a place called the Oriole Hotel —he would later refer to it as moving right out of the frying pan and into the golden goose.

The Oriole was owned and operated by a handsome young Colombian named Juan Carlos Ramirez, whom Swan met within an hour after checking in, and with whose intelligence, maturity and wealth Swan could not help but be impressed. Ramirez was twenty-eight years old, had been educated in Canada, and spoke impeccable English. His was a very casual approach to the hotel business, and he and Swan became friendly almost immediately. It would not be long before Swan would introduce him to Vincent, a man with whom Ramirez had at least one thing in common, Swan noted, Roberta Flack notwithstanding—Ramirez, whose own room at the Oriole was decorated with Day-Glo posters and outdated acid art, was always throwing parties. Vincent would certainly have approved. To his parties, it happened, Ramirez invited many of the hotel's guests, his favorites among whom were the young Americans and Canadians who seemed to abound there, and at least two of whom, Swan soon discovered, were definitely cocaine smugglers. One of them was Canadian Jack.

Canadian Jack, about twenty-five years old, with blond hair, blue eyes and a passion for rock and roll, had been making regular trips to Colombia for well over a year. When he was not in Bogotá, he was hanging around in Jamaica smoking dope with the freaks at Strawberry Fields or chasing his own brand of music in one direction or another—what little cocaine was available at Woodstock in the summer of 1969 was his. Arrested on a charge of smuggling a large shipment of hashish from Turkey through the Toronto airport, he had jumped bail and was wanted in Canada. He was supporting himself in Bogotá on the steady income he derived moving small amounts of cocaine into Canada and the United States, either using mules or running it himself, getting himself in and out of North America on a false passport. He managed to get home quite often. Jack had a lot of valuable connections in Bogotá and a lot of valuable information even on those people with whom he was not connected. He was not the most professional smuggler around—he seemed to get by more on luck than on any experience he might have gained over the years—but Swan liked him right away. He thought he was a "good kid." They became friends quickly, and soon after their meeting, Swan introduced Jack to Armando. Perhaps it was because Jack was not a professional—he never had a lot of money—that Swan did not put anything on the price.

Through Canadian Jack, Swan met Black Dan, another Oriole guest, an American from San Francisco who Swan would later learn was smuggling large quantities of cocaine into the United States at a rate that was remarkable for a strictly one-man operation. He was the most professional smuggler Swan would meet in Bogotá. About thirty-three years old, laid back, Dan smuggled his coke across two borders, and he had been doing it the same way for almost two years. He traveled via Mexico with the coke strapped to his legs —a dangerous and somewhat foolhardy procedure for an ordinary man. But Dan was far from ordinary. A former heavyweight boxer, he was as strong a man as Swan had ever met—he was tall, had to weigh at least 250, and his muscles were strung like bridge cables. He did not say much and was not the kind of man you wanted to spend a lot of time with if you were looking at him over a Customs counter or an airport gate barrier. Black Dan was friendly, a good man to blow coke with and a good man to have on your side, but he was frightening to look at if you were looking for more than a smile. It would be a while before he and Swan became friends.

By the end of his first week in Bogotá, Swan had put two new smugglers in touch with Armando. He, Jack and René were now waiting to score from the Cuban. And Armando, who had promised delivery within a week, was late—the delay, Swan would learn, was characteristic. Armando had a lieutenant named Raoul, who, in addition to running underlings like Lallo, was employed to handle the Indian women who walked the pure across the mountains from Ecuador. Raoul would meet the couriers on the Colombian side of the border, pay them their wages—twenty dollars a trip if they were lucky—pick up the coke and deliver it to Armando in Bogotá. As a matter of course, however, Armando was forced to keep his customers in Bogotá waiting while Raoul, on the border, went out of his mind for a few days with the two young Indians and the fresh shipment of cocaine. Deliveries were made about once a month out of Ecuador, and Raoul saw them as vacations. When Raoul was not making everyone wait, he was making everyone laugh.

Raoul was short and fat, in his middle forties; always dressed in a rumpled business suit—Swan was convinced he slept in it—he looked like a cross between a racetrack tout and a flood victim. He was a Cuban and was always referred to as such—even Armando called him a Cuban. He often made deliveries for his boss, acting as a link to the smugglers, and on these assignments he liked to meet in ice cream parlors. Whenever a smuggler went out to deal with Raoul, he went prepared to watch this one-man sideshow knock off at least two double-dip cones in a sitting. When meets were scheduled elsewhere, say in a hotel room, Raoul drew on a repertoire of other entertainments, one of which Swan became party to when Raoul delivered a kilo to Swan's room at the Continental.

Swan told Raoul the kilo was not pure. *"No es pura,"* Swan said. Raoul's eyes flashed open—they went on like Lucas lamps. *"Pura! Pura!"* he said, pointing to the cocaine. Swan shook his head solemnly. *"No es pura."* Raoul grew indignant. He picked the coke up in his hands and began to throw it all over his face as if he were sampling an exotic aroma of some kind. He splashed it around his nose, nodded and yelled *"Pura!"* While Swan shook his head, Raoul continued to throw the cocaine lovingly into his face, then into Swan's. *"Pura! Pura!"* he sang. It was when Swan started to laugh at the suggestion that Raoul started to go a little bit crazy. Raoul bent over like an ostrich, buried his face in the cocaine as if it were a bouquet of roses, shook his head from side to side, then, inhaling the coke, jumped around the room screaming *"Pura!"* He waved his arms and jumped up and down and screamed *"Pura!"* to the world at large. Swan, who did not intend to buy the coke, was really not obliged to offer an excuse for not buying it, but he found the show exhilarating—he continued to shake his head. Raoul continued to jump, then wheeled around to face Swan with cocaine clinging to his moustache and eyelashes—he looked like he had just come in from Vermont. *"Pura!"* he screamed. Swan waited for him to catch his breath, then, timing his shot perfectly, referred to the coke as "shit." This drove Raoul almost insane. By the time the Cuban finished arguing the merits of his product, he was covered with cocaine from his head to his shoes and panting like a racehorse. He put his hand over his lungs as if he were about to collapse. Swan handed him a glass of water. He looked Raoul in the eye. With a nod of his head, Raoul picked up the kilo and put on his hat. He left with a polite goodbye and, mumbling *"pura,"* went directly to an ice cream parlor.

It was Raoul, in a more sober moment, who told Swan that you only get two years in the trade—"You can't run for more than two," he said, "after two years, quit." Two years after he began smuggling cocaine, Swan was in the Riverhead Jail—he would not know until later that Raoul had learned the wisdom of his own words the hard way.

A week after Vincent's cocktail party, Swan kept an appointment with Rudolpho. He had been invited to visit the ranch and meet Evelyn and the children —he arrived bearing gifts. He had brought flowers for Evelyn and candy for the children—he had brought two long rolling pins for Rudolpho. He was there to talk business. The agreement that he and Rudolpho would ultimately reach was born of two complementary goals: Rudolpho wanted money; Swan wanted Angel the carpenter. Rudolpho got what he wanted. Swan got much more.

Angel was no simple carpenter. He was a master craftsman who employed four apprentices. In his shop, which was located in a large garage on the outskirts of Bogotá, he had two lathes, a table saw, electric sanders and several power drills, in addition to the manually operated tools necessary to his trade. When he and Rudolpho went to work for Swan, many of the tools were moved from the shop to the top floor of Rudolpho's house—subsequently, the entire shop was transferred. Rudolpho and Angel split $1,000 on every kilo Swan moved out of Colombia. Angel handled the woodwork, and Rudolph handled the paperwork. It was Rudolpho's job to mail the packages. Each package had to be mailed separately and from a different Post Office. In the event of trouble, Rudolpho was always given a hundred-dollar bill with which to buy his way out. Both he and Angel would accompany Swan on the score, acting as backup men, and Rudolpho, who knew cocaine, would help judge the samples. Rudolpho spoke a little English, thanks to Vincent, and until Swan had been working out of Bogotá awhile, Rudolpho would also provide a necessary linguistic link, not only to Swan's suppliers, but to Angel as well.

In addition to Angel's tools, one other piece of apparatus—a monster—was evident in the packaging plant upstairs at Rudolpho's. As soon as he had cemented the deal with the two Colombians, Swan had done some shopping. He had bought a press. A hand-operated, flat-bed, job printer, it was six feet high with a metal stand and cast-iron impression levers. With two handles and a torsion screw to operate the platen, it was an archaic device, suitable only for hand embossing—and with the metal frames and adjustable jigs that Angel designed, it was perfect for cocaine compressing. Swan had seen it in a print shop—he paid eighty dollars for it. He, Rudolpho and Canadian Jack were on hand to cart it away, but without Black Dan, who happened to be walking by at the right time, they would never have managed to get it into Rudolpho's car. It was big and it was heavy—they had to remove the rear seat to load it—and only Dan was able to move it more than an inch at a time. The press was essential to the business that followed; it, more than anything else, was responsible for increasing the weight Swan was able to move through his network in New York—it cut his volume by 50 percent.

Because of the weight, density and desiccated condition of the wood involved, loading a store-bought rolling pin with cocaine was impractical. What Angel would do was fashion a duplicate out of fresh Madeira wood, saw it longitudinally down the middle, hollow it out, line it with plastic, fill it, close it with glue and clamps, then paint and finish it. In New York, Swan would find that the rolling pins Angel made were about as hard to open as they were to build. But the manufacture of any item was child's play compared with what went into the compressing and packing of the cocaine—when Armando finally came through, Swan took a *kilo y medio,* 1,500 grams, and he, Angel and Rudolpho went to work.

Working in the glass-enclosed room on Rudolpho's roof was like working in a greenhouse. Though high in the mountains, Bogotá is less than five degrees north of the Equator, and when the sun was high, it was directly overhead. Compressing the *kilo y medio* took hours—in the months to come, three kilos would be the minimum load. When the sweat was running and the coke was flying off the press under the drop of the impression plate, the three bandits looked like snowmen, soaking the powder up through the pores of their skin. Wearing gloves to keep fingerprints off the merchandise, they plastic-wrapped the cocaine before filling the souvenirs. They worked stoned most of the time, and drank beer to fight the heat. The impression levers on the press were always breaking, and the three men spent a good amount of their time just sitting with the coke—under the sun, gloved and sweating and drinking beer—while they waited for the broken parts to come back from the machine shop. When the job was done and the souvenirs packed, a package was made. It had to be addressed in block lettering to disguise the handwriting—the address was often printed by all three men, one man taking every third letter—then tied with string and kept clean of prints. In the case of the Lothario's packages, love letters had to be enclosed. Rudolpho handled those. And each package had to be mailed separately to account for the odds against more than one going through.

It would work like this on all subsequent trips but two—Angel and Rudolpho would be as essential to the South American operation as the ounce-dealers were to the New York network. And Armando would continue to deliver pure. In the months to come, Canadian Jack and Black Dan would avail themselves of Swan's equipment and imagination. Raoul would begin to offer kilos on his own and other cocaine dealers would emerge. And Vincent van Klee, a good friend, would be consulted on every sample that came Swan's way. Before a year was out, Michel Bernier would return, Juan Carlos Ramirez's parentage would yield secrets, and René Day, the prince of players, would rejoin Swan to participate in what would be known as the Boat Move. Swan had gone from 300 grams on his first move to 600 grams on his second. After the kilo and a half moved on this, his most recent trip, he would never move less than three keys. He left Bogotá with nowhere to go but up.

10

Alkaloid Annie/ Power of the Press

SWAN STROLLED through United States Customs in New York with three rolling pins in his luggage—red, white and black, respectively, each a duplicate of one he had mailed from Bogotá. None of them was examined. Shortly after his return home, he got a call from Davis, who phoned from a booth on the street below his office.

"I've got a visitor," he said.

The package was in. Swan took a subway to midtown, carrying a blue canvas AWOL bag folded under his arm. From the lobby of Davis's building he took an elevator to the eighth floor, then walked the fire stairs to the tenth, examining the stairwell and the hallways for a stakeout before proceeding to Davis's office on the ninth. He looked the package over for signs of a search and found nothing blatantly wrong, but conducted a trial run anyway before leaving with the load. He put a heavy catalogue into the AWOL bag, left the building with it, and took a walk around the block. Satisfied that he and the package were clean, he traded the catalogue for the cocaine and took the coke home.

Before breaking the load down, he called Anthony to say that he had just returned from "down South." Allowing himself time to collect the other two packages, he made arrangements with Anthony to deliver a sample. The next morning the Lothario called. "Why don't you come and visit me?" he said.

He gave Swan an address on West 90th Street. Swan walked it. He paid the Lothario $500 cash on the spot and switched the rolling pins—they were white.

"What did she say?" Swan asked.

"Not much. It was pretty routine. She gets presents all the time."

"I thought so."

"How much are these things worth?" the Lothario asked, taking the rolling pin from Swan.

"I'll find out soon," said Swan, taking it back.

"Yeah? Well, when you do, let me know."

"Yeah. I'll let you know."

(Later, when the Lothario learned how much the packages were worth, his fee was boosted to $650.)

With two packages at home, Swan started breaking the rolling pins down. He cut out a sample for Anthony —pure—and put the rest on a twenty-two and six, hitting it with borax, adding about 300 grams of powder to the kilo of pure and packaging the ounces in plastic. He moved into the Lincoln Square Motel with 45 ounces cut and ready to move through his ounce-dealers. He was out in a week with $31,500. (He moved the cocaine at $700 an ounce. Soon he would be asking $850. In a year it would be going for $1,000.)

The third package came in late. The Lothario called Swan from an apartment on East 79th Street which belonged to a young woman in whose direction the Lothario channeled the greatest share of his romantic energy. The Lothario was in love. The young woman was a very famous model and a part-time actress—her worldwide exposure and the Lothario's constant company, both taken for granted, accounted for two subsequent shipments to her address. Her favorite color was red. Swan walked into her plush apartment and found the rolling pin on the radiator. Bad news.

"Jesus fucking Christ."

"Well, I didn't know," said the Lothario.

They were surveying the damage.

"Heat destroys it, man."

"I'm really sorry."

Swan tossed the souvenir onto the couch and shook his head.

"God damn it."

The rolling pin was hot. The Lothario was sincerely sorry. Swan was running out of ways to take the Lord's name in vain. When he regained his composure, he assured the Lothario that it was his, Swan's own fault.

"Forget it, man. I'll straighten it out."

Swan paid the Lothario and went directly to Anthony with the load. They had decided on $11,000 for 500 grams of the pure Anthony had sampled. Swan explained what had happened. It was painful. He and Anthony opened the rolling pin together (in keeping with Swan's earlier promise to deliver the coke in its original container). They used a hammer and chisel, cracking the pin on the floor of Anthony's billiards room. What they found was discouraging. The cocaine had turned brown—another five hours on the radiator and it would have converted to paste. They spread it out on the floor over newspaper and put lamps on it, trying to dry it out, hoping to bring it back. When it was as dry as it was going to get, it looked somewhat improved, but was still brown and crusty. Anthony got on the phone and within twenty minutes he had a customer waiting in the living room. He went out, leaving Swan with the stash, and came back shaking his head.

"I don't know what the fuck to do with it," Swan said.

Anthony left again. He kept going and coming until the price went from $11,000 to $9,000 then finally to $7,000. Swan was glad to get it. In order to complete the deal, Anthony needed a piece of evidence —unorthodox in the extreme.

"We need the rolling pin," he said.

"What the fuck do you need the rolling pin for?" Swan wanted to know—things were getting a little bit out of hand.

"He wants to know why there is sawdust in his coke," Anthony said.

"Shit."

Swan's total take on the *kilo y medio* was $38,500. He stashed most of it in a safe deposit box. As the amounts of money he made on cocaine increased, so did the amount of time he spent devising safe ways to hide the cash—he kept safe deposit boxes in several banks around the city, but could not trust them to stand up to an investigation. What evolved was a ready-cash system which in its most extreme example owed much to Swan's love affair with wood and his disdain for the conservation of human energy. He started secreting the money in logs.

His apartment in New York and every house he rented on Long Island had one thing in common— each had a fireplace. From the woodpile in the living room, Swan would select a sympathetic-looking log and soak its bark off—the process required a good deal of work. He would float the log in the bathtub for two or three days, now and then adding a knife or spatula wedgelike to the imposing piece of flotsam, hammering the implements gently into the interface of the bark and wood, and wait for the bark to soak free in one piece. Baths and showers were shared with what ultimately resembled an anchorless underwater mine, floating at the surface with its trip devices exposed. When the bark was finally worked off, Swan would chisel a hole in the log just large enough to encase the money he was hiding. The hole, carved in the shape of the currency, looked something like a robbed grave. When the money was laid to rest, the bark was replaced with glue, clamps and ropes. Swan would sand and sawdust the ends of the log, wipe off the excess glue, then stick the log back onto the woodpile. A hearth fire would cost him $30,000. He sometimes hid dope in the same fashion.

"I had nightmares about people burning logs. I made

it a point never to let anyone stay in my house and burn fires while I was away."

What it all amounted to was the Zachary Swan branch of the Chase Manhattan Bank. The hours were terrible—there were many people who were of the opinion that if he had ever run across a time-and-motion studies man, Zachary Swan would have been a millionaire.

What not a few considered to be the loose wires in Zachary Swan's head sparked him down other dubious paths. Raoul, Armando's man with the ice cream habit, had told Swan that one of the waiters at Victor's Café —the Cuban restaurant in Manhattan which was Ellery's HQ and one of Swan's favorite neighborhood hangouts—owed him, Raoul, $80,000. When Swan asked what for, Raoul assured him it was not for ice cream.

"Once I tried to talk to the man about it—to do a favor for Raoul, to see if I could get any of the money for him. From then on I got very bad tables at Victor's."

Swan's Mail Moves, as they were called, were the bread and butter of his operation. In a way he was very much like Sears Roebuck—no matter what scam he was working on to cover, say, a four-kilo move, he always had at least one package in the mail. Many times he would simply send the money to Rudolpho and let the efficient Colombian handle the South American end of the deal. In order to sustain the mail-order branch of the business, he had to keep updating his New York pickup and delivery service. Davis's was the cornerstone scam. And the Lothario was very important. But there were others.

On one occasion, Swan mailed a statue of Saint Anne to Iona Prep in New Rochelle—a donation from "an alumnus." He and Charlie Kendricks showed up at Iona to photograph this beautiful piece of Colombian craftsmanship, which they expected to find in the chapel. For some reason it had been relegated to the cafeteria—they had to wait for the lunch hour to come and go before they could get to work. The photographs never appeared anywhere, but the original statue appeared that night on the floor of Swan's living room under a chisel. The duplicate left in its place suffered only the penance of the Christian Brothers.

Less difficult than the Saint Anne switch but a bit more harrowing was an experience with one of the Lothario's lovers. She was a very superstitious woman, a fact Swan had not taken into account when he sent her, as a gift "from my country," a tribal head instead of a rolling pin. The head was so frightening she nearly threw it out the window. The Lothario was on hand to prevent the defenestration, but was even more severely taxed after the switch was made. Swan had been unable to find an exact duplicate of the souvenir—the snarling face that had prompted the woman's hysteria he had replaced with one sporting a benign smile. The Lothario had to keep *her* from going out the window when she noticed that.

Zachary Swan, in his pursuit of the perfect formula for drug running, had made enough mistakes and come up hard against enough misconceptions to mistrust intuitively the folklore surrounding cocaine. There was one bright fable in the prevalent street mythology which he learned to discount early—it offered as its moral the celebrated principle that rocks in the coke you buy guarantee the purity of the sample you sell.

Rocks, in cocaine lore, are the lumps that appear dispersed throughout the sample. They are what account for the meticulous chopping which serves as the bizarre Introit to any coke-snorting ceremony. The truth about lumps is that they are simply lumps, like the lumps in damp sugar (in a gram sample of street coke, chances are better than average that the lumps *are* damp sugar), but the lore of the street holds them to be crystals of pure cocaine. A dealer, who will chop the rocks in the cocaine he snorts, will leave them alone in the cocaine he sells, and he will always point to them, if they are there, to show the quality of his product.

Pharmaceutical cocaine, that manufactured legally (1,057 kilos in the U.S. in 1969—twenty dollars an ounce), is sometimes sold in the form of a rock, one large, lambent crystal, like rock candy, 100 percent pure. And illegal cocaine can sometimes be found, in its pure state, to crystallize in a similar fashion, but not so completely and not nearly so often. Pure cocaine of the illegal variety, though chemically crystalline, appears as a flake (as does *most* pharmaceutical cocaine). Rocks in cocaine are more often than not due to moisture, and the moisture will lump any of its impurities and any of the ingredients with which it has been cut. Zachary Swan became aware of this early. Moses Wellfleet, on the other hand, was as devout as they come.

Moses had been dealing coke for years, and he had been dealing it on the street. No one was going to tell Dr. W anything about rocks. And so when Zachary Swan began pressing his coke for shipment, he had trouble with Moses. Compressing the coke essentially pulverized it—the crystals disappeared. After his first shipment using Angel and Rudolpho, part of Swan's pressing ritual included sprinkling crystals on the top of the load for Moses. It was no more than a gesture, and it kept Moses happy. Moses was getting fluff from the blender and rocks from the top of the load, and his customers never complained. The ounce-dealers occasionally got questions from new customers, but the impact of the pressing upon their end of the business was minimal. Compressing the load hurt sales maybe 5 percent.

"Most people don't know what they're blowing anyway—they know what they've been buying. You offer them pure and they won't meet your price—they say it's shit because it doesn't look like what they're used to. So you hit it with some borax and they pay your price. But that takes time. After you unload most of it at an honest price, then you can fuck around with what's left for the sucker trade."

In the months between his first trip to Bogotá in the winter of 1971 and the Brown Gold Move which he made in the summer, Swan made two trips to Colombia. He used Angel and Rudolpho on both and mailed three kilos of cocaine to New York on each occasion.

11

Horse Latitudes

BROWN GOLD COFFEE, imported and packaged by the Andes Coffee Corporation of Palisades Park, New Jersey, is, as its label points out, "100% Colombian." A unique blend of the Medellin Excelso and the Armenia Excelso coffee beans, the label adds, it is "worth its *taste* in gold." Cocaine, on the other hand, a blend of coca leaf alkaloids and neutral crystals, very often 100 percent Colombian, is worth approximately its exact *weight* in gold—and that is before it crosses the border. The mathematics of this coincidence appealed to Zachary Swan, who over his morning coffee was scanning the travel page of *The New York Times*.

"Perfect," he said.

"Find what you were looking for?" Alice asked.

"Avianca Airlines is offering a ten-day excursion. Santa Marta, Barranquilla and Cartagena. Leaves from New York. It even names the hotels."

"Lucky you."

Alice, at this point, was the only person in whom Swan had confided. But to assure the success of this, his most Byzantine move, Swan would need the help of at least two others. He would use Davis on the New York end and Canadian Jack in Cartagena. He needed an office, a telephone number, a few jars of coffee, a handful of printed material, and a lot of luck. He moved fast.

The office was a small one near Lüchow's restaurant on 14th Street. He rented it on a month-to-month basis. Into it he moved an old desk, a new filing cabinet, a swivel chair and a coffee percolator. While he waited for a telephone, he worked on getting the printed material he needed. This was not hard. As a former packaging executive (in essence a printing salesman) he had very little trouble coming by the necessary four-color work and stationery. Most of it he ordered from the Andes Coffee people himself—labels, poster ads, and packaging paper, all stamped with the Andes logo and address: ANDES COFFEE CORP., S. A. Schonbrunn & Co., Inc., Palisades Park, N.J. 07650. What he did not get directly from Andes, he got from business associates who had access to the Andes printing buyer, and what he did not get from them, he had printed on his own. The most important piece of original printing was a miniature folded brochure stamped with his new office number.

He decorated the office in appropriate bad taste with all the trappings he had accumulated—posters on the wall, coffee cans adorning the desk, subway ads, supermarket art, labels glued to everything—bought the coffee and moved in to work. It was difficult work, but after a while and several containers of coffee, he finally managed to remove the vacuum seal from a four-ounce jar of freeze-dried instant without tearing it. He inserted his brochure, replaced the seal with rubber cement, capped the jar and drove to Queens to put the jar in a grocery store. Before he returned to his office, however, he experienced a head-on collision—running hard up against America's free-market system. The coffee in Queens was cheaper than the coffee in Manhattan. Bohack was selling it for less than D'Agostino's. The price tags were different. But Swan was undaunted. In the proud tradition of Yankee know-how and a typical consumer's respect for our nation's supermarkets, Swan switched the lids and moved his jar to the front of the shelf. It was as simple as that. He was leaving nothing to chance.

He walked out, wondering who had shoplifted whom, returned to his office and waited. For days.

Mrs. Vagelatos called at about 4:30 in the afternoon.

"Brown Gold Company."

"Hello."

"Hello."

"I am Mrs. Vagelatos."

"Yes, Mrs. Vagelatos."

"I am number 21-27-37-31-32."

"Are you calling about the contest, Mrs. Vagelatos?"

"Yes. The contest. Yes, I am."

"And what is your number again, Mrs. Vagelatos?"

"Number 21-27-37-31-32."

"Did I hear you correctly, Mrs. Vagelatos? Will you repeat that number?"

She did. (Swan's filing system was quite simple: there was only one number—it was printed into the brochure, it came with the order. There was only one number, and only one of the brochures was in circulation. If Mrs. Vagelatos had not called, Swan would have waited and tried again—he did not want too many copies of the brochure floating around.)

"Mrs. Vagelatos. Mrs. Vagelatos, you are a winner. You have won a prize. You have won *first* prize. You have won a free ten-day trip to Colombia."

Mrs. Vagelatos said she was old and that her husband was retired. He was old too, she said. She spoke English poorly. Mrs. Vagelatos had, however, lived in America for some time.

"Can I have the money, instead?" she asked.

Swan explained the rules of the contest to her— essentially, "It doesn't work that way, lady." Mrs. Vagelatos said she would think it over. She called back the next day, having talked it over with her husband, and told Swan that she and Mr. Vagelatos would take the trip.

"You will enjoy it, Mrs. Vagelatos. Yes. What? Of course. And in addition to the vacation, there will be many gifts and souvenirs."

Of course.

Swan opened a checking account in the name of S. A. Schonbrunn & Co., Inc., and bought tickets for the Avianca tour in the Vagelatoses' name. He enclosed the tickets in a Brown Gold envelope, added a letter of congratulations and an itinerary typewritten on Brown Gold stationery, and mailed them to the couple in Queens.

The itinerary: Santa Marta, Barranquilla and Cartagena. Swan knew where the Vagelatoses would be, and when they would be there, all the time they were were in Colombia. In his letter of congratulations he had informed them that a representative of the company would meet them in Cartagena to present them with their gifts. He called Armando from New York and told him he would be down in a week. He needed three bottles of Chanel.

"And no fucking around, Armando, I must have it. If you've got it there, hold it. I will definitely be down."

Two weeks later he took $22,000 cash from a safe deposit box on the East Side and flew to Bogotá. (Whenever Swan carried large amounts of currency —and sometimes cocaine—he wore a special jacket, the lining of which had been designed specifically for that purpose by Alice. Essentially the jacket was lined with pockets. They were distributed evenly around the back and sides to prevent bulging, they were invisibly tufted so that the lining itself appeared smooth, and they were hemmed with Velcro, that miracle of the Space Age, to facilitate access and obviate the necessity for zippers or buttons. At any time, but especially when Swan traveled South, the jacket was a very expensive piece of tailoring.)

Armando delivered. He charged Swan six thousand a kilo for the three keys, a five-dollar increase per gram, partly for holding the load and partly because at the time the price of cocaine was going up all around the world. Angel and Rudolpho made the fill. Swan tracked down Canadian Jack, gave him $200, a few grams of coke, and a ticket to Cartagena. The two flew north together, Swan with the souvenirs, and Canadian Jack carrying a brand new Polaroid camera.

El Caribe Hotel, where the Vagelatoses' tour was booked, is located in Cartagena's Bocagrande district, at the tip of a peninsula which separates Cartagena Bay from the Caribbean Sea. Remote from the Old Town, decidedly distant in statute and spiritual miles from any of those things which may distinguish Cartagena from the other cities of the world—out there, across the harbor—Bocagrande, on the ocean side, is devoted almost exclusively to tourists. The Caribbean front of the peninsula is covered with neo-Miami concrete-and-Formica firetraps which go by such names as Americar, Flamingo, El Dorado and Las Vegas, every room of which offers Inquisition-in-walnut furniture, a pastel, circular sink in bas relief, and a view of the beach. Under construction when Swan worked out of Cartagena, and now a second-thought-provoking reality, these wonders of modern architecture are designed to make South Americans feel they have come a long way and make North Americans feel at home. The principle governing their birth is the same one as that which presumes the drinking of Coca-Cola in Bordeaux. Social historians call it progress.

Tucked away out here in the trees, a lush array and ample variety of trees, on a vast expanse of protected real estate, is the Hotel Caribe. A faithful rendition of Spanish architecture, old, stately, a kind of one-man Environmental Protection Agency, El Caribe supports its own arboretum and tropical gardens as well as an animal population of modest scope. Much of the fruit served here is grown on the grounds, and most of the grounds, obviously, are devoted to nothing more than the simple pleasure of being on them. A back gate opens onto the beach. A marina fronts on a bay to the southeast. The hotel itself, if not as large as some of its treeless and sunscorched upstart neighbors, affords its clientele a greater degree of comfort, and a variety of luxury that all but disappeared with the advent of terrazzo lawns and vertical expansion. Perhaps because it is impossible for a swimmer to drown in an upright position within sight of Cartagena—the Caribbean here is just too shallow for too great a distance out—or maybe because walking the beach at night, like walking anywhere in South America, is taking your life in your hands—the Hotel Caribe was blueprinted around space for an Olympic pool, shaded by palm trees on two sides, bordered by an enclosed restaurant on one and an open-air poolside dining area on the other. It was by the pool, amid these lavish surroundings, that Swan staged his awards ceremony.

Swan and Canadian Jack took a midweek, morning flight from Bogotá to Cartagena and checked into the Hotel Caribe. Shortly after he arrived, Swan called the Vagelatoses' room and asked the couple to meet him at the pool to receive their gifts. While Swan, sporting a full beard and dark glasses, awarded the Vagelatoses their prizes and made a big show of certifying with the waiter that the coffee they were drinking was 100 percent Colombian, laughing all the way, Canadian Jack dashed around with the camera. As usual, Swan and the Canadian were stoned, so it made no difference to either one of them that the Polaroid was empty and showed no signs of developing and ejecting the pictures it was presumably taking.

Swan loaded the Vagelatoses down with rolling pins, statues, wall hangings, hammocks, blankets, *ruanas,* straw hats, leather bags—about forty pounds of paraphernalia that cost him close to $150 and which would retail in the United States for over $500, all of it dragged out of two great, overflowing plastic bags. In his room, Swan had a duplicate of every one of the souvenirs. He asked the Vagelatoses to sign an agreement by which they were bound to be photographed again with their presents in the New York office. He made an offhand joke, unacknowledged, about Greeks bearing gifts, gave them a copy of the agreement to keep, and wished them a safe trip home.

The Vagelatoses were due back in New York two days later. Swan left a day early and made a dry run with his duplicates. They were not examined. The Vagelatoses were supposed to call Swan's office as soon as they returned. They did not. Swan waited. He worried. He had to call them. They were tired, it turned out—they had arrived on schedule. Swan groaned out loud over the phone. He dispatched a limousine, which he paid for in cash, to pick them up at their home in Queens.

Davis took the New York photos. And while Swan bought the Vagelatoses lunch at Lüchow's, Davis made the switch. The Vagelatoses returned to the office, picked up their gifts, Swan wished them health, wealth and happiness, escorted them to the limousine, and sent them home. He closed down the office the next day and never saw the couple from Queens again.

Quidquid id est, timeo Danaos et dona ferentis . . .
The Customs man, obviously, had never read Virgil.

With the Brown Gold Move, the supposed foundation upon which Swan had based his entry into smuggling was first called into question. His claim that he would never endanger a carrier or throw an innocent individual to the lions was challenged on the basis of his use of Mr. and Mrs. Vagelatos, a couple who had no idea of the trouble they might be walking into, two innocent Greek immigrants whose faith in America was reflected, for better or worse, by the faith they placed in its institutions, whether these be its supermarkets, its coffee companies or its Treasury Department, and the trust they placed in its citizens, whether they be honest Customs agents, as innocent of the facts as they, or alleged felons like Richard Nixon and Zachary Swan. The evidence in Swan's favor, however, is significant.

In the first place the Vagelatoses *were* innocent, which in itself is anyone's greatest asset to getting by a Customs check. In their favor also was the fact that they were traveling with a tour, a group of Americans who are predominantly middle class and middle-aged and who are supervised almost every step of their way through a foreign country—their luggage is even handled differently. But it begs the question to say that the Vagelatoses had a better than average chance of making it through Customs without a search. After all, Swan's idea was to get the coke through—it was what the scam was designed for. In the event of a search, then, and assuming the even more remote possibility that the cocaine was discovered (Customs did not break open Swan's souvenirs, which were identical to those Mr. and Mrs. Vagelatos were carrying), one must ask how well the Vagelatoses were covered.

Swan claims they were covered well. He had insisted that they save the contest number; he could assume that they still had the coffee jar. In addition to these two items, the Vagelatoses were in possession of two Avianca tickets purchased by a check accounted to S. A. Schonbrunn & Co., Inc., whose office address was on 14th Street. On their persons at Customs they had a letter of congratulations and an itinerary typed on Brown Gold stationery. And in the same envelope they had a signed agreement to appear at the 14th Street office with their gifts upon arrival in the United States. In the absence of everything else, they had at least thirty witnesses poolside in Cartagena. The evidence of their innocence, then, was overwhelming, as Swan saw it. If the Vagelatoses suffered at all, he assumed, it would be principally by way of embarrassment and perhaps temporary detention at the airport while the evidence was examined; and he supposed that the free ten-day vacation and the unconfiscated souvenirs would be sufficient compensation for that. As it turned out, in fact, everyone but Uncle Sam made out on the deal.

Swan was moving fast now. The Brown Gold Move was such an overwhelming success, and his confidence in the wake of it so buoyant, that his roiling imagination began to generate more blueprints than he could follow. He had to throw them away. One outline that was carried through to success without his knowledge was one that he threw away in the company of Canadian Jack and Black Dan on a rainy night in Bogotá, when the cocaine express was taking its curves on the high side.

Black Dan had been living at the Oriole for almost two years when Swan first met him. He loved it in Bogotá. He left only once every six weeks, and he was always back fast. His visits to San Francisco were brief. Although he did not open up to Swan until a year after their meeting, it was pretty obvious all along that he was a smuggler. It was what you were in Bogotá if you were not manifestly anything else. And Dan always had cocaine. It was Dan who told Swan about *Mannite,* the Italian laxative, the cocaine-cutting agent of choice and that with which Dan always cut his own coke before snorting. He preferred it that way to pure, for reasons which were unclear to Swan, and he preferred it out of a spoon, a taste Swan attributed to hours in the back rooms of Mission District bars.

Dan's closest friend in Bogotá was Canadian Jack, a friendship, in Swan's mind, distinguished chiefly by its sharp contrasts. Beyond the obvious one (Canadian Jack was a blond) was the almost polar difference in their approaches to smuggling. Black Dan was thoroughly professional. He found no need to acknowledge that he was a smuggler, even to Swan, a smuggler himself, whose professionalism was exemplified, if in no other way, by the fact that he never questioned Dan. Black Dan was a pro, and he had been going for years. He moved in quantity, unlike Jack, whose moves were small, and he was consistent. Every six weeks he flew to Mexico City with the coke strapped to his legs. From there he would fly to Matamoros or Tijuana, or whatever border town was convenient to his needs, and walk the load across, reentering the States with the bullfight crowds on the weekends, intimidating every official in his path by his mere presence. He never wasted time, and the closest he ever came to trouble was the trouble out of which he was always bailing Jack.

It was an evening in the early summer of 1971, six months after he had helped load Swan's press into Rudolpho's car and still six months before he would open up and apprise Swan of the Mexican route, that Black Dan, Swan and Canadian Jack were doing samples in Dan's suite at the Oriole, talking about the upcoming Summer Games in Cali.

"That's going to be a smugglers' convention," said Swan.

"You think so?"

"Well, just think about it for a minute. Number one —the pickpockets. Every dipper in the country is going to pack up and leave home. The thieves will be coming out of the woodwork, and they'll all converge on Cali when the games start. There'll be a million tourists there and another million people connected with the games in one way or another. Don't even count the Colombians, and that's a hell of a lot of money floating around. This country is as famous for its pickpockets as it is for its fucking coffee, and every one of them will be in Cali next month. So a smuggler doubles his money before he starts."

"I don't get the connection," said Jack.

"Can you picture the activity at the American Express office? Everybody and his mother is going to be there replacing stolen traveler's checks—'I just got to Cali and my traveler's checks have been stolen'—and they're not going to ask them any questions. 'Of course they've been stolen, this is Colombia.' So what do you do? You sign 'em, sell 'em . . . use 'em . . . and then you replace them. You can do it every day, and the banks aren't going to pick up on it. Barclay's, Bank of America, First National City, Cook's, they're all going to be giving money away. So you double your money . . . triple it . . . before you begin."

"And with all the traffic in and out," said Dan, "Customs will be that much easier."

"Or tougher," said Jack.

"So you hire a jock. Or get a crewcut. Steal a couple of warmup jackets with emblems on them and walk through Customs carrying your equipment. Soccer balls would be perfect. Or javelins, if they're made of wood, though they might be making those out of metal now. You name it. You know what I'd do?"

"What's that?" asked Dan.

"Starting blocks. You know, the wooden blocks they use for the dash. Perfect. Who would think of cracking a starting block? And you can get a couple of kilos in there easily. It's perfect."

"It is perfect," Dan agreed.

"Let's have another blow," said Jack.

Canadian Jack told Swan that the Brown Gold Move was the most beautiful piece of business he had ever witnessed. It inspired him to christen Swan with a nickname, one that stuck, and one which gained immediate currency among the borderline elite. From then on Swan, because Jack thought he was sly and because everyone thought he was old, was known as the Silver Fox.

"The feeling after putting one over is indescribable. In the beginning, they all laughed at me, at all my long, intricate plans, my maps, my charts—my over-development, they called it—Vinnie, Mickey, all of them, they all thought I was dumb, but pretty soon they all ended up working for me . . . eventually they were all either investing in me or working *for* me.

After that one I had so many ideas, I couldn't use them all. I gave them away. [Some, like the flourish he worked on Adrian, he sold, but he did, in fact, give many of them away. One of these was the Duplicate Bag Switch, which he gave to Canadian Jack on his next trip to Bogotá.] I wanted to keep moving, and I wanted that boat move."

Before leaving Colombia to await the Vagelatoses in New York, Swan bumped into two old friends. Somehow having drifted down from Santa Marta, at the whim of whatever currents prevailed, Jane and April had ended up on the beach in Cartagena, and they were as loose as ever—Swan was always reminded of Halloween when they were around. Assuming that they had eaten little but mushrooms since he had last seen them, he smuggled them past the guard at the back gate of the Caribe and bought them dinner. He tried to get as much protein into them as he could.

Jane was looking particularly unwell. April's voice seemed to have dropped about an octave in the past six months, but Jane was strung out to the limit. Swan saw tombstones in her eyes. She had found a pair of old walking shoes and a broken conch shell on the beach and was carrying them around with her wherever she went. They were for her brother. For his birthday. He lived in Brooklyn, she said.

Swan offered to take her home.

"No," she said.

She wanted her brother to come down and get her: "Tell him where I am and tell him to come down and get me."

Swan said: "Please."

"No."

She gave him a note and the old shoes and the shell. He carried them back to New York with the Vagelatoses' souvenirs. He called her brother in Brooklyn, and when her brother came to pick up his birthday presents, Swan told him he had better go down soon.

"Well," he said, "you know what kind of girl she is. She ran away when she was fifteen, doesn't give a shit. And I don't give a shit. Did you give her money?"

Swan just stared.

"She probably spent it on dope. That's what kind of girl she is."

"You're not going?"

No.

12

Why Did You Write
My Name in the Snow?

WHEN ZACHARY SWAN was introduced to Harry Morgan, he laughed out loud.

"What's so funny?" asked Sea Gull Billy.

Sea Gull Billy was a Hotel Caribe boathand. If he was needed, and he often was, he could be contacted at the hotel marina. If he was not working the marina, Billy could be found at any of several locations around the hotel, either making a connection of one kind or another or waiting for a connection to make him. Billy was a promoter, a fixer. He was the man to see at the Caribe. He knew what was happening, where, when it was happening, and who was making it happen. *I'm Sea Gull Billy. You need anything, you come to me, I'll take care of it. I'm honest. You get a good deal. You need a woman, something to smoke, you name it, esmeraldas, coca, I'll take care of it. Just ask for Sea Gull Billy.*

Swan had asked for Sea Gull Billy on several occasions. When Uta ran off with Ramón Greco, Swan gave Billy $200 before he left for New York with the driftwood: "See that she gets it when she comes through again," he told Billy. Billy did. If Swan wanted to know the whereabouts of Canadian Jack or René Day, or if he needed information—current activity, traffic in and out of Cartagena, government surveillance—or if he needed a connection he did not have, he went to Billy. Billy was the man to see.

Billy was Colombian, about forty-five. He was short

183

and wide with a weatherbeaten face. His brown eyes were constantly working, keeping up with whatever the action happened to be, jumping from side to side behind the tinted glasses he always wore. He spoke English well, would never smoke anything but his own brand of cigarette and always wore a boatman's cap. He was dressed in khaki, wearing deck shoes, and passing the pool at a good clip when Swan stopped him. Their conversation was brief.

"Billy, I need a boat captain."

Billy nodded. He looked around. Across the pool he spotted what or whomever he was looking for. He looked back at Swan.

"Tomorrow morning. Nine. At the marina," he said. He moved on, chasing whatever it was he was chasing.

A hot breeze was blowing in off the bay. Sea Gull Billy was still waiting for an answer. The boats, their boards swelling in the heat, were rocking gently, tugging at their bowlines. The temperature was approaching 90 degrees, and Swan was standing on the pier at the marina, in his bathing suit, with a towel over his shoulder. Billy was staring at him quizzically. Harry Morgan, smoking Chesterfields, knew what was so funny.

"His name's Harry Morgan, Billy."

"That's right."

"And he's a boat captain."

"Right."

"In the Caribbean."

"Right."

"Well, you see, Billy, that's very funny. Harry Morgan is a very famous boat captain."

"Harry's not famous," Billy said.

"Not this Harry, another Harry," Swan said.

"And that's funny?"

"Not anymore, Billy. Thanks."

Swan paid him, and he and Harry Morgan walked back to the hotel for a drink.

* * *

Harry Morgan, thirty-five, boat captain, was not making money working for a thief in Miami. He wondered where it was he had gone wrong. And he was interested to know what it was he could actually do to make money working for a thief from New York. He listened to Swan. Harry, an American, was from Florida, just south of Coral Gables, where Swan had gone to college. He had grown up on a number of boats, and had made a living at one time taking fishing parties from Miami to Bimini—a piece of biographical information that Swan found attractive. In Cartagena, Harry was working for an American who owned several tourist boats, which he chartered out, through Harry, to scuba divers and deep-sea fishermen. Harry's American employer was a smart operator. He owned another boat, in addition to the ones Harry managed, which he skippered himself out of Miami, an 80-foot schooner in which he had at one time invested about forty thousand dollars and converted to use as a treasure hunter. Having converted the boat, he opened an office in New York, incorporated, sold shares in the corporation, and sailed to Colombia, where he bought gold doubloons, pieces-of-eight, salvaged pottery, anchors and various bits of recovered chandlery, which he then threw overboard and slowly re-recovered, reporting a magnificent find to the shareholders back home. He then went public with his corporation and made a killing on the common stock. Because he was doing so well, Harry's employer devoted all his resources to the salvaging scam, and Harry's paychecks in Cartagena were coming in three weeks late when they were coming in at all. Harry was looking for work.

Swan had been working toward a boat move, in one way or another, from the beginning. He wanted it to be big. When he was finally ready to engineer it, he went to Anthony for backing. The agreement was that Anthony put up the money for one kilo, front Swan a thousand toward expenses, and guarantee the sale of

Swan's first thousand grams. If the move was a success, they would parlay their money and do it again. Swan had nowhere to go but up. In the summer of 1971, he laid out the plan.

The key to the move was Harry Morgan. He not only knew the waters off Colombia, but he knew Florida and the Bahamas as well. Bimini, a sportsman's paradise, would provide the cover, and the Florida coastline, somewhere north of Miami, would provide the drop. The cocaine would travel, as usual, in wood —gaffs, boat hooks, belaying pins—whatever was appropriate to the vessel they used. The trip would be a long one, but the load would be big, and if the move required a lot of preparation, that was all right too, because they would use it again if it worked.

Anthony considered the details and insisted on one change, a major one. He wanted a man of his own in on the move, a man who could follow the load all the way through. And he had the man he needed, a boatman in Miami named Jimmy. Swan could have him for free. Jimmy was Anthony's man, and he would be looking out for Anthony's interests all the way down the line. Swan accepted the deal and headed for Florida to get the operation under way.

Jimmy reminded Swan of a young, but still fat and jolly, Burl Ives—if you nail Burl Ives, you've got this guy, he would tell Harry Morgan. Jimmy must have impressed some others the same way, because in the off-season, when there were no boats to captain, he made good money playing the banjo in various clubs around Miami. Swan met Jimmy at home and went to work on him right away—Swan ran his man through a fundamental security procedure, his own brand of speed clearance, something on the order of a reverse Pinkerton investigation, an intensive, counter-FBI check. It relied heavily on instinct, experience and the remarkable insight generated by the imperatives of self-preservation. And it had to be done fast.

Jimmy's wife was a waitress. She introduced Swan

to a woman she worked with named Nina, and that evening the four of them went out. It gave Swan the opportunity to observe Jimmy from several angles. Swan brought some coke, and Jimmy came across with some transplanted, home-grown, Gainesville Green from his tomato garden. Swan was beginning to like him already. He and Jimmy got stoned together, and very drunk, foraging through the neon wilderness of Miami Beach. They had a wonderful time. When the party was over, Jimmy stumbled home with his wife, Swan spent the night with Nina, and by the time he got around to his second cup of coffee the following morning, Swan was sure about his man.

"Jimmy was completely trustworthy. You know a guy right away . . . whether he's going to do you or not do you . . . and if you have any reservations about him, you'd better stick to those reservations, because if you don't you are really in trouble . . . in jail or dead. I know guys who wouldn't shoot me for ten thousand dollars, but for fifteen I wouldn't turn my back on them. I had no reservations about Jimmy."

Jimmy and Swan spent the next couple of weeks looking at boats. There were several old shrimp fishers available, but most of them needed work, and there was no way Swan could work out buying any one of them without having his or Jimmy's name appear on the papers. Swan evaluated his options, discussed the problem with Jimmy, and the decision was finally made to pick up a boat in Colombia—the original plan was going to be altered. Swan called Avianca and made reservations for two to Bogotá. With three days to go before their flight, Jimmy began thinking about *his* man.

"Do you know how to handle a piece?" he asked.

"No. Not since the Marine Corps," said Swan.

"I think we better do a little practicing."

"O.K.," Swan said.

Sure.

Jimmy drove to a firing range on the Tamiami

Trail that was open to the public for two dollars an hour and the price of ammunition. He was carrying four guns, three revolvers and an automatic. He wanted Swan to try them all. The clubhouse reminded Swan of a golf shop, but where he was used to seeing Slazengers and Spauldings he saw Smith & Wessons and Colts. Out on the range, in the hot late-afternoon sun, Swan shot first, firing from the hip.

"Jesus, this is ridiculous," he said when they examined the target; he had missed it completely with all six rounds.

"Like this," Jimmy said.

Jimmy went into a crouch, held his firing arm rigid, and braced one wrist with the other, sighting along the barrel before squeezing the trigger. It was what Swan had seen done often in movies made after Jimmy Cagney had retired—when the cops became the identifiable heroes.

"That's terrific, Jimmy, but by the time I get into fuckin' position, we're going to have to shoot from close range or forget it."

"Look," Jimmy said, "I know exactly what you ought to do. I've got this fine Colombian back in the car. Go to the parking lot and smoke it, and when you come back, things will be different."

Swan was never one to say no to a good hit of dope. He started for the parking lot.

"On your way back in, pick me up some more bullets," Jimmy shouted.

Swan nodded. He found the joint in one of the hubcaps of the car, stood in the shade, and took his time smoking it. He stared at the sunset. Swan liked Florida. Probably, he thought, because he associated it with the sea. He knew he could never live inland. No surprises. He thought of the island he would buy someday with the money he made—someday, he thought, if he did not get shot first. He listened to the gunfire on the breeze and watched the smoke rise over the coconut palms. It looked as though it might rain. He crushed the roach out with the heel of his shoe and headed for the clubhouse to pick up Jimmy's ammunition. At the counter he ran into four policemen. He smiled. They were buying bullets, .38 calibre service rounds. He headed for the firing range.

"Well?" Jimmy asked.

Swan just nodded. He fired more slowly this time, but still from the hip.

"Not bad," Jimmy said.

"Not bad," said Swan. "It's not bad. I can see the bullets coming out of the gun now. It happens much slower. I can see it and feel it.

"Jimmy," he said, turning to his friend, "I'm really shooting good."

"You're doing fine, baby," Jimmy said with a smile.

Swan was pretty well jammed up by now.

"Jimmy, what are those fucking cops doing over there?"

"Well, you see on the other side of the clubhouse there, that's the police firing range."

In Swan's drug-addled mind a couple of transistors failed.

"Are you kidding me?"

"No."

"Well, Jimmy, I happen to make that guy we scored coke from last night." Swan pointed. "You see, he's down over there, shooting."

Jimmy looked. "Oh, yeah," he said.

"And these two guys shooting next to us, Jimmy, they don't look like they're on the side of the law, do they?"

"Nope," said Jimmy without having to look.

"Well, I got a great idea for you, Jimmy. Let's go make a deal right now."

"What?"

"I'm going to go over and talk to the police and I'm going to tell them that if they see me, don't shoot me because I'm not out to kill anybody—you know, it was all a big joke. And as far as I'm concerned, man,

it's cool, I ain't going to shoot at them if they ain't
going to shoot at me, and I want to let them know, so
let's go make a deal right now."

Jimmy laughed. And then Swan laughed. And the
lawmen on one side of the fence and the outlaws on
the other all fired their guns into the approaching
darkness.

Two days later Swan and Jimmy went South.

"Bogotá at your feet," said Swan.

Swan had taken Jimmy to the top of Monserrate,
the more accessible of the twin peaks that overlook
the capital. They stood on the steps of the shrine
facing west. Guadalupe, a hard climb by mule train,
rose on their left. Directly in front of them, two thousand feet down, beneath the eagles and the wind, was
Bogotá. Jimmy sighted along the funicular cables to
the *barrios* at the foot of the mountain. Beneath the
funicular and to the right of it ran the tracks of the
older cable car, disappearing here and there into a
ravine, reappearing out of the trees, and gone again,
emerging finally at the terminal below. Beyond the
terminal and the *barrios* was the city. The air was
clean and the sun was directly overhead.

"It sure looks different," he said. "It's really beautiful. And you can breathe up here. The smog down
there is incredible, isn't it? I mean, just look at it."

"There are three million people down there," Swan
said, "and every one of them thinks he's rich if he
owns a '58 De Soto. They've never heard of PCV
valves or smog control—you figure it out—at eight
thousand feet above sea level you don't have much
oxygen to start with. And we think L.A.'s bad."

"Three million?"

"And tonight I'll introduce you to a few of them."

Jimmy nodded.

"You in a hurry?" he asked.

"Nope."

"I think I'll take some pictures."

"Take your time."

"Do they ever use that one?" Jimmy asked, pointing to the cable car tracks.

"When they're busy. In the off-season they alternate them."

Jimmy aimed his camera.

"One's the funicu-li and one's the funicu-la," Swan said.

That night at the Oriole, Swan introduced Jimmy to Juan Carlos Ramirez and Canadian Jack. While Jimmy and Juan Carlos talked, Canadian Jack took Swan to one side. They conversed quietly for a while, and Swan nodded when they were finished. Jack sat down, and Swan motioned Jimmy away from the bar.

"Jack wants in on our move," Swan said to Jimmy.

Jimmy looked at the Canadian, who was talking to Juan Carlos now.

"He ain't gonna like it," Jimmy said, referring to Mr. Big.

"He doesn't even have to know," Swan said.

Jimmy looked at Swan. He shook his head.

"No," he said, "he's a kid."

Swan shrugged. He did not feel like arguing. He motioned to Jack, and together they walked outside.

"I'm sorry," he said, shaking his head.

"Why not?" Jack wanted to know.

"I got robbed in New York. All my money's gone and I'm working for a guy, somebody else. And he hasn't got any room. I'm sorry, Jack."

Jack sighed. "Well, what am I gonna do?"

"Well, what have you got?"

"I've got a girl down here."

(Customs was knocking mules over now.)

"Well, what *were* you gonna do?"

"Stick it on her back or up her cunt."

"Does she know you?"

"Yeah, I've known her a long time."

"Will she stand up?"

"I don't know. She's getting shaky."

"Well, you're in trouble, aren't ya?"

"Yeah."

"Yeah."

Swan shook his head. He liked Jack and he felt bad about having had to lie to him about the setup.

"Look," he said, "let me do some business. I don't have anything right now, but I'll think about it, and I'll meet you here tomorrow night. O.K.?"

"O.K."

Swan nodded. He turned to go.

"Thanks," said Jack.

"Don't mention it," Swan said with a wave of his hand and walked back into the hotel.

Jimmy wanted to go on the score. Swan said no. He knew he had to keep Jimmy away from Armando. He had to assume that giving Armando to Jimmy was giving him to Anthony, and with a sizable slice of his New York operation at stake, that slice of his business which was represented by Anthony, Swan was determined to keep Jimmy away from his contacts, especially Armando, his principal supplier. But Jimmy insisted—and with Anthony behind him, there was nothing much Swan could say. So Swan took him to Luís.

Luís was a connection Swan had made on a previous trip to Bogotá, a friend of Rudolpho's from whom Swan had accepted a kilo once when Armando was short. He was a Ford auto parts dealer, trying to make it in the cocaine business, and Swan was always accepting *muestras* from him. Luís was not as reliable as Armando, and his quality was not always there, but he was usually good for a kilo in an emergency. So Swan gave him to Jimmy. Swan and Jimmy scored Anthony's kilo together, after Swan had made the deal with Luís and had put five hundred on it. Swan scored his own three keys from Armando—alone.

(Swan used several suppliers in Bogotá—after his

first two moves he scored only in that city—and he accepted *muestras* from everyone. His pockets were always full of the white paper packets he picked up in the course of a day, and he and Vincent spent many evenings together, destroyed, sitting around the coffee table in Vincent's living room, snorting up the day's samples. Swan would score from Luís again, and on his last move he would score from Jago, the Hawk's man. But Armando would always be his number one connection, and the reasons for it were simple: "His weight was always there, his product was always good or superior, and he'd get me all the grass I wanted free.")

Through Armando, Swan found out that René Day was back in town. He would be at the Marguerita that night. Before going to the Marguerita, Swan dropped in on Canadian Jack.

"I got one for you," he said.

"She's coming now," said Jack, and the door opened.

Swan turned his head away, his back to the door.

"I don't want to meet anyone," he said.

But by then Susan was in the room. She was tiny, no more than an inch over five feet, and she was beautiful. She had big brown eyes. Swan was reminded of a Keane painting—he said later she should have been carrying in a cat. He shook his head.

"O.K.," he said, giving up, "bring her in."

All the things you say you're never going to do, he thought. Susan sat on the bed and kept her mouth shut. Swan looked at her, then at Jack. They were both wrecked.

"Well," he said, "I'll give you a perfect one."

Jack smiled.

"Evidently we've got to prop up the chick," Swan said, "so let's give her something she can't get scared on."

"O.K., but keep it easy," said Jack.

"You know, you're not giving me room to work," said Swan. "I've got something set up so that if she gets caught, she walks out."

"An excuse?"

Swan nodded. And then an exasperated look came over his face. He stared at Jack. Susan had jumped up—and she was prancing around the room, singing, "The Silver Fox is gonna give us an excuse . . . the Silver Fox . . . the Silver Fox . . ."

"Can you get her to cut that out?" Swan said.

Susan sat down. Jack got serious.

"Now, here is how it works . . ."

And Swan gave Canadian Jack the Duplicate Bag Switch. Like all of Swan's flim-flams, the Duplicate Bag Switch is designed not to protect the goods, but to protect the carrier. The goods are taken care of in the usual manner. The cocaine is packed in Madeira wood, chosen for its high specific gravity—a distinctive physical property of that wood which, after all is said and done, is nothing more than Nature's way of telling us: it is heavy. When a Madeira rolling pin or statue is hollowed out, it does not *feel* hollow. Neither does it feel suspiciously heavy when filled with cocaine. So whenever he could, Swan used Madeira. And he used Angel, who was more than a carpenter—Angel was an artist, and his work was flawless.

So from the time it is packed, the coke is on its own, protected as well as it can be. There is no guarantee in the smuggler's handbook that *everything* that passes through Customs will not be opened (that is why Sicilians and Corsicans dealing in hundredweights of heroin go *around* Customs). The only thing that encourages or discourages a Customs man from cracking anything he finds—apart from the fundamental consideration of the time it requires—is the carrier. And if the carrier is not a consummate actor or actress (and often even that is not enough), then he or she is going to need propping up. Propping up a carrier can be done with coke, or it can be done with a foolproof smuggle. There are other ways, but the point is that if a carrier is propped up (confident, unafraid, i.e., not suspicious looking), the chances are that the Customs agent will not be any more curious than usual. Given the odds on the coke (and when you mule it, no matter where you put it, those odds conform to nothing more profound than the law of averages) and taking for granted that *there's no way you can deny it's yours, man, if it's strapped to your back,* then the Duplicate Bag Switch is the perfect scam.

". . . you have to buy two suitcases, and they have to be exactly alike, in every way," Swan said.

"Right," said Jack.

"Have Angel and Rudolpho pack the load for you —a statue, a rolling pin, anything. It should look like a souvenir."

Jack nodded.

"Now the suitcases have to open like this"—he drew his arms inward—"at a right angle. No zippers. And it's got to stand up—she has to be able to open it away from her—so that when it is open and the inspector is going through it, she can't see what he's doing, the top's between them. O.K.? I'm talking about a standard suitcase, very simple, nothing fancy. The other shit won't do."

"O.K."

"O.K. Now, in one of the suitcases, she puts everything she owns, all her clothes, her shoes, anything that fits, and a few things that will identify her. And *she* packs it. O.K.?"

"Got it."

"Now, the other suitcase, the duplicate, is where the load goes. And *you* have to pack it. Her fingerprints can't be anywhere near the duplicate bag. *You* pack it, and you pack it with a lot of women's clothes, all size ten . . . what size are you, Susan, about a six?"

"Six," she said.

"Good. So all the clothes in with the load are size

ten. Shoes to match. Cosmetics, everything. Just as if it were a woman's suitcase like any other. Everything two sizes too big, all of it clean, no prints, and none of it hers. She never touches this particular bag. Understand?" he said to Susan.

"I understand."

"O.K. You take the same plane and you don't sit together. Both bags are checked aboard and they are exactly alike except for a scuff mark on one of them. That's the loaded one. When you get off the plane, Susan, you pick up the loaded bag—this is the first time you've touched it—and you carry it through Customs. Jack, you're delayed. Susan opens the loaded bag—away from you, Susan, you undo the clasps and pull the top up toward you—and she can't see what the Customs man is doing. The lid of the suitcase is between them. She's short, so that helps; the counters are usually high at Customs. And, while the agent is examining the contents of the bag, she's fiddling with the rest of her stuff—whatever else she's carrying. She's not looking at what he's doing. If that bag goes through, Jack, you just pick up her real bag and carry it through yourself.

"*If* the man cracks the statue, Susan, *if* they nail you, you've never seen that bag before in your life. 'This isn't my bag. That must be mine running around all alone on the conveyor belt over there.' And it is. Jack has left it there. Everything fits. No way they can put anything in it with you, no fingerprints, no belongings, no nothing, you got the wrong bag, you moved in on somebody else's hustle, no record, no nothing, out. You walk away."

There was silence.

"What do you think?"

"Unbelievable."

"You like that one, huh?"

"I like it."

"It's a giveaway, a winger, no planning, nothing, I just thought of it last night."

"It can't fail," Jack said.

"It can't fail."

(And it did not fail. They got the load through. If they had not, they could have tried it again and again until the money ran out. The Duplicate Bag Switch, if handled correctly, is arrest-proof wherever the rules of evidence apply.)

When he left Canadian Jack, Swan picked up Jimmy and headed for the Marguerita. Like every discotheque of any standing in Colombia, the Marguerita had a neo-cave quality about it. It was loud and dark, always jammed, and a good place to plant yourself if you wanted to be either lost or found in a hurry. The acoustics, like the drinks, were bad by design. The strobe lights were out of phase by accident—or incident—the kilocycle-per-second realities of South American power not entirely blameless. It was the kind of place second-rate film directors were always looking for in the 1960s in which to shoot "now" footage. It was not the kind of place that especially impressed René Day.

René was at the far end of the bar, nursing what he thought was Scotch. He was wearing a tan suit, no tie; he looked happy, and Swan was glad to see him.

"Hey, Rainy."

"Hey, man, it's good to see you."

"Good to see *you*, Rainy."

They shook hands.

"This is Jimmy. He's a friend of mine."

"It's a pleasure."

"Glad to meet you," said Jimmy.

"When did you get in?" Swan asked.

"Last night."

"I talked to Armando."

René looked at Jimmy. He said to Swan, "Yeah, I'll see him again on Friday."

"Going North?"

René nodded.

"What are you drinking?" Jimmy asked.

"I think it's Scotch, but I wouldn't bet on it."

Jimmy bought drinks all around. "Here's to a good trip North."

Everyone drank.

Then Swan lost Jimmy for two days. He left him at the Marguerita bar and did not see him again until forty-eight hours later, when he turned up alive (no small wonder in Bogotá) with René, stepping out of the half-light of dawn through the doorway of an after-hours club Swan was leaving. Which of them—Jimmy or René—looked worse was hard to say. Neither one of them was as stoned as Swan.

"Jimmy . . . Rainy . . . Rainy . . . Jimmy . . ."

Swan was fumbling with three hotel keys he had drawn out of three different pockets from beneath his *ruana*, trying to figure out which was which. He was living at the Tequendama, stashing his coke at the Continental, and keeping his money at the Hilton. And as an edge, he had taken the plastic identification tags off each key.

"Jesus, this is difficult," he said.

"You need a drink," René said.

"A drink will fix you right up," said Jimmy.

Swan turned around, and the three of them went inside for a drink.

"Rainy wants in on our move," said Jimmy, picking up his drink.

Swan looked at Jimmy. Then at René.

"I told him it was O.K.," Jimmy added, downing his drink.

Swan shrugged his shoulders, nodded his head, turned to René, lifted his drink and smiled:

"Anchors aweigh."

Angel bought the lumber. Rudolpho flew to Barranquilla to buy the hardware for the gaffs and boat hooks. While the coke was being packed, Swan sent Jimmy with a note to Harry Morgan in Cartagena.

Harry had found a boat, a 55-foot ketch with two aux-
iliary diesels, the *Buccaneer,* docked at the Club de
Pesca. The owner would rent it for $1,500 a month.
There were legal complications, something to do with
smuggled liquor aboard, but Harry knew the dock
master and was well attuned to the technical lies, paper shuffling, and Customs procedures involved in getting a boat out of Cartagena—any boat. With Harry
Morgan's help, Jimmy rented the boat for two months.
Where required to show a reason, he wrote: *buried
treasure.* When Angel finished the packing, Swan and
Rudolpho carted the load—gaffs, boat hooks and the
rest—from Bogotá to Cartagena in a rented pickup
truck, an adventure in itself, given the numerous
breakdowns that attended their journey. The truck
was more than twenty years old. With René's thousand
grams the load came to five kilos, and in a moment of
rare pique at the technological realities visited upon the
host country, Swan entertained the notion that one gaff
was worth three Cadillacs. It took them two days to
go the last 250 miles. When they reached the coast,
the *Buccaneer* was ready to go. With René Day signed
on as first mate, and two assistant seamen aboard, she
sailed out of Cartagena with Jimmy at the helm. Swan
and Harry Morgan flew to Miami.

In Miami, Swan stayed for a time with his sister.
Harry Morgan stayed at his aunt's house just north of
Matheson Hammock. Neither of the women was particularly surprised to see her prodigal relative. Swan's
sister never asked questions, Harry's aunt was happy
enough to see her nephew to leave him alone, and under the circumstances—not unlike those of a long-
forgotten summer vacation—the days of waiting were
not as hard as that kind of hard time can be. Perhaps
that is why it was not until the boat was a full week
overdue, with no word from anyone aboard, that
Swan, at the end of his patience, finally called Anthony
in New York.

"Anthony, where's the boat?"

"I haven't heard anything."

"Nothing?"

"Not a thing."

"Well, I'm worried."

"There's nothing to worry about. Jimmy can take care of himself."

"It's been three weeks. They were due in two."

"What does your captain say?"

"He says two and a half on the outside."

"Well, Jimmy had instructions to call me if there's any trouble. If he's alive, I'll hear from him."

"Oh, that's terrific."

"Jimmy's a good captain. He'll make it."

"That's a lot of water out there, Anthony."

"He can handle it."

"Can he swim?"

"Don't worry."

Five days later Jimmy called.

"Where are you?" Swan asked.

"Where do you think I am?"

Jimmy was in Bimini.

"We're on our way."

Harry's aunt's house was situated on one of the many inlets which give onto Biscayne Bay. A hundred yards from the back door of the house was a dock, and, like many of her neighbors, Harry's aunt had a boat. Hers was a ChrisCraft. According to the plan, Swan and Harry, aboard the cabin cruiser, would meet the *Buccaneer* in Bimini, transfer the load to their own boat, and bring the coke in at Matheson Hammock. And they had an ace: Harry had sailed often from Bimini to Miami, and often he had brought his fishing parties home late at night, sometimes as late as three A.M. He had been told more than once by enraged Customs officials to dock for the night, *for Christ's sake,* and come back the following morning to check in. It had become standard procedure, and on this run it would pay off. So with rods and reels aboard, Swan and Harry stopped at the fishing station, bought ice, bait and fishing hats, and set out for Bimini.

"What the hell took you so long?"

Jimmy, a little bit drunk, put up his hand and, before answering, finished his drink.

"We had some trouble," he said.

"What kind of trouble?"

And Swan finished his own drink.

"We're not out of the harbor an hour and we get stopped by a patrol boat."

Swan ordered two more Martinis.

"What did they want?"

"Well, let me tell you what happened. They held us up for six hours. They drilled the mast, ripped open a couple of life preservers, and went through the bulkheads. In fact they went through almost everything on the boat. Now, I wonder what the hell they were looking for?"

"Damned if I know," Swan said with a shrug.

The drinks came.

"Well, anyway, we took a different route than we had originally planned, hoping to avoid any more of *that* shit. A little bit more circuitous. We had one motor breakdown and we ran into a storm. Add it up."

"Jimmy, I swear, we thought you were dead."

"Not even a cut."

"Well, I'm glad you're safe, man, it's good to see you."

Swan raised his glass. Harry Morgan looked at his watch and said:

"Jimmy, it's your turn."

Jimmy nodded, finished his drink, and went out onto the pier to relieve René, who was guarding the load. The four men drank all night, retiring to the boats when the bar closed.

The boats were docked eight feet apart, and the following morning, their heads swelling with hangovers, Swan and Harry and René and Jimmy carted the boat hooks and the gaffs from one boat to the other, going back and forth now and then with fishing gear, trying to look as cool and casual as the anglers and boat freaks who spend their lives in ecstatic fealty to the hardware of their hobbies. If the ecstasy was not there, they had certainly drunk enough the night before to look authentic. It is not hard to look crazy, anyway, awake at six o'clock in the morning. With an occasional "ship ahoy" as they passed each other, they got the job done, not the least taxing aspect of which was removing the gaff clamps from the *Buccaneer* and attaching them to the smaller boat to accommodate the larger equipment.

"We don't want the stuff just lying around," Swan pointed out. "It has to look like it belongs on the boat."

And so Harry kissed about forty dollars' worth of equipment goodbye, and they set out for Miami.

Somewhere along the line it had escaped Jimmy that, being the only captain available, it was up to him to sail the *Buccaneer* back to Cartagena.

"Oh, shit."

"Harry's got to get us through Customs, Jimmy."

And René was going to follow his kilo.

Harry and the two smugglers left Jimmy in Bimini. By eight o'clock they were off Matheson Hammock, where Swan had spent the better part of his college career swimming, and by nightfall they had made Harry's. They all had a drink with Harry's aunt, and when she asked how the fishing in Bimini had been, Swan, with a straight face, said, "Divine." When she went to bed, they unloaded the boat. Harry borrowed her station wagon, and they took everything to the Key Motel in Coconut Grove, where Swan had a room. They broke the load down, had a sniff, then René picked up his kilo. He had a connection in Miami, he said, a Cuban.

"Be careful, man, those dudes are dangerous."

"They pay top dollar," said René.

"The price sounds too high," Swan told him, and they said goodbye.

By the time Harry Morgan made Customs in Miami, Swan was boarding a New York bound train with Nina, the waitress to whom Jimmy's wife had introduced him. The cocaine was in his luggage, broken down and double-wrapped in clear plastic bags. He handed his luggage over to a porter and followed it through to his compartment. The baggage was never out of his sight, as it would have been on a plane, and there was no weapons search to worry about, as there surely would have been at an airport. And as if the safety of this form of travel were not enough, Swan was confronted, immediately upon entering his compartment, with a wide array and variety of handles attached to the walls of the Pullman, which, when taken into account with the expansive mirror opposite the bed, brought all of his sexual fantasies home to roost. He looked at Nina and smiled. They had just entered what, in Swan's mind, amounted to a playpen. Nina smiled back.

Together they explored the train. There was a fashion show scheduled for that evening. There were cocktail parties and bingo games. Nina would win a sack of oranges with O-63. They drank and laughed with their fellow passengers, many of them elderly and afraid to fly. And between Miami and New York, between smoking and sniffing, staying high on Colombian in one way or another, they covered every inch of their compartment, flying like beatific trapeze artists, from wall to wall to open window, where the sights and sounds and the semiprecious smells of Cupid's Circus drifted out and shared themselves among the people of America.

"Drivin' that train, high on cocaine
Casey Jones, you'd better watch your speed
Trouble ahead, trouble behind

And you know that notion just crossed my
     mind."

"Casey Jones," from Workingman's Dead,
THE GRATEFUL DEAD

Swan arrived in New York with four kilograms of
cocaine, three revolvers that Anthony had ordered
from Miami, and several boxes of ammunition. It was
getting heavy. He said goodbye to Nina, went immediately to see Anthony and unloaded everything but
two of the kilos. Anthony paid him $25,000.

"Excellent stuff," Anthony said later, after he had
tested the coke.

And the Boat Move was over.

Swan distributed the remaining two kilos, with a
good cut, through his ounce-dealers in New York.

Two months later, Anthony got a message from
Jimmy. He passed it on to Swan.

Swan:

". . . Rainy left me that night in the Key Motel.
That's where we broke it down and we had a sniff.
He left maybe about midnight with his stuff, and that
was it, I never saw him again. Later on, Jimmy got
word, when he had come back from Cartagena. I didn't
even know what had happened. If I had known who
it was or what it was, I would have done something,
because I really liked him . . ."

René Day, three hours after leaving the Key Motel
in Coconut Grove, was found shot to death on a dark
street in the Cuban section of Miami. He had been
wearing his white suit, and he had found someone who
had wanted his cocaine. He had taken the ammunition in the face. Rainy Day, his knife in his boot,
had made his connection, and the last thing in this
world he had seen was the wrong end of a gun.

Running Blind

13

Back to the Border

THE BOAT MOVE, the cargo from which was distributed by the early fall of 1971, marked the end of Swan's first year as a cocaine smuggler. In that year he had been to Colombia six times, increasing his duty-free quota with every import subsequent to the first Santa Marta package, and had not been hit, either by the Federal government, by local authorities, or by people in the employ of other, civilian, thieves. None of his carriers had been endangered, nor had they been as much as incriminated by agencies of either the American or Colombian governments. He was doing well. He was making a lot of money, spending most of it, giving some of it away, investing very little and snorting the rest.

In Bogotá he had developed an apparatus for the procurement, packaging and dispatch of his cocaine, an efficient assembly line that began with the ever-dependable Armando and ended with Rudolpho, the mainstay of the Bogotá operation. Since the driftwood package, he had used nothing but wood and no one but Angel, who in addition to the boat-hook hafts and belaying pins had wrought duplicates of everything he was unable to open and close cleanly, such as the base of a bowling trophy, the shaft of an occasional wall hanging, and more than one rolling pin. Rough-hewn statues, such as the Madonna and the tribal head, he cut, hollowed out and reassembled. (He once drilled a set of chessmen—it was more trouble than it was worth.) Swan had so streamlined the

Bogotá operation that on occasion he would simply mail the money to Rudolpho with instructions on how and where to mail the package.

And in that year Swan had established a sound network of ounce-dealers for the distribution of his cocaine in New York. What remained after Anthony bought his kilos went directly to Ellery, Roger, Mickey, Moses and Charlie. The demand for cocaine had increased significantly in a year, and the price had climbed, both north and south of the border. Soon kilos would cost close to $7,000 in Bogotá and command $30,000 in New York. Swan was turning it over fast and spending his leisure time experimenting with new and outrageous gimmicks. Some of the experiments were costly. He invested $1,000 in the failed attempt to saturate a handkerchief with an aqueous solution of cocaine—twenty grams converted to gum on the supposition that he might do the same with his clothing, wait for it to dry, then wear the cocaine through Customs. He pictured himself crossing the border in a white suit, wearing a matching hat with a broad brim and a long, white, not unsullied plume. It had worked with salt. He experimented with cocaine's miscibility in other liquids, but with no greater success. In a room in Barranquilla he had sampled a preparation of cocaine in solution with an alcoholic beverage, the inventor of which was still experimenting with ways to extract the coke after it was smuggled and in the meantime selling exclusively to shooters and drinkers. Swan later said of the drink that it would "knock you on your ass," but was unable to track down its name or ingredients.

On his seventh trip to Colombia, Swan's plan was to get in and get out fast. He established a new mail drop, having exhausted the Lothario's supply of models, and went South to buy four kilos, two scheduled to go to Davis, two to the new address. The new address was close to home. It belonged to a young woman whom Swan had known since his grass-dealing days, to whom he had sold an occasional ounce and whom he had dated briefly. She had an across-the-hall neighbor, a young man who was often out of town and who left his keys with her when he went—she fed his cats and watered his plants. Also with a key to the young man's apartment was the doorman, who, at the tenant's request, rather than store his mail in the building lobby's package room, would deliver it to the apartment. Swan would mail the package to the young man at a time when it could be picked up by their mutual friend, the Cat Lady. If the package were followed (and for some reason delivered under those circumstances) she would be in no way suspect. Swan paid her $500.

Swan was staying at the Hotel Bacata, an upper-echelon hotel on Calle 19, avoiding the action and waiting for Armando to come across with the coke, when Uta showed up in Bogotá. The last time he had seen her she had been standing alone on the beach at Cartagena and he had been hurrying to see a boat off. The time before that had been almost a year earlier—she had been standing on the same beach with Ramón Greco, getting ready to disappear. This time she was standing in the doorway of his hotel room with her biggest surprise yet. She was with Vinnie Pirata. If Swan had been awakened in the middle of the night and asked to choose the one person in the world he would least like to see when he woke up in the morning, he would have rubbed his eyes, thought for a minute, said Vinnie Pirata, and gone back to sleep. Asked now, he would have said Pirata, standing in the doorway of my hotel room with a tour guide that looks very much like the woman I lived with for six years. Give him an hour and he would say Pirata and the woman I mentioned, in Bogotá looking for a cocaine connection.

Pirata had $6,000 which had been given to him by a small-time hood in New York named Crazy Leslie, and he was looking to score a kilo.

"Terrific."

Swan fixed Pirata up with Luís, two stuffed dolls and a seamstress. He put a thousand on Pirata's kilo, the bulk of which came out of Pirata's pocket. The seamstress overcharged him too. Armando came through with Swan's coke a day later, and by the time the fill was made it had become old-home week in Bogotá—Michel Bernier showed up. With Bernier and Pirata in town at the same time, Swan saw it as inevitable that the law of the jungle would soon assert itself. By the end of the week, Bernier was trying to steal Pirata's coke, Pirata was trying to steal Swan's, and Swan was trying to get out of town with Uta. The carnival culminated in a midnight assault on Monserrate, when Swan, Rudolpho and Uta set off in Rudlpho's De Soto in search of Pirata's cocaine, buried somewhere on the mountain according to Uta, who had accompanied Pirata earlier that night along the same roads in the same rain to wherever, in his growing paranoia, he had stashed it. They returned six hours later, sleepless, soaking wet, and empty-handed. Swan left town, Uta left Pirata, and Pirata, not about to trust Rudolpho, was left with no one but Bernier to mail his cocaine for him. Pirata addressed the package, followed Bernier to the Post Office, and watched him hand it to the clerk. It was over in a matter of seconds. In a matter of hours, Pirata left town.

Swan picked up his packages in New York, unloaded a clean kilo to Anthony, cut what was left and moved into the St. Regis. Staying at any other hotel in New York, Swan would store his cocaine in the bathroom—perhaps disguised as bath salts in a jar on the tub—close to the plumbing, where it would have been easy to get rid of fast in the event of a bust. At the St. Regis, however, the Feds would never have been able to get past the lobby. The security was excellent, there was never a hassle, never an arrest, and the bellhops and chambermaids were honest. Staying there, Swan could leave the coke in his locked suitcase in the bedroom. After a week and a half, having unloaded all but forty-five ounces of his stash, Swan moved from the St. Regis to a hotel on Central Park South. From the St. Regis he had been making daily visits to the Chanticleer Bar a few blocks away, where Moses was hanging out. He would call Moses at home in the morning, ask him how many ounces he needed, and make the delivery in the afternoon—they were snorting lunch together every day from the chopping block in the Chanticleer kitchen. The ounce-dealers were making regular pickups at the St. Regis, and the turnover was fast, but Swan figured a week and a half was long enough to stay anywhere. He moved to the Essex House.

Swan's first afternoon at the Essex House, a Sunday, he watched the football game on television. Nice Mickey was there. After the game Swan left to meet Alice, Roger and Angela for dinner at a Chinese restaurant on Broadway, and had the cab driver drop Nice Mickey off at 79th Street on the way. He did not enjoy his dinner. He apologized. He passed up the fortune cookie, said good night and dashed back to the Essex House. He was too late. His room had been hit. The lock had been worked and his suitcase was open. Gone was $45,000 worth of cocaine.

"Now, *here,* you see, it takes all the running *you* can do, to keep in the same place. If you want to get somewhere else, you must run at least twice as fast as that."

The Red Queen in the Garden of Live Flowers,
from *Through the Looking Glass,*
Lewis Carroll

Swan sat on the bed, immobilized by his own adrenalin, drained of the power to think by fear,

frustration and anger, staring for a full five minutes
at the open suitcase. All he could do was shake. He
had been hit. Violated. Suckered and taken off hard.
The honeymoon was over. From now on things would
be different. All the slick had been taken out of him.
All the flash and style was history. He was vulner-
able now. His territory had been invaded, his delicate
manhood tampered with, and he sat amid the evidence of his frangibility like a raked and exposed
mast in the wind of all the heavy dues he had never
paid.

He figured Pirata for the job. And that made it
worse. But as painful as was the suspicion that Pirata
had hit him was the thought that it might have been
Nice Mickey who had set him up. As far as Swan
could figure, only Nice Mickey had known he was
at the Essex House. But more incriminating than that
was the hard-to-swallow certainty that Nice Mickey
had known, better than anyone, exactly when he was
not at the Essex House. Swan took it to Ellery. The
only way he was going to find out was to see whether
Mickey was moving ounces. If Mickey was, then Swan
would know.

Ellery arranged to meet Mickey at Victor's. Swan
parked his car two blocks away, watched Ellery go in
and kept his eye on the door. He would give Mickey
until the corner, then pick him up from behind. He
waited only a half hour before Mickey hit the sidewalk. Nice Mickey stepped out of Victor's, paused
for only about thirty seconds to light a cigarette, and
started walking. He went, without haste, directly to
the passenger door of Swan's car, opened it and
stepped in.

"Look, I know how you feel," he said.

Swan should have guessed there was no way he was
going to catch Mickey off guard. Mickey had made
him as soon as he had hit the street—he was the best
there was. Swan conjured up visions of the Scarlet

Pimpernel. Mickey even looked like Leslie Howard. Swan was embarrassed.

"I know how you feel, and I wish there was some way I could convince you."

Swan liked Mickey, liked him a lot, and from the beginning had been hoping to find a piece of evidence, any evidence, however slight, that would vindicate him. He wanted to be told he was wrong about the man. But Mickey was right—there was nothing but his word, and Swan would either believe him or he would not. And there was nothing Mickey could say about Pirata—Swan knew that—he was Pirata's friend, and more than its not being his place to say, it was not Swan's place to ask. But Swan did ask him about Ellery. (Swan knew where Ellery had been every minute of that Sunday—there was no question about Ellery. There never was. There never would be.)

Mickey said: "Absolutely not."

"And Vinnie?" Swan asked, as if by way of an afterthought.

"I couldn't say," Mickey replied.

Mickey's answer was enough. Taken in light of how he had answered with regard to Ellery, combined with Swan's suspicions and added to the evidence of Vinnie's recent behavior, it was enough to convince Swan. Pirata was the man. Swan would never know for sure about Mickey, but he would always try to believe the best. He would have to be content with it as it stood.

Swan had options. He made a decision. And with his response to the robbery at the Essex House, he took his first irretrievable step into the cold, compelling nightwater which led from the Byronic banks of adventure land into the dark, adult realities of the cocaine trade. He took his problem to a friend named Pepe, one of that seemingly inexhaustible supply of maître d's at Maxwell's Plum, New York East Side saloondom's answer to Versailles. Pepe made a phone call. It was brief:

"I got a friend—he's been South—ya know? He lost a couple packages."

There was a pause. Pepe nodded and hung up. He turned to Swan, who was standing with Uta—always good for public relations.

"He's gotta come in from the Island. He'll meet us later. Not here."

An hour later they were sitting in a bar on 34th Street.

"When he comes in, talk to him," Pepe was saying.

"How will I know this guy?" Swan asked.

"You'll know him."

"Yeah?"

"Yeah."

Yeah. Swan knew him. He walked right by the table. Walt Disney could not have created a man who looked any more evil, threatening or downright dangerous than this man—mean and rotten and a real *big* son of a bitch. He passed them without saying a word and took a table in the rear. Swan did a slow take in Pepe's direction.

Pepe said: "Okay, go back and talk to him."

Swan swallowed hard. They discussed Pepe's percentage. He and Uta went back.

"Hi," he said.

"Hi."

No names.

The man waited for them to sit down. He ignored Uta. He eyed Swan. Then slowly he spoke:

"Well, Mr. Prep School, here's how it works . . ."

Awesome. Blood and raw meat.

". . . If the guy has it, I'll get it. But if he didn't do it, you'll never see him again—because I never leave anybody to come back at me."

That was all. Swan said: well, Uta and I, we'll have to talk it over. Sure, Swan, that makes sense. Idiot. He crept back to Pepe's table. No sale.

"Pepe, do you know anyone maybe a little bit *down* the ladder, someone who'll just go *beat up* the guy?"

With Pepe in the lead, they set out for Pemble's, a bar on the other side of town. There they met Mike, medium heavy, who after a few blows of pure said he and his partner, Frank, would be glad to take the job. Swan paid Pepe. He filled Mike in. Within two days, Mike and Frank knew who had made the hit and how it had been done. A creeper named Joey had gone in. He had been seen later hanging around with Pirata. They were friends. Pirata had been seen sitting in a car outside the Essex House at the time of the robbery. The money was gone, blown at the track.

"I think you need a partner," said Mike. "You wouldn't want anything like this should happen again."

Swan had heard that line before. On television. A lot.

"I'll have to talk it over with Pepe," he said, thinking fast.

You know Pepe. My partner. The one with connections from Disneyland.

Mike left. He did not come back. Swan said a few ill-remembered prayers of penance, abandoned all his contingency arrangements, the last of which would have been going to Anthony with the facts, and wrote off the robbery and its aftermath as an education, inexpensive at twice the price, a naïve man's look at the realities of his business, a breath of smoke from the back room. Welcome to the real world, Mr. Prep School—the sink. In here there are only the quick and the dead—he who hesitates is lunch. Eat or be eaten. Or move to Pennsylvania. This is where Fantasyland ends.

Swan's awakening was rude and abrupt. He opened his eyes and found himself looking down the throat of a beast disguised as the American Dream. And his troubles had just begun.

Two months later, Swan would be asking Michel Bernier: "How did you do it?" And Bernier would answer: "It was simple." He had merely written his own name and address on a gummed label, carried it into the Post Office in his breast pocket, and with his back to the door withdrawn it, licked it and slapped it into place on the package. "It was very simple," he would repeat. "I did not even stop." And Swan would smile, very much impressed, and say: "Beautiful."

Vinnie Pirata had never received his package. And if that were not necessary to explain the robbery—Pirata never needed an excuse to steal—it went a long way toward explaining why a hood named Crazy Leslie had been trying for a week to locate Swan. Swan was taking a vacation of sorts, hanging out at home, contemplating a quick trip to Bogotá, staying away from everyone but Alice, who, just prior to the Essex House break-in, had returned from a prolonged trip to Europe. Swan remembered having met, on one occasion, a man introduced to him as Leslie, Crazy Leslie if one took his Christian name into account. The introduction had been made by another individual with an adjective for a first name—Mean Mickey.

Mean Mickey, anything but mean, was a something-for-nothing small-change hustler who worked hard at making money the easy way. An Ivy League graduate and a former ad man, he came from a wealthy family in New York, hard-line WASP, and at thirty-eight he was chumming around with bookies, hookers and holdup men and living on other people's credit cards. A small-time hood himself, he was proud of his record. He had started as a swindler, dealing in lettered stock under the auspices of some West Coast religion in which he was an ordained minister. He was arrested stepping off a plane from Miami in priest's garb, carrying a kilo of mix—he dealt cocaine in drag, too—and, after the lab test, sued the City of New York to get it back.

The arrest that put him away for a while was made when he tried to sell some stolen stocks that matched a bunch found on the bodies of two young women that had recently floated to the surface of a river in Florida. He would not reveal the source of the stock—in the business he was known as a stand-up guy—he got four years, did a year and three months and went on parole. At the time of his arrest, one of the local papers nicknamed him Mean Mickey. He was proud of the name. He saved the press clippings and waved them around at parties. At Moses's Feast of the Epiphany at the Chanticleer, he would show them to all the pimps and dealers from Harlem—a big man in Crime. After his release from jail, Mean Mickey failed in an attempt to hold up Maxwell's Plum—Crazy Leslie, who was to steal the getaway car in Long Island City, got stuck in traffic on the Bridge, and they missed the payroll man—but he did ultimately manage to stick up Adrian's casino, which destroyed the myth of the Mafia protection represented by Ike and Freddy, the shooters from Brooklyn.

It was Mean Mickey who had introduced Swan to Moses. He had also introduced him to Pepe. (After leaving his job at Maxwell's, Pepe opened an office on 34th Street and started a transatlantic charter service, taking deposits and leaving people stranded all over Europe. The Civil Aeronautics Board got him.) Mickey, who made sure it was known that he was dating a prominent black jazz singer, had given marriage a try for a while—he was married to a "very big Social Register chick" who eventually divorced him to marry a Kentucky Derby trainer. Swan introduced Mean Mickey to Mike Riordan, but they never got along—Swan suspected that they were trying to rob each other and never settled it properly. Mean Mickey, during the cocaine years, was pretty much outside Swan's sphere of activity; he handled ounces now and then, but there were really only two things for which he was responsible that actually touched on Swan's business: he was directly responsible for Nice Mickey's name, and he was indirectly responsible for Crazy Leslie.

* * *

Crazy Leslie, distinguished by no special feature beyond the fact that he was several parts mad, finally located Swan. They had a talk about the package that never arrived. Swan told him all he knew. Leslie listened, and, still not satisfied, left to talk it over again with Pirata. Swan went South. He returned on November 8 at six P.M. A Monday. On Tuesday the ninth, at two P.M., he was stashing his coke in a safe deposit box in a midtown bank. Alice, at home, was putting on water for instant coffee. By the time Swan had located a phone and picked it up to call her, the water had boiled over. Alice was sitting egglike on the living room couch confronting her future—face to face—a future full of guns around the house, three of which were aimed right now at her head, and one of which was in the well-muscled hand of a man known to be crazy. The party was over. There were dues to pay.

Alice Haskell came into this world on a spring day in 1949 with nothing to recommend her to Zachary Swan but her description—she was a pretty girl. While she was struggling to see light and foraging for her first high-calcium rations, he was trading war stories with a stewardess in Coral Gables. He knew he was going to get drunk. The stewardess knew he was going to get laid. Alice did not know anything yet. The only thing she and Swan had in common at the moment was that they were both very breast-conscious. They hit paydirt at about the same time.

Swan never changed. Alice, of course, did. For twenty years she changed along the lines of most middle-class American children in the care of loving and responsible parents. Healthy, educated and not unattractive, she was quieter than most, somewhat shy, but for the most part conventional. After high school she enrolled in a junior college close to home, did not really like it much, left, decided to spend some time finding out just what it was she did like, and went about doing so in the same way many people of her age and time went about it. She split. Splitting recommends itself as a verb which does not take a direct object—it was very popular in the sixties. Alice ended up in New York at about the time Lyndon Johnson was declining the throne.

Alice met Swan through Ellery. She had met Ellery in the neighborhood—if you lived anywhere on the West Side of Manhattan between 116th Street and the Tunnel, you were bound to meet Ellery in the neighborhood sooner or later. Alice did not cheat, she did not steal, and she would never learn how to lie. When she arrived in New York, she still had nothing more to recommend her to Swan than she had ever had—she was a pretty girl. Shortly after they met, she moved in.

Alice moved in at a time when Swan's life was undergoing a gradual downshift, a life the style of which was now less influenced by gin and more by marijuana, and was more susceptible to change than ever before. He was smoking a lot of dope, and in his posh 88th Street brownstone apartment in the middle of the city he was beginning to take on the character of a country squire. He was going out less and hanging out more. Within a short time of Alice's arrival he would be sharing that apartment with several dogs. Cats would come later. And soon he would let almost anything come through the door.

"If I let Alice run things we'd be living in a zoo. We had a fifteen-pound toad living under the sink in the kitchen eating roaches. I wonder what Crazy Leslie thought when he saw *that*. Alice didn't want to use roach spray, because it was bad for the animals and for the people in the house—not to mention a roach or two here and there."

What Crazy Leslie thought of the toad and the dogs was nothing to what Alice thought when she saw Crazy Leslie and his friends. Her trip to Europe had been only one of several attempts to leave New York, a city full of crazed people, behind for good. Her experience with lower-echelon freaks was growing with every ship-ment of dope that passed through town. At the end of their second year together she and Swan as a unit were about as stable as Leslie's brain chemistry—they were living apart as often as they were living together, chan-neling their emotional energies into one casual affair after another. Alice was asserting her womanhood through the use of cocaine. Neither of them was going anywhere but nowhere, and when the oblivion express occasionally slowed down it was simply to wait for the sky to fall in. Crazy Leslie provided the first rent in the firmament.

Alice put water on for coffee and opened the win-dow for the dogs (the apartment was on the ground floor—it was from the same window that Swan had run his curb service a few years earlier, passing marijuana ounces to his friends). The doorbell rang. Through the eyeglass, Alice recognized one of the three heavies who had come the day before looking for Swan. She threw the bolt and ran immediately into the living room to close the window. She was too late. Crazy Leslie was halfway in.

"The doorbell is ringing," he said, grinning. "Aren't you going to answer it?" In addition to everything else, Leslie was a notorious comedian.

Alice tried to push Leslie out. She failed. He threw her off and shoved her in the direction of the kitchen. When she screamed, he drew a gun.

"Shut up."

It was cold and blue—like the eye of a snake—in off the November streets and aimed right at her brains. She would never do acid again.

"Open the door," he said, and she began to cry.

Leslie closed the window and pulled the curtains to. Alice opened the door, and two men came in, any dis-tinguishing features they might have possessed over-shadowed by the fact that they, too, were carrying pistols. They threw Alice onto the couch and told her to stop crying. Alice continued to cry, and the dogs continued to bark. She was told to lock the dogs in the bathroom. She did. She kept crying and Crazy Leslie and his friends kept telling her to shut up. They wanted to know where Swan was.

"I don't know," she kept saying.

They searched the house and found nothing but two amyl nitrates and a small sample of coke. After an hour Crazy Leslie said, "Watch her, she keeps looking at the window," and went out. He returned five minutes later with a Patty Cake and a quart of milk. He offered Alice a bite of the cake. While Alice remained seated in one position, her knees against her chest and her face buried in a pillow, the tough guys walked around her, circling the couch, talked of killing Swan and twirled their guns, now and then resting the barrels against her head. There was always at least one gun aimed at her all the time they were there. They listened to music, and when they tired of that, they decided to watch television. They agreed on a movie. It was between commercials when the phone rang.

"Tell him to come home."

Alice answered the phone. It was Swan. He asked what was wrong. She said everything is O.K. but please come home. When he asked again, she cut him off. She said goodbye, and hung up the phone. One of Leslie's heavies waited outside in the car. The other stood by Alice in the living room. Leslie stood by the door. They waited.

Swan did not step right into the apartment. He kicked the door open and called Alice's name twice. She whimpered in reply. Leslie stepped from behind the door, showed Swan the gun, and told him to come in quietly. He pushed Swan onto the couch and waited for his partner to come in from the car. When the man arrived, Leslie asked:

"Was there anyone with him?"

"I didn't see anyone," the man replied.

"Did you close the door?"

The man nodded.

Leslie turned to Swan:

"Are you alone?"

Swan said yes. Leslie hit him with a right uppercut, gun first, in the mouth. He asked:

"Did anyone follow you here?"

Swan shook his head, and Leslie hit him again, this time above the eye. He asked the question a few times, using the gun, and Swan kept saying no. Soon there was blood all over his face. Leslie used a rolling pin to ask where the cocaine was. Swan kept giving him the same answer—the coke would be in town in two days, they could have all they wanted—and Leslie kept calling him a liar. When they ran out of things to talk about, Leslie said:

"You're coming with us."

They were going to lock him in a garage and chain him down until the coke arrived.

"You can come if you want," he said to Alice.

Alice could not stop crying.

"Ah, you'd only be in the way, anyhow," he said.

Swan's clothes were covered with blood. He would have to change them, Leslie said, to get by the doorman. Swan leaned forward on the couch and the blood dripped onto his shoes. He would change them too.

When Swan was taken away, Alice threw herself down on the couch and cried. And she prayed. She called Trude Daniels to ask Trude to chant, but there was no answer.

As soon as Alice replaced the receiver, the phone rang. It was Swan. He had escaped.

"Get all the mix you can find, pack a bag, and go up to Jeannie's. I'll be home real soon, and we're going to split."

Alice collected the mix (half a kilo of borax), grabbed what she thought she would need in the way of clothes, and went upstairs to her neighbor's apartment. Swan showed up twenty minutes later. He explained in a hurry how he had gotten away.

When the four men had reached the car, Leslie's heavies got in ahead of Swan. Very unprofessional. Leslie had Swan by the arm and released his grip long enough for Swan to get in after them. Swan had other ideas, none of which was spending the next two days with Leslie and the boys. He had bloodied his shoes for a reason—the shoes he had worn home had leather soles, the ones he had changed into, rubber—and it was now or never. He broke free and ran, heading for Broadway and screaming for the police. (A familar cry on the West Side—not worth much.) Leslie, in pursuit, gained on him, and when he was a foot away, Swan went into a crouch. Leslie tumbled. Swan grabbed a cab in front of the New Yorker theatre and said, "Get going." He had called Alice from a corner phone booth while the driver waited.

Swan had only a chipped tooth to show for the night's work. Within an hour of his return, Ellery showed up. Then came Charlie and Lillian. Lillian helped Alice clean the house and pack. Nice Mickey arrived. Then Roger and Angela. Suitcases were packed, and all the animals were jammed into Alice's Volkswagen. She was finally leaving New York. That night she stayed with friends. The next day, she and Swan moved to Long Island. In Amagansett, where Swan had spent so many summers, he would now set up business.

14

Journey of the Magi

IT WAS FINALLY the cats—two black and white American shorthairs, cantankerous and corpulent, neither with the benefit of a legitimate name, sometimes called "my little Babunchkas," more often referred to as just "the fat cat" and "the skinny cat," because as fat as the skinny cat was, the fat cat was fatter—these two sinfully spoiled but not unloved brats, that finally prompted Trude Daniels to turn to Zachary Swan.

"I've got to get out," she said.

Swan had known Trude for years, her husband longer, and there were few people in the world for whom he would do more. She was the kindest person he had ever known, the gentlest and most generous, a woman who sought nothing but tranquillity, a kind of earth-mother sorcerer's apprentice who knew all her friends' sun signs and drew on an eclectic collection of prayers for everyone she met. Swan was an old friend and a friend in need when Trude's husband committed suicide, throwing Trude into the depths of depression, the embrace of heroin, and the small West Side apartment of her mother. With an infant child, she was a broken woman at twenty-eight.

Now in her thirties, free of her heroin habit but not of unstable men, Trude, jobless, was still living with her mother, not an unpleasant woman but a mother nevertheless; her brother, whose disdain for work of any kind, especially work that might render him self-supporting, was exceeded only by his passive and passionless love for music—this week it was classical; and her daughter, Elaine, the reason for Trude's moving in with her mother in the first place and, at five years of age, the only thing that made explicit sense at this moment in Trude's young life. And there were the cats, aloof and self-indulgent, obviously ready for analysis, and Trude blamed this on the adverse living conditions which she and they had suffered for so long now. She was ready to move.

Swan was still lying low after his run-in with Crazy Leslie. He was living in Southampton and distributing his coke through Charlie Kendricks. It was Charlie's responsibility to get the coke to the ounce-dealers. Kendricks and Swan met regularly at the Red Coach Grill off Exit 57 of the Long Island Expressway. Charlie liked the roast beef there. When the transfer was not made there it was made at the McDonald's parking lot in Riverhead. Swan liked the hamburgers. Swan would park his car next to Charlie's, leaving a sack of groceries on the front passenger seat with the cocaine packed in dairy substitute jars, and buy a hamburger while Charlie made the transfer. They never talked to each other during these meets; messages were transferred to Charlie via the grocery bag and to Swan by way of the money bundle with which Charlie replaced it. Business was taken care of over the phone. Swan would call Kendricks in New York from a pay phone, ask him to call back, and give him the Long Island number with the last two digits reversed. Kendricks would call back from a pay phone. It worked the same way if Kendricks wanted to reach Swan. Over the phone, Swan was always Jonathan, Kendricks, the Hungarian. Meets were scheduled often when the coke was moving well. On a meet early in December, Charlie showed up at the Red Coach Grill with a bundle of money and a message from Trude Daniels. She wanted to see Swan.

"I know the risks involved."
"Are you sure?"

"I'm sure."

"Can you tell me why, Trude?"

"I need the dough to get out and get my own place."

"I can lend you some dough."

"I can earn it."

Swan nodded.

"Well?"

"Couple of weeks."

Swan did not want Trude in a hotel, near any trouble, or near any of the action. He had Juan Carlos Ramirez, owner of the Oriole, write Trude a letter, inviting her to Bogotá. It was her first piece of cover. When she arrived she would stay at Juan Carlos's girl friend's house, out of the way. Swan would fly first on Avianca. Charlie Kendricks would follow a week later on Pan Am. Trude and Elaine would travel the third week. Swan wanted Trude and the baby to stay down there at least a week after they arrived.

When Swan arrived in Bogotá, as he passed through the airline gate, he saw Canadian Jack trying to get out. Jack was trying to board a flight to Kingston, Jamaica, and was being held up by two immigration officials—his papers were not in order. He looked scared. (Canadian Jack's papers were never in order. Having jumped bail in Canada following a big hash bust, he faced a ten-year sentence at home, and he was moving in and out of the country on false passports, sometimes hitchhiking in from the States on U.S. credentials. On this particular occasion he was doing what Swan called one of his triple-border routines—smuggling his coke into Jamaica, where he would hang out for a while at Strawberry Fields, crossing the U.S. border on his way home, and finally smuggling it through Canadian Customs for distribution in Toronto—according to Swan, a sucker move.) Swan walked over to see what he could do, and as soon as the immigration people averted their heads, Jack handed Swan a package. Swan moved on.

That night at the Hilton, never having made it out of the country, Jack picked the package up in Swan's room. It did not contain a lot of cocaine, but it contained enough to get him in a lot of trouble. He had the rest strapped to his legs.

"When are you going to grow up, man?"

Jack shrugged.

"It's going to come down on you, Jack. You gotta get smart."

Before trying to leave the country again, Jack sent Christmas wishes to all his friends in Canada. Using a small wooden press with a hand screw, which cut his volume by about 30 percent, he compressed a kilo and a half of cocaine into flat ounces, placed each ounce between the two halves of a folded piece of paper, and inserted one piece of paper into each of about fifty Christmas cards. The cards, which he mailed first class, more than one to a customer, earned him an average of $1,000 apiece and read, *May All Your Christmases Be White*. He signed them, *Frosty the Snowman*.

By the time Trude Daniels arrived in Bogotá, Swan had mailed a package of his own. There were two kilos of cocaine in his hotel room. He was staying at the Hilton, Charlie Kendricks was at the Tequendama, and Trude was now on her way to stay with Ramirez's girl friend. They stayed away from one another for a week, giving Trude time to establish her cover. At the end of that week, Swan and Kendricks visited the house. Kendricks arrived first. Swan arrived soon after. Swan was wearing the cocaine, and under his arm he was carrying a large stuffed white rabbit.

Angel had compressed the coke, and now Trude stuffed the rabbit, sewing it carefully back together along its original seams when she was done. Charlie took the rabbit back to the Tequendama, where he kept it on top of the dresser in his room, innocent and evident to anyone who might enter. He, Swan, and Trude made separate reservations on a midweek, off-peak flight to New York. They arrived at the airport separately.

On uncrowded Avianca flights, passengers may sit where they want. Their seating assignments are simply a formality. Charlie Kendricks, carrying the rabbit in a shopping bag, boarded first, choosing a window seat over the wing in the coach compartment. He removed the rabbit from the bag and stuffed it under the seat, careful that it was not visible to anyone who might sit behind him. Trude Daniels, with Elaine, boarded next, sitting across the aisle from Kendricks. She and Kendricks did not speak. Swan followed close behind

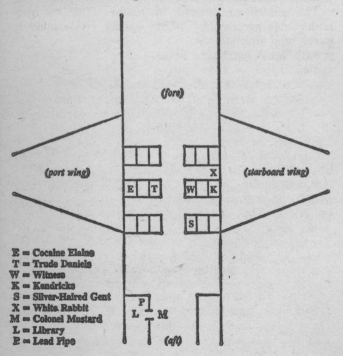

E = Cocaine Elaine
T = Trude Daniels
W = Witness
K = Kendricks
S = Silver-Haired Gent
X = White Rabbit
M = Colonel Mustard
L = Library
P = Lead Pipe

Trude and chose a seat behind Charlie on the aisle. A stranger, whose name and address Charlie managed to get, in writing, in the course of the flight—he was good that way—sat directly in front of Swan, in the aisle seat between Kendricks and Trude. He was a free witness.

The jet was not in the air five minutes when Charlie Kendricks, making sure the stewardess was nowhere around, "found" the bunny.

"Oh, look what I found."

He held up the bunny and called for the stewardess. The stranger shrugged. Before Kendricks could call a second time, the silver-haired gentleman in the seat behind the stranger tapped Kendricks on the shoulder.

"Why don't you give it to the baby?"

The gentleman pointed to Elaine. The stranger nodded his agreement. Charlie smiled. He handed it over.

"Oh, thank you," said Trude.

> "Cocaine Elaine, she never complains
> She's so aware, you know, she likes to share
> It's such a shame, she's not to blame
> Let's cry for Cocaine Elaine."

> "Cocaine Elaine,"
> Isis

Kendricks, Trude and Swan walked through Customs in New York in the order they had boarded the plane. Trude preceded her witness.

When he laid out the plan, Swan had asked Trude: "Who are they going to arrest?"

He was unable to find anyone to answer the question.*

Before he left Bogotá with Trude Daniels and the rabbit, Swan bumped into Back Dan at the Oriole, and Dan invited him up to his suite for a drink.

---

* See Appendix VIII.

"I've been using your press a lot," Dan told him, "and I'd like to pay you for half of it."

The news did not come as a surprise to Swan (everybody had been using the press), but the fact that Dan had finally opened up—admitted he was a smuggler—did. Swan took it as a compliment.

"No sweat," he said. "We're both making a lot of money."

"Well, let me give you some of this, then," said Dan, reaching for a package on the coffee table in front of him, and he opened up a brick of the strangest-looking marijuana Swan had ever seen. It was white.

"Where the hell did that come from?" Swan asked.

"*Rubia de la costa,* the blonde from the coast, the finest, complete dynamite 'up' grass in the world. Take a hit."

"Be glad to."

While Swan explored the wonders of *rubia,* Black Dan gave him the rundown on the Mexican route. Over a second joint, Swan outlined the Trude Daniels Move and described the immense white rabbit he had found after searching all over town.

"Stick this in the bunny," Dan said, nodding in the direction of the brick.

Swan smiled, a bit confused. He figured the *rubia* must have hit Dan a little hard. Taking his own condition into consideration, he had to assume that Dan was seeing pseudoscopic holograms where he should have been witnessing the work of the world's hardware. A typical Delta-9 problem. Incidence-and-rebound was becoming a problem. Perhaps Dan was telescoping. The brick weighed a pound—Dan could not have meant what he had said.

"I want you to have it," Dan nodded. "And I've got something else I want to give you."

Dan handed Swan a hard, white, luminescent rock, uneven at the edges, about the size of a Slazenger 3.

Swan reached out slowly and took it in his hand, which was shaking a little now, along with his other appendages and the rest of the world—a complement of nerve endings just about shot with the latest toke of high-voltage Colombian blonde—and under the cool, familiar touch of the rock, his fingers began to flicker. The rock weighed about a quarter of an ounce.

"Jesus Christ, Dan."

The rock was cocaine—through and through. As pure as it gets.

"My compliments," said Dan.

"I don't get it, Dan, what's this all about?"

Did Dan want something? Could this 250-pound black son of a bitch with the eyes of a killer and arms like mahogany trees be a bellowing lunatic pansy? Dan? My idea of the complete professional? Is this the end of the line . . . the doors locked, my mind wrenched . . . thrown to the floor by a faggot spade heavyweight with the thighs of a Roman war horse? What will Alice think?

"The Games," said Dan.

"What games?"

"Cali. The Summer Games at Cali."

"Yeah?"

"Yeah, I used your scam."

"Yeah?"

"Yeah."

"No shit."

"It worked. Best load I ever moved."

"No shit."

"I figure I owe you."

Swan laughed (at the expense of a third "no shit").

"Thanks, Dan."

"My pleasure. Thank *you*."

"How'd you do it?"

"Like you said. Had a couple of friends come down. Short hair. Athletic. We put on warmup jackets with the U.S. patch, and we walked through with equipment."

"What did you use?"

"Baseball bats. We had a bunch of baseball bats and Angel made us a bat rack—filled that too. It was perfect. They didn't even stop us."

"Unbelievable."

"Well, you were the one who said it would work. You were right."

"And they let you right through?"

"Right through," said Dan.

"That's unbelievable, Dan. It's perfect. How absolutely beautiful."

"Nothing unbelievable about it," said Dan. "It was a perfect scam. How could it fail?"

Swan smiled.

"Dan," he said, "they didn't have baseball at the Summer Games."

Dan's eyes shot to about sixty standard candles.

"No shit!"

"No shit."

Dan rolled another joint. Swan wrapped the rock in his handkerchief.

"I know just the man to give this to," he said. "Thanks a lot, Dan."

"My pleasure," said Dan.

The rock and the *rubia* went into the rabbit with the cocaine.

In the United States of America, where Zachary Swan lived, worked, distributed cocaine and occasionally paid taxes in the 1970s, the term *Black Culture,* where it was acknowledged at all, was treated by most as an oxymoron; as recently as today, in fact, the word "nigger" accounts for a greater part of the national vocabulary. Before the term gained currency among journalists and advertising copywriters, who had no idea what they were talking about when they used it—they saw it as a kind of pig-knuckle-and-chitlins equivalent to whatever Little Richard had meant when he sang *Good golly, Miss Molly, sure likes to ball*—it had been grappled with by a number of America's unctuous and minimally educated politicians, who had felt it coming like shit against the fan, some odoriferous blend of all that was red, white and blue about Jesse Owens and certifiably "pink" about Eldridge Cleaver. Up until recently it was embraced to no further end by certain tenure-seeking sociologists and a few blackboard-bound Ivy League Ph.D.'s as part of an end-of-the-rainbow answer to the irrelevance of Marx—they were destined to eat crow, as it were, when Angela Davis began doing public relations for Herbert Marcuse. Persisting was the reality that somewhere out there, between first base and the foul line of the Fourth Estate, growing, was this phenomenological monster known as *Black Culture*.

In whatever way, if ever, its aesthetic and ideological validity was to be affirmed, it was certain that New York City was going to be the Florence of what was soon to be called a *black renaissance* in America; and by the time it became a recognizable force in the United States, this renaissance would have its Botticellis. Long before that day on which everything that was Black became as a consequence Beautiful, John Coltrane and Charlie Parker were legends. If it was music in which this flowering was going to be cultivated, jazz was its *disembodied line*. Stevie Wonder, it was tacitly agreed, made white man's music, so cultural elitism had already begun. About the time Lincoln Center discovered that the Alvin Ailey Dance Company was a force to be reckoned with, the Theatre, which was pretty nearly dead at the time in New York, struck up a brief romance with Melvin van Peebles. And while James Baldwin was struggling from abroad to demonstrate that he could write at least as well as any member of the New York Jewish Authors' Cabal, a young man from Harlem named Claude Brown was writing a book called *Manchild in the Promised Land* which was going to be the last word on just where this groundswell was coming from.

And where it was coming from was the only place it could come from in Harlem: the street. The street was where everything was beginning to happen. It was where money was being made. It was where respect was being gained. It was on the street, and by his influence on the street, that a man was being measured. On the street in Harlem, and only on the street, according to Brown, was a man able to come by . . . *status*. And status, the predeterminant of . . . *re-spect* . . . *man* . . . was not something you earned working for somebody else. If you were able to get a job, and coming from Harlem your chances were slim, you were not going to find one that paid for anything beyond the rent. If that. Wall Street was a long way off —it was going to take more than the Broadway Local to get you there. So you were not going to make big money legitimately. And you were not going to make it running numbers for somebody else. Or fencing— to somebody else. All that second-story jive and bagholding was for losers and junkies; self-employment, capital gains . . . *this is a business, man* . . . is what paid for the El Dorados and the quadraphonic sound . . . *get your shit together, Jack* . . . *do not be a fool* . . . *you got to look out for your* . . . *self!* And if you were going to take the initiative, you had to use the tools at hand . . . *look around you, man* . . . *you grew up on this street* . . . *you know where the cash is*. And when the cash comes home, you do not put it into tax shelters . . . *brother* . . . you advertise. Clothes, cars, shoes, women, jewelry . . . power . . . and cocaine. A thousand dollars an ounce . . . *suck-er*.

And a man had something to work for in Harlem. Street status. No more steppin'-fetchit-nigger-yessuh-nossuh heroin or reform school got-to-get-out-of-the-ghetto-or-die-young blues. After all, Walt Frazier was driving a Rolls Royce, making a million dollars a day playing basketball for the Knicks. There were alternatives. Harlem was becoming a place to *be*. And be from. Downtown was O.K. if you wanted to eat at the Plaza or something—they could not throw you out anymore . . . *We Shall Overcome* was history, and they were kicking down the doors at City College to prove it—but Uptown was the place to show it all off. Everyone was coming off the tenement roofs and out of the alleys. It was as if a carnival had come to town. To stay. The prevailing mode was flamboyance. Extravagance. Why be outraged when you can be outrageous. Pimps, local policy heavies, dealers, and just plain *hustlers* were showing themselves off now, unashamed, flaunting it, every man outdoing the next, throwing the new money around. Status. Only in Harlem could you get a reading on the word "hustler" . . . *hey, baby, how is that nigger fucked up, I mean, what does he . . . do? He is a hustler . . . Fred . . .* and that could mean he was doing everything or he was doing nothing, but whatever he was doing . . . *man* . . . he had bread. He was heavy and he had influence, and . . . *baby* . . . if you did not know where his bread was coming from, that was his business . . . The dude's wearing eighty-dollar shoes, so he ain't working for a living, and that's all you gotta know.

"Once I lived the life of a millionaire
Spent all my money, I just did not care
Took my friends out for a good time
Bought bootleg whiskey, cocaine and wine . . ."

"Nobody Knows You When You're Down and Out"
JIMMIE COX

And the vibrations coming out of Harlem moved south across 96th Street, and they were picked up all over the city. Now there is fascination and awe . . . *I mean, how outrageous can you get . . . take a look at that Spade, Stanley . . .* because in New York City only a black man knows how to . . . *walk* . . . on the street. You *know* where he's coming from. This man

has turf sense . . . an air of territoriality . . . he's got
. . . *moves*. This man is fluid. There is a hydraulic
principle at work here that you do not understand, and
you have to call it something, so you call it . . . *funk*.
Everywhere you look there is this new standard of
cool. And you pick up on it. And if your man is stepping out of a Rolls Royce, you *know* he's doing something right. Add to that the fact that he's got knife
wounds all over his body and in America you have got
yourself a culture hero. Here is a guy so downright
virile, and sure of it, he can afford to dress like a
woman. He's wearing a mink coat, a contoured silk
shirt and high-heeled crocodile shoes . . . he's got
diamond rings up and down his hands . . . he's . . .
the fucker's wearin' pearls! . . . He's got on a white
felt hat with a brim as wide as the Astrodome . . . and
maybe there's a feather in it . . . velvet trousers with
a twenty-eight-inch flare . . . and shades . . . always
shades . . . three A.M. and shades . . . he's got lace
cuffs . . . and . . . *Jesus Christ . . . a cane . . .
with sterling silver brightwork.* And the son of a bitch
is six-four. He never bends his knees or his back . . .
he folds at the waist . . . he pivots from the hips and
struts like a bayou water crane. He has a tall, fragrant,
fox-furred woman on either arm, calling him *baby* . . .
or *sir!* And this motherfucker's wearing a sixteen-
hundred-dollar, gold and ivory, emerald-encrusted
coke spoon around his neck.

Step aside, suck-er.

Now, you *know* your girl friend is going to bed with
him tomorrow. All day. Broadway Joe has let you
down. Budweiser is a thing of the past. You have been
sold down the river. And all you can say is *shit . . .
suck-er.*

And, brother, you have got *Black Culture.*

And you have got cocaine.

And so it was special, and it was somehow fitting,
on an unseasonal night in the winter of 1972, that a

white man's cocaine should bring the Uptown, street-heavy, Harlem elite from 125th Street to midtown, to the Chanticleer Bar at 57th Street and Lexington Avenue. Something was happening. And it had to be big.

"Where is it happenin' tonight?"

"At the Chanticleer."

"There's a *thing* at the Chanticleer?"

"That's where it is happenin'."

"Is that right. And *whom* is it, Fred, that is makin' it happen?"

"Moses."

"Say what?"

"Moses."

"Moses?"

"At the Chanticleer."

"Moses is the man that is makin' it happen at the Chanticleer."

"Tonight."

"And do you know what is it that is happenin'?"

"I do."

"You do?"

"I do."

"Then when are you goin' to cut the jive and tell me?"

Moses, who would never again in his life know a night like this, was having a "showing." Moses had the *rock*—one-quarter ounce of snow-white, self-evident purity, a dealer's dream and a gift from his man, Swan, who had known when he had first seen it that there was no one in the world who would appreciate the rock more than the good Dr. W. The rock had belonged to Moses before it had left Bogotá. A *beau geste,* and Moses would never forget it. For one night in his life, at the Chanticleer Bar, New York City, America, Moses Wellfleet Esq., who would never be President of the United States, was God.

It started late, as it always does upstairs and in the

back at the Chanticleer, an after-hours bar once the lights go down on the street floor. It is a night like other nights, with one or two Cadillacs hogging the curb out front. But tonight is different. Tonight something is happening. Tonight something . . . real . . . is in the air. Something is coming. Tonight 57th Street is holy.

They begin to assemble at around three A.M. . . . white El Dorados, two-tone Lincolns . . . with sculptured rear windows, white sidewalls, custom-cut sunroofs, TVs, telephones, blue interior lighting, leopard upholstery, ermine . . . chrome everywhere. Everyone is double-parked. Limousines are pulling up, and stepping onto the curb are the most elegant, outrageous and flamboyant men and women that ever adorned a sidewalk . . . five, ten, a hundred street-wise birds of paradise . . . a fluid mix of all that is Harlem street status . . . a blend of flash and sparkle and slow-movin' funk . . . and East 57th Street lights up like a loose neon Christmas tree . . .

. . . *Ecce advenit Dominator Dominus: et regnum in manu Eius, et potestas et imperium* . . .

. . . the procession continues.

Past the jukebox, up the stairs, and in the back. Private. The place is coming to life. There is music. Blue light. Saxophones and silver spoons. The women smell good. There is cocaine in the air. Moses is seated at a table against the wall. He is wearing an apple-green suit with a broad-lapelled jacket and high-waisted trousers flared wide at the ankle. His yellow silk shirt is open at the neck, its collar overlapping the lapels. His coke spoon is platinum. His serpentine legs are crossed knee-over-knee to show off his two-hundred-dollar alligator shoes. He is wearing a white felt hat with a soft brim the size of a Cadillac fender. He is leaning back in his chair. He is accepting praise. On the table in front of him, for everyone to see, is the rock.

* * *

. . . Behold the Lord, the Ruler is come, and the kingdom is in His hand, and power and dominion . . .

. . . There is awe in attendance at this badass Epiphany . . . the Mass is Solemn High . . . the journey is ended. Moses was not kidding.

Seated next to Moses, on the right, is Swan, dressed in a Paul Stuart glen plaid suit, a blue silk, four-in-hand tie with foxes *courant*, and a white broadcloth shirt. Cufflinks. Folded handkerchief. Wing tips. Madison Avenue all the way. The only thing jiveass about this freak, beyond the forty-candle-power cocaine burn in his eyes, is the bejeweled black hand on his left shoulder.

"This is mah *ma-an*," Moses is saying. "He is my ace number one *brother*. And this is my product," pointing to the rock on which he had built his church, "the purest flake on the street."

Moses sang this tune until eight in the morning, and not once, as long as the party lasted, did he or Swan come close to ego saturation. They sat there, smiling, sharing the coke, shaving it with a scalpel and passing it around, riding the crest. There were always drinks on the table, compliments of admirers, and there was always one more street-heavy admirer to outdo the last. At five o'clock a tall, lanky, ostrich-like pimp in a tapered calf-length cashmere coat—navy blue—approached the table. His hat was white. His collar was fur. He carried an elaborate cane. He wore gloves. He was accompanied by two intoxicating, statuesque women in satin evening dresses who entwined him like Paris at midnight. Each was enveloped in fox. They were good to look at. If they were hookers, they were expensive. They were not unacquainted with the imperatives of respect. The man was cool, not in a hurry. He reached into his overcoat pocket and pulled out twenty Federal Reserve notes. He placed them on the table.

"Two thousand. I want it."

Moses looked up. He glanced at the women. He leaned back in his chair and acknowledged the pimp. He turned back to Swan, and as he turned he spoke to the pimp, with a wave of his hand:

"Take a little blow. Sit down someplace."

Dr. W was ridin' high.

"Now, where was I?" he asked Swan. "Oh yeah"— he straightened Swan's tie—"you don't dress bad . . . for a white man."

15

Blues in the Bottle

WHAT ALICE HASKELL, in her diary on November 9, 1971, referred to as "the Catastrophe"—the sudden appearance at the apartment on 88th Street of Crazy Leslie and the boys—and its concatenations marked a kind of turning point in Zachary Swan's career as a cocaine smuggler. The effect the deracinated B & E man had upon the immediate conduct of Swan's business was negligible, but his impact on Swan's psyche was nothing short of profound. An examination of that impact, even a superficial investigation, leads one across a minefield of subtleties.

Swan, by his own admission, is a "classic case of immaturity." Now, the self-awareness implied by that admission does not really go very far toward proving he is any less immature than he ever was—if it does anything at all, it merely shows that his regressed development is somewhat more unusual than he gives it credit for. In fact, though he would bitterly deny it, the truth is that today he is as ethically loose as he ever was—and having come this far in his life, the chances of his ever growing up are pretty slim. Nevertheless, he has achieved a certain level of self-awareness, and he is quite candid in his evaluation of those answered impulses which accounted for his becoming a drug runner in the first place. He would be the first to admit, for example, that cocaine, like motorcycles, machine guns and White House politics, is, among many things, a virility substitute. Its mere possession imparts status—cocaine equals money, and money equals power. And, as if in mute imitation of its symbolism, cocaine's presence in the blood, like no other drug, accounts for a feeling of confidence that is rare in the behavioral sink of post-industrial America. The *sang-froid* with which Swan walked into that room up against a certifiable lunatic and a loaded revolver, when all he had to do was slam the door open into the freak's face, was no more than the residual belief in his own invincibility that came with hanging around cocaine for a year, smuggling it past everyone in sight and living to tell about it.

Curiously, it was that one poorly calculated act— he was sure he could talk his way out of any trouble he might find on the other side of that door—that set him free to explore the true potential of his manhood. Or so he claims.

"After going up against the gun with Allie, I knew I didn't have to smuggle anymore."

Whether the statement is merely a gratuitous piece of hindsight is probably something not even Swan will ever know for sure. And how much of what followed was actually attributable to Leslie, and how much to mere fatigue, is probably a question he will never entertain—in less than a month he had been hit by the news of René's murder, the theft of his kilo at the Essex House, the holding hostage of Alice and his own near-kidnapping. But the fact is that after this last brush with the realities of his trade, Swan's attitude toward smuggling became far more businesslike and significantly less cavalier. He lay low on Long Island, meeting fewer people, satisfied to move most of his cocaine by mail, flying to Bogotá alone and getting out fast. The fun never went completely out of the work, and the impulse to embroider never left him, but over the following year Swan became increasingly more professional. He was making a lot of money, and he would continue to do so for the duration.

His thinking in the beginning had been that an arrest on a first offense, especially in light of his background, his age and his record—a clean one—would cost him little. He would smuggle until they nailed him or until he had made enough money to buy his way out of ever working again. In light of the professionalism he demonstrated over two years of smuggling and the reputation he had established for being extremely shrewd and calculating, and in light of the fact that he got better at what he did with every kilo he moved, the amateurish blunder that accounted for his arrest in the fall of 1972 invites the suggestion— one he readily entertains—that he *wanted* to be caught. But the manifold subtleties of *that* psychological gem are too dizzying even to begin to ponder. And anything Swan might add to an analysis of his motivations, it seems, must be taken *cum grano salis*; his self-awareness quotient is appreciably mitigated by the very components of that self-awareness—and here the gymnastics really begin.

"You learn to lie as a smuggler. You have to if you're going to be safe. After a while, it's all you do. You don't know what you told the last person, and you don't stop."

Who is conning whom? And why? A hardened shrink would turn in his license.

Whatever one divines out of the residue of years spent on the edge, whether they be one's own years or those passed through the prism of another's imagination, certain thematic patterns recur. A man on the run does learn to lie. There is no clearer evidence of this than the example given by a man who will lie when there is no ostensible reason to do so. Ask Zachary Swan what color his eyes are, and he will tell you they are brown. Tell him you know they are blue and he will tell you you are colorblind. When he trusts you, he will tell you the truth—maybe. It is all a matter of self-preservation. His is not a voluntary exercise at deception—it is reflex. A man with something to hide also learns to forget. He forgets names, dates and numbers And really forgets them. He becomes skilled at autogenic amnesia. If he forgets enough, he will beat a lie-detector and a perjury conviction. It is just another part of staying alive.

And there is more. A man on the run develops an intuitive sense, the dubious merit of which separates him from the rest of us—he can always spot someone else on the run.

"I can look around a plane and tell who's doing something. It's a feeling you get. You can sense it."

Flying out of Bogotá once, he struck up a conversation with a young woman seated in the international departure lounge at Eldorado Airport. He asked her how she liked Colombia. She claimed not to have seen too much of it; she was married to a minister and taking only a brief vacation, and she had kept pretty much to herself, she said. She was wearing her only souvenir, a bright red *ruana*.

"You lie," Swan said.

The cocaine was strapped to her back.

Swan bought her a couple of Bloody Marys and learned she was a judge's daughter from Westchester, New York. She was taking the load she was muling to Buffalo. She told him she thought he was very good cover because he looked so distinguished—she generally stayed away from older men, she said, because they inevitably put an arm around her and inevitably felt the kilo. She and Swan flew to New York together.

"You're underpaid," he told her.

He explained that carrying it through was a sucker move. They exchanged addresses and made arrangements to discuss her working for him.

"You can't deny it's yours, if it's strapped to your back," he said.

In New York they separated.

"Break a leg, Ellen," he said as they parted.

He tried calling her a month later. She was away.

He did not leave his name. Six months later he heard she was arrested.

Whatever new sensation Crazy Leslie brought to the funhouse of Swan's mind, and whatever cumulative toll finally made itself felt after a year of running blind, there is one exhibit in evidence of Swan's altered behavior that cannot be dismissed lightly. And it is pretty much what all the preceding introspection and second-hand analysis serves to introduce—within hours of his escape from the three hoods who had abducted him, Zachary Swan bought a gun. A .32 calibre revolver. And if, indeed, everything he did afterward was mingled with a desire to be caught, it was done with a desire to be caught before he had a chance to use it.

Swan overpaid Trude Daniels for the White Rabbit Move. He gave her $2,000 a kilo, twice the going rate. When the overweight bunny (five pounds with the two keys of coke and the pound of *rubia*) was disemboweled, he made a quick call to Anthony. They arranged to meet in the backgammon room of Le Club, where Swan was a member. It was the perfect place to do business—there was no way to get in unless one was a member or a guest of one. The deal was for one kilo.

"Thirty-two thousand," Swan said.

"It better be good," said Anthony.

It was. Anthony put a full hit on the kilo, turned it into two, and sold the two keys for $20,000 apiece that night. Swan put a half on the second kilo and moved the fifty-two ounces through Charlie Kendricks and the New York dealers at $850 an ounce. His total take, before expenses, on the cocaine Trude Daniels moved was $76,200. The rock went to Moses and the *rubia* went to the wind. The kilo he mailed never made it through—it was bust number one.

* * *

Between the end of February and the first day of summer, while Alice—on the run again—was living alone in New Orleans, Swan made only two trips to Colombia; he relied on Rudolpho to handle the Bogotá end of the other spring shipments without him. In July, when Alice returned to New York, Swan planned a five-kilo move that would take the two of them to Cartagena on a busman's holiday—he was ready for a big move, and he figured a Caribbean cruise was just what his and Alice's unstable love affair needed. Among the cruise ships in town at the time was the *Leonardo da Vinci*. She was scheduled to sail on a hot Saturday morning.

Swan and Alice, carrying gift-wrapped packages with *bon voyage* cards attached, left Long Island early that day and drove into Manhattan to see the Italian liner off. Once they were aboard, they climbed to the upper passenger deck and strolled the corridor outside the starboard cabins until they encountered a steward leaving a vacant stateroom. They exchanged smiles with the steward as he passed, and as soon as he was out of sight they entered the cabin he had just prepared. There they unwrapped their packages.

Alice's gift was a plastic Clorox bottle, Swan's a Deer Park Mountain Spring Water container—each was filled with two-point-two pounds of sugar. While Swan craned his head through one porthole, Alice dropped the containers through the other. Though Newton and Galileo were nowhere around, their laws were enforced by Nature—Swan saw the bottles hit the water and disappear beneath the surface of the harbor. He did not see them emerge. Deeming it unwise to linger, he and Alice hurried out of the cabin, down to the gangway and off the ship.

From the pier below, Swan looked for the answer to the last of three questions. The first had been answered when he saw that the bottles would in fact fit through a porthole. The second question was tied to the third

—would the bottles, when dropped to the sea, if necessary from the highest passenger cabin of an ocean liner, break under the impact? And if not, would they float? Swan, standing straight-backed on the pier, with a cigarette in his mouth and his car keys in his hand, turned to face the south. He looked at Alice and winked—the bottles, floating midway between the anchor chain and the stern of the *Leonardo da Vinci,* had given him his answer.

Swan would make his move in the Verrazano Narrows. As soon as the ship had cleared the Bridge, he would drop the coke. He would need two power boats, one on the Brooklyn side and one on the Staten Island side of the Narrows, and he would need enough personnel to ensure that the pickup was made smoothly. He called Ellery and Mickey.

"No," said Ellery.

"Absolutely not," said Mickey.

They wanted no part of being retrievers.

"Carry a knife," said Swan. "If you're spotted, just cut the bottles. What are they going to do? Run a lab test on the Hudson?"

"No."

"Absolutely not."

Swan needed more personnel than he had, and there were too many loose ends—one of which was the possibility of a nighttime arrival and not the least of which was the boats—to tie together. Even with all contingencies met, he was reluctant to make the drop without Ellery and Mickey. He called Adrian the Mogul.

Adrian had been hounding Swan since Vinnie Pirata had squealed to him about the Billy Bad Breaks flourish. Swan, though he did not feel obliged to make amends for what he thought was a justified swindle, had set Adrian up with some people who were doing traveler's checks, and since that time Adrian had made double what he had lost to Swan. But Adrian wanted to get into some smuggling. Swan figured that now was as good a time as any for Adrian to begin.

"Adrian, I've got one for ya."

They met the next day, and Swan laid out the plan. He wanted $1,000 a kilo on a minimum five-kilo move. In advance. Beyond that, Adrian could handle it any way he wanted. Adrian said he would let Swan know. Swan knew what *that* meant. He heard from Adrian a day later.

"My backer wants to meet you," Adrian said.

That is what it meant.

"I don't want to meet him," said Swan.

Adrian whined for a while and Swan relented.

"O.K. I'll meet you at 86th Street. We can have coffee."

"That's not necessary," said Adrian. "We can meet in his limousine."

Terrific.

Adrian's backer looked exactly as Swan had expected him to look:

". . . jaded glasses . . . Jewish . . . fat . . . cigars . . . white-on-white . . . pinky ring . . . and a chauffeur that carried heat . . ."

Swan would learn later that he ran a VIP limousine service "in Jersey" and that Adrian had done TC's with him on more than one occasion. He evidently had some very good customers, because he was prepared to invest $20,000 in the five-kilo scam. Swan figured he was looking to make $100,000 on the deal. He listened as Swan laid out the plan. When Swan finished, the fat man looked at Adrian and said he thought it was "a little dramatic." Swan was on his way out of the car:

"Look, man," he said, "I don't really give a shit. You can use any method you want. What you're really paying for is the connection and the know-how—how to carry your money down there, how to get the load on board, how to do everything. You can take it or leave it."

"I've got a man I want to use."

"I know. Everybody's got a man."

But the man you use to follow the load cannot look like a gangster, Swan was thinking as he eyed the fat man. Adrian looked at Swan, then at his backer. The fat man nodded. He bought it.

Swan met with the fat man one more time. Adrian had called to tell Swan that his backer was bitching, and Swan made his final offer:

"Move the locale. I don't care. I don't want to know where or how, and I don't want to know who. I'm just going to show you how to get it on. The rest is up to you."

Swan knew then that the carrier was going to be Adrian.

Adrian booked a cruise to Colombia and other Caribbean ports of call with his wife and young son. The tour would return to New York with stops in Venezuela, the Windward Islands and Florida. Swan met the ship in Cartagena. He had paid Evelyn, Rudolpho's wife, $200 to sew the five kilograms of cocaine into a large stuffed panda which Adrian's son carried aboard. In addition to the $1,000-per-kilo charge for the scam, he had put $500 on each of the kilos he had scored for Adrian, bringing his total take on the deal up to $7,500. While he was in Bogotá, he had mailed a package of his own.

Adrian had booked passage on a ship with a scheduled daylight departure for New York from Fort Everglades, Florida. It was there that he made the drop. He had carried the five empty containers with him from New York—at Swan's suggestion—against the possibility of their being unavailable in the Caribbean, and Swan had seen to it that the cocaine was wrapped in such a way as to make the transfer from the panda to the containers simple. The cocaine cleared the porthole at the appointed time—Adrian waved a towel for the boatmen to target on. The pick-up was made by water skiers.

While in Bogotá, Swan was introduced to Rudolpho's cousin, Camillo, who worked in a mobile cocaine-processing lab in Leticia. Swan had heard that paste was available in Leticia for three dollars a gram—Camillo offered to handle the chemistry for a thousand dollars a kilo. The deal would bring Swan's capital investment down to four dollars a gram while prices were going up in New York. He said he would think it over.

One of cocaine's more primitive effects upon Zachary Swan was the ego problem it gave him—after he had been at smuggling a year, there were a lot of people who knew what he did for a living. He was careless that way. He could not resist the attention. He became kind of a cult hero, a guest lecturer on the crime circuit. He was approached once in Amagansett by a casual acquaintance, a man who knew Swan as well by reputation as by personal association, and offered a typical speaking engagement.

"I've got a friend," the man said. "He needs some advice."

"Send him over," Swan said.

But the man's friend, who introduced himself to Swan as Peter Crawford, needed more than advice. He had a very big problem.

"I sent a package," he said.

So, it was like that, thought Swan:

"Yeah?"

"Well, I'm not sure about it."

"Not sure how?" asked Swan. "Did it arrive?"

"That's what I'd like to find out," he said.

"Well?"

"Well, let me tell you how I did it."

"Please do."

"You know that they don't deliver the mail out here."

"Right."

"You have to pick it up. At the Post Office."

"Right."

"Well, it's there."

"Very good."

"I think."

"In your name?" asked Swan.

"It's addressed to Peter Crawford."

"Well done."

"Thanks."

"It's a good scam," Swan said.

"That's what I thought."

"What's the problem?"

"Well, I'm afraid it's being watched."

"How did you send it?"

"I don't know. However you send packages from down there."

"There is only *one* way to send packages from down there. First class."

"Yeah?"

"Yeah."

The man calling himself Peter Crawford shook his head.

"I don't think I sent it first class."

"Then you've got trouble."

"Shit."

"What did you save—a buck and a half on the postage?"

"I didn't know."

Swan nodded his head.

"Well," he said, "if it's being watched, it's easy enough to find out."

"How?"

"How do you think?"

Swan took a drive the next morning. To pick up some stamps. In front of the Post Office he saw two men tossing a Frisbee back and forth. They wore windbreakers tied around their waist. It was July. Inside, the man behind the Parcel Post window was wearing a jacket. Swan bought his stamps and left. He saw the man called Crawford that night.

"Well?"

"Well, I'll tell ya—I asked one of the Frisbee players the way to the beach. He didn't know."

"What does that mean?"

"It means he was Federal."

"Shit, it's only two blocks away."

"I know. And he looked so Ivy League."

"What should I do?"

"Hell, I don't know about you, but I'm going to go back again. I can't resist, now that I know it's there. Why don't you talk to some people? Find out where they take the packages at night. I'll find out what I can."

The next day Swan went back. The Frisbee throwers were tossing a baseball. Swan saw a car parked in the IGA lot across the street that had been there the day before. It had the same two men in it. And the same jacketed man was behind the Parcel Post window. Swan did not even bother to buy stamps.

"You're out of luck," Swan said. "It's a stakeout."

"No suggestions?"

"Where do they take the packages when the Post Office closes?"

"To the station."

"Well, then, there's only one thing you can do."

"What's that?"

"Well, I happen to know from some people I talked to that none of those guys can run seventy-five yards without collapsing—so what you do is you get yourself a track star, preferably dumb, with nothing to lose, pay him a lot and have him jump over the counter, grab the package, and then run like the Pan American games depended on it."

"I pass."

"You're smart."

Peter Crawford's package is still waiting to be claimed.

16

The Hawk and the Hired Man

"I CAN'T HACK IT," Charlie Kendricks finally said.

He was close to tears. He was shaking, and he was ashamed of it. He was completely shot.

"I just can't make it anymore," he said.

As an ounce-dealer, Charlie Kendricks was finished, beaten, taken off once too often. His nerves were shot, and he was through. Swan should have seen it sooner. Charlie had been strung out for weeks, stoned all the time, close to the edge. If it had gone on much longer, it might have killed him.

"Look, man, it's O.K., you don't have to explain a thing," Swan said, putting a hand on Charlie's shoulder.

Charlie's head was down.

"Forget it, Charlie, it's not a problem."

Charlie had lost another five ounces, this time to a dealer from Harlem and two of his friends. *Put the money on the table and get out, motherfucker . . .* either that or get your head shot off. The five thousand dollars' worth Swan had fronted him was worth thirty thousand dollars on the street—that paid for a lot of guns.

Charlie had been losing that kind of money regularly. He had once fronted five ounces to an actor friend who was going to fly to Chicago to sell the load. The actor, smiling, chatting up the personnel, carried the coke through airline security in a handbag. In the handbag, next to the coke, was a knife. (James

Bond.) It triggered the metal detector. They busted him right there in the airport. He never made it out of New York. *Break a leg, sucker.*

There were other occasions. Charlie Kendricks was always getting robbed, suckered or soft-touched by people who were just better suited to the kind of work he did than he was. It was Lillian Giles who finally pointed it out to him. Lillian had had enough—Charlie was losing his grip, and she was losing Charlie. It was time to call it off. She wanted out. If he could not pull it together, she could. And she did. She went to Swan and laid it out.

She and Charlie were going home, she said. They wanted a farm. It was now or never. She wanted $1,000 a kilo on a five-kilo move—down and back fast. Charlie would be given extra ounces to sell to his safe customers, and as soon as he had unloaded them they would split.

"We gotta go," she said. "If we don't break now, we might never make it."

If Lillian weighed an ounce over ninety-five pounds, Swan would have been amazed. She stood no more than five feet off the ground, and her blond hair was so straight it would not even curl at her shoulders—it just slid on by. Though he thought she was pretty as hell, Swan had trouble thinking of her as the nursery school teacher who had come to New York with Charlie Kendricks—the one who wrote home to mother in Brisbane every week. She chain-smoked Kents, had no threshold when it came to dope of any kind, and she had nerves that would not bend under all the stress in the world. On her own she was as serene as a sunbird, but when there was shrapnel in the air she was as cold as they come. Swan saw her as one who would easily cut your arms off for trying to get tough, then kick you in the face for bleeding on her shoes—he thought she was wonderful. He said O.K.—he could not say no—and set up the scam.

* * *

On the following Monday morning, Charlie Kendricks took a subway to West Fourth Street and put an ad in *The Village Voice:*

Help Wanted. Import/Export. Good money. Travel and Expenses. Call Mr. McCann 212-361-0555. 9 A.M.

On Thursday morning at nine, a pay telephone on the corner of Madison Avenue in the fifties rang once. Zachary Swan answered.

"Mr. McCann."

"Hello, I'm inquiring about the job advertised in *The Village Voice.*"

It was Lillian Giles. She had made the call through an operator—she had had trouble getting through. The operator had taken her number and made a record of the call. For billing purposes. The call and the *Voice* ad were Lillian's responsibilities. Swan's job was to see that the phone he had listed in the ad actually worked.

"Why don't you come over to the store," Swan said. "About noon."

He gave her the address of an establishment around the corner from where he stood.

"You can't miss it," he said. "It has a sign out front that says 'Things Colombian.' O.K.? About noon. See you then."

At five minutes to twelve, Swan walked into the store in shirtsleeves. He had left his jacket in his car, parked a block away. In the breast pocket of his shirt he carried an array of retractable pens and mechanical pencils, all clipped to a plastic pocket insert designed for that purpose and imprinted with the name of a defunct hardware store. Approaching the counter, he passed stacks of *ruanas* and woven baskets, leather sandals, pottery, hammocks and an assortment of other handmade Colombian artifacts with which he felt quite familiar—a lot of them were made of wood.

He smiled at one of the clerks and started his routine with the other.

"I've been to Colombia . . ." he began.

He chatted about his souvenirs, and theirs, and asked if they had trouble with the Customs people. Yes, they said, our crates arrive open. I know what you mean, said Swan, who appeared as if he were going to stay for a while, chattering away, a sourceless fountain of anecdotes, quips and tasteless flattery leading to boredom. He was leaning with his elbows on the counter, quite at home, when Lillian Giles walked in.

"I'm looking for Mr. McCann?" she said.

"I'm Mr. McCann," said Swan.

He shook her hand.

"Look," he told her, "things are a hassle here— let's go around the corner for a cup of coffee."

He took her arm. He turned to the clerks he had been talking to.

"Take care of the place," he told them.

They nodded.

"O.K.," they said.

Swan left them to think that one over.

Swan flew first to Bogotá. He had instructed Lillian to fly a day later and check into the Tequendama when she arrived—there would be a reservation made there in her name. When her plane landed at Eldorado Airport, Swan was there to meet it, but not to meet her. There was a change in plan. He walked up behind her as she left the Customs counter, bumped into her gently, and in place of "excuse me" said, "Go to the Hilton." He kept walking. Lillian said nothing, but continued forward in the direction of the main entrance. She handed her bags over to a cab driver and asked him to take her to the Bogotá Hilton. Swan was nowhere in sight.

The Tequendama, Swan had learned, was hot. There had been a number of arrests there in the previous month, according to Canadian Jack, and the place was crawling with agents. Stay away, Jack had told him.

"Things are getting very tight."

Things were getting very tight all around. Both Armando and Luís were keeping their inventories down. Camillo was in Leticia—Rudolpho had not seen him in over a month. After a day making the rounds, Swan found Canadian Jack at Vincent's.

"What have you got?" he asked.

"There's always the Hawk," said Jack.

Swan nodded: "There's always the Hawk."

"Tsk tsk," said Vincent.

Vincent van Klee, for over a year, had been prevailing upon his friends to go straight. He and Swan had become very close friends over that year. Always, Vincent would take Swan to gallery openings, society parties and after-hours clubs in Bogotá, and Swan, coming in from New York, would bring Vincent the modern consumer miracles unavailable to Colombians, not the least of which were the Carter's Little Liver Pills Vincent relied on for his regularity and the latest Roberta Flack L.P.—the old man was a sucker for Roberta. And Swan always brought him cocaine.

Vincent was very proud of a cosmetic skin cream he had invented, and because he looked far younger than he was, he was the product's best advertisement. He called it Vincent Dior. He would not disclose its ingredients, but he did sell it to his friends for five dollars a bottle, and they swore by it. When Vincent learned that Swan had been in the cosmetic packaging business, he asked Swan to find an American pharmaceutical company which sold chemical stabilizers—Vincent Dior had a habit of going rancid in about six weeks. He gave Swan the names and addresses of companies he had written to in the United States. Though Swan never came up with the stabilizers, he did come up with a package. He designed a box of white Kromecote which, except for the word "Vincent," would pass for a Christian Dior package. Vincent was thrilled with it—Vincent Dior had finally arrived. Swan's cosmetic dealings with Vincent—correspondence, print orders and the like—apart from everything else provided the perfect cover for his operations in Colombia.

"Vincent, may I fix you a drink?"

"I will have only a small *aguardiente*," said Vincent, pivoting his head to throw his face into profile—one of his favorite gestures.

"Vincent, you are such a faker."

"Oh, don't tell me"—one of Vincent's favorite expressions. He liked nothing better than to be told about himself. Vincent was the only man over seventy Swan had ever thought of as coy. He was a real coquette.

Swan poured the drinks, and Jack proposed a toast: "To the Hawk."

"To the Hawk."

"Shame on you both."

The Hawk was Juan Carlos Ramirez's mother. It was she who had paid for the hotel he managed. (As good a way as any, Swan figured, to keep him off the streets.) The Hawk was in real estate—in addition to the Oriole, she owned at least ten of the largest whorehouses in Bogotá. When Swan and Canadian Jack had first met, they had figured each other out fast—smuggler, they said—but Swan had never given Jack credit for his end of the figuring: Canadian Jack had had the Hawk's number from the beginning.

"I'm telling you," he said.

Even after meeting her—as a dinner guest with Jack at Juan Carlos's home—Swan would not buy Jack's story. An immense woman, in emeralds and Incan jewelry Mrs. Ramirez came on like a countess. Her husband was less than half her size, a tiny man, and he said nothing, but Swan attributed this to the man's poor command of English, nothing more. No, said Jack. The man said nothing because his wife was the Hawk. And though the nickname was apparently not so much a comment on her formidable position in the underworld as it was a comment on the formidable size of her hooked nose, the truth was this: Juan Carlos Ramirez's mother was not only the matriarch of her immediate family and of half the whores in Bogotá, but she was the matriarch of an extensive Colombian cocaine network as well. She could buy and sell Armando in a minute, and her man, Jago, would just as soon cut your lungs up as piss on the carpet. The Hawk was heavy-duty. Level-one. If you had the money, she would sell you all the cocaine in Bolivia. Swan could not help but believe the story once he had met Jago.

Swan had met Jago on more than one occasion, and though they had discussed business often they had never come together on a deal—with Armando and Luís coming through, Swan had not needed the connection. His experience with the Hawk's man, apart from the occasions on which he bought samples from Jago, was limited. Jago was not a man whose company one would seek for any reason other than a professional one. He wore a long-barreled revolver holstered to his leg, and an expression on his face that said he was not afraid to use it. He had an air of homicide about him. There was always a look in his eye which seemed to indicate that his body was metabolizing raw flesh, that it would not be long before he required feeding again. Swan could not imagine his ever throwing a dinner party. He did not smile a lot, and he was not the kind of person one would automatically be inclined to say hello to upon introduction. He inspired caution. People responded to Jago less as they would to a man and more as they would to, say, the boss's Doberman. Swan recalled that his samples were always of the highest quality. With Lillian growing old at the Hilton and the entertainment provided by the agents at the Tequendama, where he was staying, growing stale, Swan decided it was time to see the Hawk.

* * *

The Hawk and Jago together were more than Swan had the energy to make jokes about. He did notice that the Hawk looked less forbidding in Jago's presence, a conclusion which led him to a reevaluation of his initial impression of the woman: he decided that though she did behave like a countess, she very definitely looked like a hooker (so there was a pun, if not a joke)—more like three, in fact, given the hulk out of which her nose blossomed. He would have to tell Canadian Jack, he decided. Because the pressure was on in Bogotá, the Hawk could only come up with three and a half kilos overnight. Swan would have to wait a day for the rest. Swan said that would do and made arrangements to meet Jago the day after the next.

As brief a trip as it was, Swan would always think of this one as his most enjoyable. Apart from the fact that he had learned to relax in Bogotá over the years he had been visiting it, there was Lillian Giles. He and Lillian had been getting it on since the night she arrived, performing new and wonderful gymnastics for six or seven hours at a stretch behind the cocaine they lavished upon themselves, mellowed by the expense of energy and no doubt liberated somewhat by the tacit, mutual certainty that Alice and Charlie were doing the same back home. It was how things were. Everybody had his goodbyes to make.

Swan had always harbored something—call it affection, respect, or maybe nothing more than a curious appetite—for Lillian Giles. Whatever it was, it was nothing he would have indulged easily in years past. He had been married twice, and then there was Uta, and that was pretty much the story—he did not fool around much. There had been plenty of women in his life, but his love affairs had usually been sequential, very rarely simultaneous. By inclination he was monogamous, observing a pattern of sexual exclusivity because it was in his nature to do so. Until he met Alice Haskell and the sexual revolution. In the beginning, he had not been very good at spreading himself around, but with time and smuggling he developed an ease with it—Alice, Uta, Jane's friend April in Cartagena, Nina in Miami, Trude Daniels in Bogotá, off and on around Colombia with Blackie's little fifteen-year-old Indian friend Pachita, now Lillian, and others—back and forth, up and down, here and there, us and them. It was not something he would care to talk about later on, when it was over— he and Alice both left it behind rather suddenly—not because he was ashamed of it, but because he saw it as not really genuine in terms of his character. It represented a style of life that was not his. Not really. Zachary Swan, for all his skill at playing the child, was actually rather conservative.

Nevertheless, he and Lillian Giles had a wonderful time in Bogotá. Swan made a point of introducing her to Vincent van Klee. Lillian and Vincent hit it off particularly well. She loved listening to his stories, and he loved telling them.

"Tell her about the volcano, Vincent."

Vincent shook his head.

Swan always had trouble getting Vincent to tell the volcano story. It was Swan's favorite and one that Vincent was always pushed into when Swan was around. Lillian looked at Swan and then at Vincent:

"Oh, please, Vincent," she said.

Vincent did his Venus di Milo.

"Some other time," he said. "When I am excited."

Swan threw up his hands.

Vincent's volcano story has one principal character —Vincent. He is dining *al fresco* at a nightclub on the water—Swan seems to remember its being in Acapulco. The story is twenty years old. Vincent is with a group of friends, and he is stoned. The music is enchanting, there are strolling minstrels and dancers. The floor show is delightful. As the music crescendos there is a grande finale, with everyone jumping up from his table and dancing. There is a lavish fountain display. Vincent turns to his friends to comment on the beauty of the whole production. He looks up and around and discovers the place to be empty. He is the only one sitting. The band has hung in there—the music is still glorious. What Vincent soon realizes, very slowly because he is so stoned, is that the fountain display is in fact a volcano erupting. There are rocks flying and splashing splendidly in the water. The colors are marvelous. There is lava. How wonderful, he thinks. How beautiful it is.

Everybody had run away. And there he sat. Alone. In the middle of it. He thought it was grand.

"Vincent, you should write a book," said Lillian.

"I have been in two books already."

"Really?"

Vincent posed.

"What books, Vincent? I will read them."

"One you will never read. It is a terrible book. By a Colombian. He could not write, and he made me look very bad. I do not even remember the name."

"And the other?"

"It is by an American writer," he said.

"Do you remember the writer's name?"

"Yes, his name was F. Scott Fitzgerald."

There was a moment of silence.

"Vincent, he is a very famous writer."

Vincent shrugged.

"What is the name of the book?"

"The Night Is Blue."

"You must mean *Tender Is the Night.*"

Vincent twirled his head.

"Vincent, what is your name in the book?"

"I am the South American."

"Did Fitzgerald know you then?"

"When I was nineteen he took me to Berlin. I was living in Switzerland at the time."

"Vincent."

"I do not think we slept together," Vincent shrugged. "He kept me."

"Come on."

Vincent gave Lillian his profile.

"He found me amusing."

Nor was Fitzgerald the only one. Vincent was introduced to Douglas Fairbanks by a mutual friend and worked as Fairbanks's social secretary for a year while the actor was married to Lady Ashley. Lillian Giles ate it up. She was thrilled with Vincent, and she was thrilled with Bogotá. She was having the time of her life.

Swan made it a point never to meet Lillian in the Hilton lobby or anywhere near the Tequendama, but made it a point also never to leave her alone for too long. He would later say that much of it was for the benefit of propping her up for the border, but it is unlikely. What is more probable is that all of it had to do with the fact that, for the first time in almost a year, he was not alone in Bogotá. He was sharing all the good things with a close friend—the restaurants, the clubs, the mountains, the people he knew. Bogotá, for the first time, it seems, was a city he knew well, and he enjoyed opening it up for Lillian.

Lillian had been practicing her Spanish. At breakfast one morning she wanted eggs.

"Huevos," she said.

"Werewolves," said Swan. "If you ask for werewolves, you'll get eggs."

"One's as easy as the other."

"Maybe for you it is."

"Give it a try," she said.

"The waiter's coming. *You* give it a try."

"Dos huevos," she said.

The waiter looked at the menu in front of her, trying to see what she was ordering.

"See," said Swan.

Lillian looked at the waiter.

"Dose werewolves," said Swan to the man.

The waiter smiled, nodded, and left to get the eggs. Lillian was astonished.

"They can't even speak their own language," she said.

"Don't tell them that."

"My accent was perfect."

"I know it was. But somehow that doesn't carry much weight down here. Our high school Spanish teachers never understood that. For instance, they don't have much truck with consonants in Colombia. All you have to say is 'weh-woh' to get eggs. Listen closely the next time someone says hello to you—it'll sound like 'weh-a ee-a.' The *buenos* and the *días* translate that way. If you want to get by, you have to translate what they say into Spanish first, then into English. It's harder the other way around—English to Spanish isn't tough, but Spanish to whatever they speak is a killer. The only words that sound the same each time I hear them are '*coca*' and '*esmeraldas.*' "

Lillian pulled a paperback out of her carryall:

"I know what *coca* is. What's *esmeraldas?* Emeralds?"

"You got it. Stick with me, kid, I'll make a smuggler out of you yet."

"I don't remember any South American in *Tender Is the Night*," she said. "Do you?"

Swan scored from Jago in a taxicab. He carried the money (more than $20,000) stuffed in his shoes, the lining of his jacket, an Abercrombie & Fitch money belt and four pockets. It was like the Keystone Kops. After the score, he went directly to Rudolpho and Angel. The entire load was packed in one night. With the cocaine safely in the wood, he moved into the Hotel San Francisco—"*¡La Capital en su mano!*" the capital in the palm of your hand, they advertised—a lower-echelon hotel on Avenida Jimenez. The Tequendama was no place to be now that he was holding. The next morning he called Lillian Giles at the Hilton.

"I'm coming over with a bag. Get out of the hotel."

The Tequendama was within walking distance of the Hilton—just up the street—but from the San Francisco Swan had to take a cab. Lillian was out when he arrived. Rudolpho was sitting in the lobby. Swan asked at the desk for Miss Giles. When told she was not in, he asked to leave a bag with the "concierge." The bell captain was summoned. Swan handed him the bag and a note, written in Spanish by Juan Carlos Ramirez, and asked that they be given to Miss Giles when she returned. Swan overtipped him enormously. The bell captain smiled. Swan thanked him and left. Rudolpho kept his eye on the bag.

When Lillian picked up the load—she was not gone long—she asked the bell captain to read the note. He began in English:

"Dear Miss Giles—"

"Wait a minute"—she reached into her purse—"I want to write it down. I have a terrible memory."

As she searched through her pocketbook, Lillian smiled at the bell captain, asked his name—got that —and told him, in general, how wonderful he was. He was pleased.

"Let me get this right," she said.

"Mr. McCann . . . ," he read, ". . . can't make it today . . . had to go to Brazil . . . take the samples to New York store . . ."

With Lillian writing it all down, the bell captain knew the story as well as she did—call him a witness for the defense.

Swan and Lillian flew to Cartagena together on a nine A.M. plane out of Bogotá. There they played for a few days and bought more "samples"—baskets, rugs, beads, hammocks and such—two of everything.

Before leaving for Barranquilla, they ran into Uta. She and Swan spent an evening together.

"Where'd you go?"

"Out for cigarettes."

It had been just about a year again.

Uta had not changed much. She had lately been involved with some people moving stuff North by air and had been questioned by the authorities of both governments—there was heat on her. She needed looking after, and Swan wanted to help her out, but he could not take a chance while he was working. He gave her money to get to New York—she never made it. He and Lillian took a cab to Barranquilla, were stopped only once—*"Turista! Turista!"* they screamed, and paid off the border patrol—they stayed at the Del Prado and left for New York a day apart, Lillian following Swan's night flight the subsequent morning.

Lillian had been instructed to make a scrupulously complete Customs declaration. The rule was never to say "statue"; always use the Spanish name of the saint it represented, and never leave anything out. Swan went through Customs with no trouble. Lillian had less. Charlie met her flight—Swan was on hand—and the load was in Amagansett before the sun went down in Bogotá.

Three days later Swan was busted.

After the Fox

THE ALGONQUIN HOTEL in New York is one of those curious American antiques fashioned by our vagrant culture in its passing, and left behind, like a priceless cabinet in the attic of an aging house. It is an elegant relic which has survived one Great Depression and thirteen American presidents, which the dollar and the national outlook have not. An outspoken tribute to permanence, the Algonquin has somehow managed to endure the vicissitudes of a national economy heavily reliant on planned obsolescence; an economy whose principal contribution to the technology of city planning announced itself more than thirty years ago, in a typically lavish fashion, over the rooftops of Hiroshima—the A-Bomb: urban renewal the American way, a bold architectural concept introduced by the United States Air Force. Predating by more than forty years that reverberating policy statement, that direct-mail piece delivered in nuclear support of our continuing Keep America Beautiful campaign, the Algonquin assumes the significance of a legacy. At one time the landmark of cultural taste in America, it is cherished now as a souvenir, a bittersweet memento of a brief encounter with *style*, a keepsake reminiscent of the pre–Niels Bohr innocence of a new century.

The Algonquin is located on West 44th Street between Fifth and Sixth Avenues in the occluded heart of midtown Manhattan. On George Washington's Birthday, in February of 1974, while Zachary Swan was confronting American history in the lobby of that venerable establishment, New York City was entering the fourth week of its annual survival drill. January's repeated attempts at snowfall had been aborted, and the atmosphere had avenged itself by coughing up a seemingly endless cycle of ice, slush, and pH-critical rain. Manhattan was in the grip of a temperature inversion. Saturated hydrocarbons choked off the air, and periodic high-velocity winds helped reproduce the conditions of a vast decompression chamber. For weeks the light had been bad, the sky, a luminous gray, etherizing the city against anything exciting or healthy, not the least of which was the sun; and day-to-day living was one continuous Act of Contrition, spiritually draining, psychologically touch and go. By Valentine's Day the mood of the people had grown dangerously ugly. Stepping outside was like entering a snakepit. Hibernation was growing fashionable.

Today the Algonquin lobby exhibited all the charm of an autopsy room. The customers were drinking heavily. The staff was wired. The electronegativity in the air oscillated precariously between category-one violence and all-out despair. Each table took on the distinct penumbra of an armed refugee camp. Swan wondered how recently any of these people had done cocaine. It was six P.M. He had ventured into this elegant literary watering hole only once before, and it had been in the evening, at night in fact, when only the foolhardy go forth, when only the volunteer goes up against New York. Now the Algonquin was occupied by the draftees, New York's victims, impressed into combat by the requirements of commerce. And there is nothing in the world more helpless and depraved than an individual impelled onto the streets of New York City by any agency other than choice. Zachary Swan stood on the perimeter, wondering if he truly cared whether the headwaiter was going to find him a vacant table, and risked his sanity in the heroic attempt truly to understand how he had arrived at that place, at that time, and in that condition on the 242nd birthday of the congenital syphilitic who had become known as the father of our country.

He was there to talk about cocaine.

Swan's initial encounter with what the New York publishing establishment was calling writers these days was not a particularly auspicious one.

"You look just like a Fed," he was saying. "They all have long hair and wear bluejeans."

"You don't look anything like a cocaine smuggler," he was told.

He was wearing a dark gray charcoal suit of worsted wool, a white French-cotton broadcloth shirt with French cuffs, and a plush, Burgundy red velvet bow tie the size of a hummingbird, all tailored by Paul Stuart on Madison Avenue. A linen handkerchief tucked neatly into the breast pocket of his jacket matched his shirt. His dark brown cordovans matched his belt. He wore ceramic cufflinks and a gold watch. One would have taken him for an advertising executive.

"That's the idea," he said.

Swan sat facing the door, nursing a Martini, chain-smoking Kools. It had been more than a year since his arrest, and he was still awaiting trial. His preliminary hearing had gone against him. He faced fifteen years in prison for possession of the cocaine and the gun, and he had already run up $10,000 in legal fees. The IRS was investigating him—they were looking for $15,000 in Federal taxes on what they had been able to unearth already in the way of supportable income. The Justice Department wanted him too.

"What have they got on you?"

"Thirteen trips to Colombia."

"Is that all?"

"They've got a guy in a Mexican jail who they say will do business with them if they get him out of there."

Vinnie Pirata.

"A friend of yours?"

"He used to be."

"Can he hurt you on the State charge?"

"No, nothing there. But the Feds and the DA are cooperating. They are feeding each other all kinds of information. The Feds say they can make it easy for me out on Long Island if I cooperate with them."

"What do they want you to do?"

"Talk. Turn in some friends. Go South again and work as a narc. You've seen it all on TV."

"Can you stand a Federal charge?"

"The Feds are always tougher. But I don't think they can make a smuggling charge stick. I covered myself pretty well."

"How?"

"You really ask a lot of questions."

"I used to get paid for it."

"They must have paid you well."

"Not well enough."

"I've got to be careful," he said.

"You can say that again."

"I've got to be careful."

Everyone laughed.

"What do you think of smugglers?" he asked.

Everyone stopped laughing.

"You ever handle smack?"

"Never. I wouldn't have anything to do with the shit, and neither would any of my people. Was that worrying you?"

"That was worrying me."

"And I don't like Nixon either. What else do you want to know?"

"You ever pull the trigger on anyone?"

"I'm a pacifist."

"What were you doing with a gun?"

"It was purely a matter of self-preservation. Somebody threatened me. That's why I moved to Long Island. I was running. I never fired the thing. I still have nightmares."

"Another friend of yours?"

"He was a small-time hood. His name's Crazy Leslie. Last year he was arrested for beating up a cop. He escaped from the hospital by jumping out the window, but he broke his leg in the jump and they picked him up again. It made the papers."

"Do you live in New York now?"

"Yes, but I'm getting out."

"Because of the nightmares?"

"No. Because Crazy Leslie's back on the street. He's got a gun and he's looking for old friends."

Somebody hit the service bell. Between that time and the waiter's arrival, there was silence. When the waiter left, the conversation returned to a discussion of Swan's health. It was pointed out that he had recently undergone cancer surgery (for basal cell epithelioma) and faced a hernia operation in the spring. He took downs (Valium) to ease the stress responsible for periodic attacks of bronchial asthma and massive doses of Gelusil to keep his stomach together. He had a detached retina. His body was like a beleaguered city, it seemed, coming apart under assault. Today it was holding out on rations of alcohol and tobacco. And it was beginning to look like Troy. Zachary Swan III, this man with the funny name, was up against some serious odds.

"Was it worth it?"

"Not if I have to spend another night in jail."

"What are your chances?"

"My lawyer says they're good."

"First offense?"

"If it comes to that. But he thinks we can get it thrown out on the illegal search. They broke into the house."

"No warrant?"

"They didn't have any evidence. There was no way they could get a search warrant. They got one after they went in."

"What were they looking for?"

"They were looking for dope."

"Just because you were stoned when they brought you in?"

"Most of us were pretty straight by then."

"They must have had some reason for wanting to go in. They can't be that hard up for work."

"They used the dogs as an excuse."

"The dogs?"

"They said they wanted to take the dogs home for us. Humanitarians, right? We said don't trouble yourself. It was one of those things—they're smiling. I'm smiling, we all know what's going on . . . *thanks, but I know you're busy, appreciate it all the same, though . . . by the way, can I see a lawyer?*"

"But they must have had a reason."

"The newspaper said they had my name from 'a previous drug investigation.' "

"Well?"

"They had my name, but it had nothing to do with any of this. Something altogether different. It was nothing I was involved in."

"What was it?"

"One of the ironic twists of the whole story is that the house I rented in East Hampton, I rented from a narcotics detective—you like that, right?"

"Just a coincidence?"

"Just a coincidence."

"Very nice."

"I thought you'd like it. Anyway, we were friendly and I happened to overhear something once. I made the mistake of repeating it in the wrong place. It was an accident, but an unfortunate one. It blew over quick enough, but somebody remembered it and picked up on it the morning I was arrested. It was totally without relevance to anything I was involved in, a complete fluke, but it came home. You might say poetic justice caught up with me."

"Had they been keeping an eye on you?"

"I don't think so."

"They just made the connection because they had you for being under the influence?"

"No. They didn't have me for anything. They busted Lillian for driving under the influence and for not having her license. They told *me* to drive the car back to the station. After I paid her bail, and we all got up to leave, the cop says, 'We're gonna lock you all up for intoxication.' Well, shit. If I'm sober enough to drive—they *told* me to drive—how are they going to lock me up for public intoxication? Well, logic doesn't carry much weight down there, you see. It's a problem, but they're going to take care of that. The idea is to hold us until they can search the house. I demanded a blood test. A lot of good that did me. This is the part in the movie where the Fourteenth Amendment starts getting the shit kicked out of it."

"How did they 'take care of it'?"

"Are you ready for this? They lied. In court! They said a cop drove the car. Can you believe it? They lied. Now, isn't that something? I mean, that's disgusting. It's dishonest."

"You mean they broke the *law?*"

"You can't trust anybody these days."

"It's terrible, isn't it?"

"It's an insult."

"Did they feed the dogs?"

"They didn't even let them out of the car until the next day."

"So they didn't take them back to the house?"

"No."

"How did they get in?"

"Well, the Sherlock Holmes on the case was a guy named Paulsen. Detective Sergeant Paulsen. At the hearing he told the judge that he was on his way back to work that day, after lunch at home, and he just happened to be passing my house—which is like passing Anchorage on your way back from New York to Pittsburgh. Anyway, he was worried about the dogs. And I feel sorry for the guy, because it obviously ruined his lunch—he only spent about three minutes at home if his addition is correct; and then there were some typographical errors on his application for the warrant. He didn't get around to correcting them until the dogs were safe and he had had an opportunity to talk to the DA—just prior to his testimony, in fact, five months later. So, Detective Sergeant Paulsen pulled into the driveway and drove to the back of the house to see if anyone was home."

"Why didn't he go to the front door?"

"It's hard to say. I guess he didn't want to block the driveway. He did say at first that he parked in the street and walked across the lawn. But he changed that under cross-examination. If he did cross the lawn he would have ended up at the front door. You have to remember that he was concerned about the dogs. He was an animal lover. Anyway, it was through the back door that he saw a suspicious plastic bag on the kitchen table."

"What was suspicious about it?"

"He said it contained dope."

"And he went in?"

"I think he *was* in. If he wasn't, he was trespassing anyway. He got a warrant."

"Why didn't you just pay your bail and go home that morning?"

"They told us there was no magistrate to arraign us."

"When did they finally arraign you?"

"One o'clock the next morning."

"But they had a judge there at lunchtime to sign the search warrant."

"Somewhere between noon and one P.M. That was one of the typos. Hell, we didn't even get a phone call until Sunday afternoon."

"Is that the Fourteenth Amendment again?"

"I think it's the Bill of Rights."

"Do you think that would have happened no matter where you were?"

"That's a good question. The harassment, maybe.

But not the search. A New York cop would never take that kind of chance. He knows he's got to have the goods on you. New York City cops at least have a little bit of style. And they know what's going to make them look bad later."

"Do you have enough money for an appeal?"

"I hope it doesn't go that far. We're waiting for a good judge. There's one out there with a good drug record. He's also trying to get on the appellate court. My lawyer figures that if we can make a strong enough case, so that it looks like a guilty decision will be overturned on appeal, then this judge won't take any chances. He can't afford to be overturned if he wants to make the appellate court someday."

"It looks like you've got a good lawyer."

"I don't know. Sometimes I think so. Sometimes I wonder."

"Sounds to me like your chances are good."

"Well, I'll tell you one thing."

"What's that?"

"I'm not going back to jail."

Zachary Swan, determined not to go back to jail, was at the time of his trial in possession of false papers with which to leave the country in the event of a conviction. He also had money. Most of it in cash. He had not been idle in the year and a half since his arrest. On the "Things Colombian" smuggle, Lillian Giles had walked through U.S. Customs in New York with five kilograms of cocaine. Prior to the costly celebration of that event, which took place two days later at Swan's Amagansett beach house, Swan had managed to move 1,500 grams of the load—he had met Anthony under the Maxfield Parrish painting in the King Cole Bar of the St. Regis Hotel and picked up a quick $48,000. What the Amagansett police busted was most of the 500 grams Swan had withdrawn from the head he cleaved that evening. What they missed were the three kilos shared by the Madonna sitting on the mantelpiece in the living room and the rolling pin hanging over the stove in the kitchen. They confiscated Swan's gram scale, his marijuana, and an assortment of pills along with over 500 grams of mix, most of it borax. Taking the coke and the mix together (if the lab techs at headquarters were smart they used Swan's Ohaus), they estimated the bust at a kilo. Of cocaine.

What the Amagansett authorities did not do—to their credit—was waste their time dealing with newspaper people. What they might have done to help their case was take a tip from the Feds. When Federal agents make a cocaine (or marijuana or heroin) bust, they not only overestimate the load for the benefit of the press, but they quote inflated gram prices. If they bust a smuggler at Customs, for example, carrying three kilos of pure, for which the smuggler has paid a total of, say, $18,000 and on which he stands to make anywhere from $80,000 to $100,000 profit, they will estimate their haul at $2 million, as if the weirdo they have captured were going to go home, buy a truckload of Reynolds Wrap, sixty pounds of lactose and a gram scale and devote the rest of his life to putting 30,000 packages together—not one of which is any larger than a stick of chewing gum, each only 10 percent of which is cocaine—and *then* go out and sell the snow for $75 a gram. It is the same logic that presumes bituminous coal is worth $3,000 a carat because someday it will be diamonds.

What the cops in Amagansett did was merely overestimate the weight. They hit Swan with a couple of possession-one drug felonies—they were worth fifteen years apiece—and a felony charge on the gun—worth five. The judge let everyone else go, and the DA went for the limit on Swan. Charlie Kendricks and Lillian Giles left for Australia as soon as the heat was off, and Alice stuck around to help Swan through the wringer.

Swan's first move, when his bail came through, was to get the three kilos out of the beach house. He made a couple of dry runs before making his move, then carried the load out under the cover of darkness, driving it northwest to his stepmother's house in Greenwood Lake, where he stashed it in the basement behind a couple of snow tires. He then rented an apartment in the name of Zachary Swan on West 84th Street in Manhattan and laid out some money at Radio Shack on a pair of walkie-talkies. He gave one to Roger.

Roger Livingston's living room window, giving southern exposure to his apartment on West 85th Street, was visible from the bedroom window of Swan's apartment on West 84th. In the weeks that followed, Swan maintained radio contact with Roger, who was in touch with Anthony, Moses and the other ounce-dealers, and through Roger and the radios he moved the cocaine by Thanksgiving. The three kilos, which had become four and a half with the hit, he moved at $1,000 an ounce, bringing his before-expenses total on the broken load up to over $200,000. He spent the next year and a half postponing his trial.

While Ernie Peace was submitting notices of motions to reargue and hard-nosed memoranda of law to the Suffolk County Court, claiming that his client was being railroaded beyond belief, Zachary Swan was out meeting his legal fees. In the year and a half between Swan's arrest and trial, Angel the carpenter made at least two trips to New York carrying peculiarly bound books. Armando was meeting people in Bogotá who introduced themselves by saying, "I used to play for Detroit." (If anyone had used Swan's name without the code, Armando's reply would have been something like, "God, I don't know *what* you're talking about, man.") Old friends were coming and going. Moses, still in business on the West Side, was getting visits from people who knew Swan: "We're back-to-back buddies," they would say. (Swan and Moses had matching scars on their backs, Swan's as a result of his surgery—he called it a knife fight in Bogotá—

Moses's as a result of a gunshot wound he received working an East Side saloon.) There were marijuana moves out of Miami and consultant's fees on two-border boat moves through Mexico. The code words were flying back and forth, and the cloak-and-dagger back-stairs forget-me-not cocaine blues carried Swan back to the border again and again. And there was always that one big move he had never made.

Two weeks after his interview at the Algonquin, Swan, walking down Broadway in the direction of a newspaper stand, felt a tap on his shoulder.

"Hey, don't I know you?" asked a voice from the fog.

Swan, whose face was buried in the collar of his trench coat and whose drenched hair covered his eyebrows, shook his head and mumbled something like "No, I don't think so" to the man. He grabbed his newspaper and walked away. Fast. When he looked back, Crazy Leslie was gone. But Swan suspected it would not be for long. A week later, he left town for good. New York City was a thing of the past.

Swan and Alice, who had been living together for a year in Alice's apartment on 87th Street, moved out of state with the permission of the court. They rented a house with a garden, and in the spring Swan took up organic gardening. Alice was pregnant. She would never go back to New York. She put down roots. Swan and Ernie Peace, having failed in repeated attempts to have their case thrown out of court, prepared for trial.

Six months after Swan's trial, Alice gave birth to a boy. Nine pounds five ounces—and five days before Christmas. Swan had said that his son—he was sure it would be a son—would never in his life do anything illegal. Old Geoffrey would live off the land. He would learn to farm and he would do his own carpentry and he would never go near New York. Swan had assured

Alice that after all the years of running he was determined to go straight.

"Things are going to be different," he said.

But for all one knows Swan may still be planning the big one he never made. On June 10, 1974, Swan went to trial. On June 26 he was found innocent on all counts of possession of a dangerous drug. He was put on three years' probation for misdemeanor possession of a dangerous weapon. He was told to go home and behave himself.

Ernie Peace had said from the beginning that the gun would be the problem, and he went to great lengths to demonstrate that because the patio, where it was buried, was enclosed on two sides, the patio was a part of the house—possession of a gun in one's house in New York, he pointed out, is a misdemeanor, not a felony. The legal memos he submitted, in which he cited drug decisions that the judge's law clerk could not ignore, won the acquittal on the cocaine charge.

Choosing to go without a jury, choosing to go before a judge who could be counted on to resist pressure, and gambling on the judge's ability to respond clearly to the technical and legal merits of the case as it was presented on both sides ("He's got a damn good law man behind him," Peace said afterward), Ernie Peace had beaten the DA.* Swan's character witnesses, Iona Prep boys who had gone straight, and the letters he submitted from influential friends, one of them a judge, were too much for Amagansett's finest, who came off looking bad. Swan, himself, at the trial, was 100 percent Zachary Swan. Outraged and indignant, he testified in his own defense, entertaining the judge and the DA at the same time. Posturing and appealing, he played the innocent fool, but when he appeared for sentencing two weeks later he was as frightened as hell. He thought they had lost it (particularly when the DA asked the judge to lay down the

---

* See Appendix IX.

maximum). Facing the judge, all Swan could think of was jail.

The sentencing took less than five minutes. Swan was instructed to report to a probation officer. He was free to go.

As he left the courtroom he kissed Ernie Peace. And as he left the building he said:

"This is just like walking through Customs."

Epilogue

I NEW YORK

Vinnie Pirata dropped out of sight sometime in 1973. He was not heard from again until DEA agents in New York threatened Swan with his testimony, which Pirata allegedly offered them in exchange for his extradition from a Mexican jail. If Pirata was there, he was never extradited. His closest friends have not heard from him in years. The best one can assume is that Pirata, if he is alive, is behind bars in Mexico. If he is in for drug running, he is in for a minimum of six years.

Billy Bad Breaks, sentenced to a stretch in Federal prison after his Brownsville bust, returned to New York, where the breaks got worse. In the summer of 1974 he was on the run.

Adrian the Mogul is by every account a producer who is still not producing.

Ike and *Freddy,* the shooters from Brooklyn, are still renting crap tables to the local houses of worship in Queens.

Nice Mickey lives in New York, where he shoots pool, plays backgammon and makes the best fudge Alice Haskell has ever tasted. Currently, he makes his money legitimately—in 1975, for a month, he operated a concession at a New Jersey department store stitching names on Christmas stockings. He made a bundle. Nice Mickey has never been busted.

Mean Mickey was last seen by Zachary Swan popping an amyl nitrate while on water skis. He is on parole in New York and still proud of his press clippings.

Moses, who offered to have Crazy Leslie eliminated by two fifteen-year-olds who would do anything for $100—"That's a hundred apiece, you understand"— in 1973 was shot in the back in a bar on the East Side, and lived to advertise it. The manager of a bar on Eighth Avenue in New York, his business is better than ever.

Roger Livingston, busted on a marijuana charge, lives in New York with Angela De Santis. She is a children's clothing designer. He teaches biology in the New York City school system. Angela got the cocaine out of the house; now she is working on the snakes.

Charlie Kendricks and *Lillian Giles* are married and living on a sheep station in Australia.

Davis has not been near a package from South America in years, and he intends to keep it that way.

The Lothario, who has never done anything illegal outside the company of Zachary Swan, has a steady girl and "a business here in New York."

Trude Daniels got her apartment. She lives in New York with her daughter, she has a steady job, and if she is not as happy as some of her friends, it is because she does not have a friend that makes her as happy as she makes them.

Honest Ellery, who once owned a Maserati but never a driver's license (he took it as collateral on a loan to Pirata, then rented a garage where he visited it every day for months—Ellery had always loved Maseratis but had never learned to drive), was busted in July of 1973 for selling two ounces of cocaine to New York narcotics agents. He stood up—he did not reveal the source of the coke. He beat the Rockefeller law by a few months and got probation. He lives in the Bronx and holds a legitimate job in Manhattan. He dreams of laundromats—Pirata stole the Maserati back.

Anthony was last heard from shortly after Swan went to trial. "He has a problem," Ellery said. Anthony's problem kept him busy for a year. He could not be reached. At the end of a year he went to Federal prison for three and a half. He can be reached there.

Crazy Leslie is walking the streets of New York, frightening people. Alice Haskell, who should know him as well as anyone, thinks of him only rarely: "I wonder if his mother knows what he does for a living?" she asks.

II SOUTH AMERICA

Uta Dietrische was never seen again after her final appearance in Cartagena. Swan continued to get word of her, however, and continued to send her money. The last he heard was that she was living in the Canary Islands. It was Alice who suggested: "Why don't we have her come and stay with us for a while?"

Vincent van Klee, having moved out of his suite at the Continental, lives in a posh apartment complex at the foot of Monserrate. As of the spring of 1975 he had given up liquor and cocaine, deeming them detrimental to a lifestyle that has changed no more since his seventy-second birthday than it has since his nine-teenth. He makes occasional visits to New York, where he monitors his investments and keeps in touch with old friends, and when Swan last saw him, in Bogotá in May of last year, he had just returned from Cartagena, where, Vincent said, he had taken the part of "a faggot ballet instructor" in a big-budget Italian movie.

Michel Bernier is selling himself to the highest bid-der in Brazil.

Rudolpho is keeping his nose clean in Bogotá, where he spends money for Vincent van Klee.

Angel was last heard to be doing honest carpentry in Bucaramanga.

Armando began feeling the heat in Bogotá shortly af-ter Swan's arrest. As of May 1975 he was not answer-ing his telephone.

Raoul, who told Zachary Swan that a smuggler's luck is good for only two years, is doing a life sentence in Florida for running cocaine. He gets ice cream once a week.

Harry Morgan and *Jimmy the boat captain* are in the Caribbean, doing what they do best.

Sea Gull Billy can be contacted at the Hotel Caribe marina.

Blackie and the beach people in Santa Marta and Mad Walter's Haight-Ashbury transplants are still playing hide-and-seek with the local police around the coastal resorts of Colombia.

The Hawk is playing hide-and-seek with the authorities of more than one South American government. It was Vincent van Klee who said: "She has a problem."

Jago, the Hawk's man, who had fronted Swan the fifth kilo on the "Things Colombian" Move, a year and a half later was looking for Canadian Jack, who had disappeared with a fronted five. In May 1975 the pistol-packing flesh eater was on the run himself. Having double-crossed the wrong people on his own end of the business, he was last seen heading in the general direction of Ecuador.

Canadian Jack was last in touch with Zachary Swan in the summer of 1974. In the year between Swan's arrest and Jack's last letter, the young smuggler had been in and out of the United States and had stepped across into Canada at least once. He was known to have been in Jamaica and eventually in Mexico, where his lieutenant, a twenty-four-year-old Canadian named Roy, was arrested and imprisoned on a cocaine charge. In May 1975 Juan Carlos Ramirez told Zachary Swan that Jack was married to a young Indian woman and living in Cartagena, where he owned a leather shop. Swan was unable to find him. Jack is still wanted in Canada, where he faces ten years on his hash bust. Said Swan, shortly after he stopped hearing from the young Canadian: "He knows how to run."

Black Dan, known for being a professional, was not seen in Bogotá after the heat came on. Last seen at the Oriole, he just disappeared one day, and was never heard from again. Everyone's guess is that he is alive and well and semiretired, living either in San Francisco or somewhere in Colombia. Zachary Swan suspects that wherever he is, he is in touch with Canadian Jack.

Rainy Day—R.I.P.

Zachary Swan and *Alice Haskell,* married a week after Swan's acquittal, are living under their own names on a half-acre of land on the East Coast of the United States. The growing season is a long one there, and Swan raises organic vegetables, the surplus of which he sells to the local health food store. He also deals in antiques, he and Alice making weekly roundups of available merchandise at local auctions and selling them on the flea market circuit. (Swan occasionally raids the neighborhood Good Will depository, faking a drop-off to pick up choice items.) While Swan monitors the New York Stock Exchange and the National Football League, Alice cans and sews and devotes the best hours of her time to hanging out with their year-and-a-half-old son, Geoffrey. The three dogs have rooms of their own, and they like the country just fine. They treat the towheaded Geoffrey as if he were one of the family—a very remarkable golden retriever. Swan, in the two years since his trial, has been on probation. He has a perfect record and a year to go. He likes his probation officer, and his probation officer likes him. He is a family man and a model of industry, and as far as the probation people are concerned he has been rehabilitated. Recently they have pointed out, and particularly applauded, his growing interest in carpentry.

Appendices

I QUAALUDES

In the late 1960s, at about the time Richard Nixon was taking over, downs became the most popular drug on the American pill-popping market. Acid was on its way out, and speed was killing everyone in sight—it was natural that under a Republican administration young dopers would turn to the favorite drug of their parents. Just as meprobamate (Miltown) had been the drug of choice in the Eisenhower years, so barbiturates would assert themselves in the years of the "silenced majority." The most popular barbiturates at the time were Seconal (sodium secobarbital—*reds*), Nembutal (sodium pentobarbital—*yellows*), and Amytal (sodium amobarbital—*blues*), the second manufactured by Abbot, the other two manufactured by Lilly. The newer, and far milder, sedatives, Librium and Valium —Roche Laboratories' bid to take the sweepstakes— were still in their infancy.

Barbiturates, known to be habit-forming, hit the college campus with a reputation. Though marketed chiefly to domestic addicts and made available by the drug companies to the occasional thoroughbred, it was known that they were manufactured principally for suicides. Toying with them ensured status . . . *if they were good enough for Jimi Hendrix, they are good enough for me*. The pharmaceutical houses worked overtime—reds put Lilly on the map and, by themselves, could be counted on to take up the corporate slack for a long time after the Darvon patents ran out.

"What in the world ever became of sweet Jane
She lost her sparkle, you know she isn't the same
Livin' on reds, Vitamin C and cocaine
All a friend can say is, 'Ain't it a shame.' "

> "Truckin," from *American Beauty*,
> THE GRATEFUL DEAD

A couple of years later, while Nixon's back was turned—call it Ziegler's mistake—the newspapers managed to get hold of some truly electrifying national news. A new drug had hit the campus. (Yawn.) All they had to do was call it an aphrodisiac, and their advertising revenues would triple. *Great Caesar's ghost!* It was a celibate city editor's dream. It, too, was a down, this pill, but not only would they attribute deaths to it, they would attribute WILD HIPPIE ORGIES IN FLORIDA and BARE ASSED RUTTING IN THE STREETS to this miracle drug. Get ready, Mom and Dad. (Do you know what your children are doing tonight?)

Quaaludes.

Quaalude is the brand name given by William H. Rorer, Inc., to a sedative and hypnotic agent known pharmacologically as methaqualone—2-methyl-3-o-tolyl-4(3H)-quinazolinone—a new, nonbarbiturate hypnotic, useful, according to the Physician's Desk Reference, in the treatment of insomnia, and designed for those cases in which barbiturates are contraindicated or where other hypnotics have failed. Because of its side-effects, or absence thereof—methaqualone is not physically addictive, though psychological addiction is almost guaranteed to the heavy user—methaqualone is in many ways preferable to the barbiturates.

Adverse neuropsychiatric reactions include headache, hangover, fatigue, dizziness and torpor. Of course, it is these reactions and others that the serious doper looks for—an absence of side-effects altogether would throw the drug off the market. Two things which make methaqualone as popular as it is are its availability over the barbituates and its ability to knock you down without knocking you out. It goes right to the central nervous system and turns you to jelly—you are loose in about twenty minutes. The exact mode of its action is unknown (of course), but methaqualone apparently acts on a different CNS site than that of the barbiturates. The tactile sensitivity it promotes makes lovemaking preferable to baseball for a good eight hours—that is what the newspapers mean by an aphrodisiac—but after the first hour, nothing is preferable to sleep. And if you happen to play baseball the next day, you might slouch a little, off and on, at second base, as the bends come and go. It is that kind of dope.

The prescribed dosage for sleep is usually 150–300-mg at bedtime. The maximum will set you up for anything you have in mind. An overdose—a very important factor, without which its popularity would slide significantly—can get you off on anything from spontaneous vomiting, delirium and convulsions to something as far out as cutaneous or pulmonary edema, hepatic damage, renal insufficiency and bleeding, shock, respiratory arrest, coma and death. Dig it. Two-point-four grams will throw you into a coma. Eight grams will kill you—reds are faster—and most fatal cases have followed ingestion of overdoses accompanied by alcohol.

Quäalude comes in a scored white tablet in two sizes, one containing 150mg methaqualone, the other containing 300mg—the famous "714." Both bear the manufacturer's name.

Sopor, manufactured by Arnar-Stone Laboratories, Inc., is the other popular source of methaqualone.

Sopors come in green, yellow and orange, 75mg, 150mg and 300mg respectively.

Parke-Davis (Parest) and Cooper Laboratories (Somnafac), as did Wallace (Optimil), market methaqualone bonded to a cation—methaqualone hydrochloride. A rose by any other name . . .

II   CREDIT CARDS AND TRAVELER'S CHECKS

In New York City, as in any major city in the country or around the world, there is a lucrative traffic in bad traveler's checks and stolen credit cards. Credit cards are marketable because the mechanism for listing the card number of any account against which theft or loss is reported is a very slow one, and it is made slower by the reluctance of many people, especially the businessman whose cards have been lifted by a hooker in a hotel room in the Tenderloin, to report the theft immediately. Traveler's checks are marketable on the same basis, but with traveler's checks there is a bonus.

The traveler's check scam (if someone is doing TCs, he is dealing in traveler's checks) works off the guarantee given by American Express and the respective banks that a customer's checks will be replaced immediately in the event of loss or theft—the no-liability clause, which makes the checks preferable to cash, streamlines crime in this area because it eliminates the weakest link in the chain, the thief. While credit cards have to be stolen, traveler's checks can be bought.

If a man like Adrian the Mogul wants some fast money, he can buy $5,000 worth of traveler's checks from First National City Bank, and Swan will give him the name of someone downtown who will pay him $2,500 for them. Adrian will pick up the $2,500, then redeem the $5,000 from FNCB. The trick with the traveler's checks is that a customer has to report them lost or stolen immediately to cover himself. New York cops know the swindle:

"Officer, I want to report stolen traveler's checks."

"Sure. You owe me a new hat or I'll misspell your name."

"Thieves! Thieves!"

The success with which the traffic flourishes is amplified by the scope across which traveler's checks and credit cards are honored—if a credit card stolen at the Americana in New York shows up the next morning in San Francisco, the odds against its having been listed, which are slim to begin with, are slimmer still over the distance. Not only does the listing mechanism, which is heavily computerized, function poorly, but chances are very small that a clerk on the West Coast is going to question a well-dressed tourist who can duplicate the signature on the card, especially if the out-of-towner is carrying corroborating identification.

The man who makes the traffic go controls two networks. He operates a centrally located headquarters where he buys credit cards from thieves, and traveler's checks from either their owners or the same thieves, and he operates an apparatus by which he can get the cards and checks out of town fast with teams of professional penmen. A good penman, man or woman, dresses well, speaks well, and can forge a signature as blatantly not his as John Hancock's without raising suspicion.

At 2:30 A.M. in one of Manhattan's larger pool halls, Nice Mickey will be shooting nine-ball. At three A.M. they will start coming in—hookers, pimps and cab drivers; the creepers and second-story men who work the hotels with the help of the desk clerks; the pickpockets, the stickup men, and all the thieves who have called it a night. They get $100 a card. Traveler's checks—half the face value.

"Now, God forbid a guy should give him a card that's three weeks old and is on the list. The guy never does any business again, ever, and it takes a while for his arm to get straightened. So it's got to be fresh, and it is fresh—no more than a day or two old."

From the poolroom the cards and the traveler's checks go to a man named George—he owns several flower shops in New York. In one of his offices, George has electric typewriters and blank social security cards, automobile registration forms and driver's licenses from every state in the Union. He calls in the teams. They get two or three cards apiece, and by the following morning they are all leaving town in different directions. They go to banks first, then to the retail stores. George takes 50 percent on whatever the teams bring in. He gives his man at the pool hall a percentage on every card, a flat fee for the checks.

And *that* is what Mean Mickey and Vinnie Pirata were doing.

III MEXICAN BROWN

In 1973, for the first time on record, the New York City Police Department's Narcotics Division reported making more cocaine than heroin "buys" through its agents on the street. Though the statistic attests to the current availability of cocaine, it is much more an indication of the heroin shortage that was brought on in 1972 by the American-instigated foreclosure by Turkey on her poppy fields. (The Turkish government prohibited its farmers from cultivating the poppy in return for $35.7 million in U.S. aid.) The Turkish ban was a temporary one, lifted in 1975, and one which more than any single factor accounted for the popular emergence of Mexican Brown on the streets of New York and other large American cities. The Mexicans, who learned to cultivate the opium poppy during World War II, were encouraged to do so by the United States government, whose legal stockpiles were threatened by the fighting in Europe. The brown heroin coming up from Mexico, though not as pretty to look at, is sold on a shorter cut than the white imported from Turkey and Southeast Asia. An addict shooting white runs the risk of an overdose if he main-lines an equivalent quantity of brown; of course, if you are spiking anything called heroin, your days are numbered to begin with—the scag may as well be blue for all the difference it makes.

IV SPEED

Speed, in the counterculture, is affectionately known as that which kills. Misused correctly, it can burn you out faster than smack. It was the methedrine shooters who were dying all over the Haight in San Francisco and up on the corner of Hazelton Street in Toronto in the late 1960s: speed, a kind of white man's scag, the young middle-class loser's own hat full of rain, coming off the street cut with anything that would melt in a spoon, bleach, rat poison . . . *anything, man, just give me the spike.* The speed freak was a culture hero, the last daredevil cowboy—guaranteed to vanish. He had an air of death about him.

A good, hard-line methedrine habit is the electro-motor Grand Prix of suicide drug use—out of the needle, speed will throw your insides into overdrive and take you out on the high side. It is the ultimate challenge to tolerance, dying with your boots on the American way, vital organs pumping the limit, synapses firing—you redline. In the death house of modern chemistry, where barbiturates are the gas chamber, speed is the chair—one high-voltage electro-orgasmic jolt and the lights go out. Overload. Oblivion express.

It was methedrine that was responsible for all those strange autopsies coming out of the drug underground in the Leary years—sixteen-year-olds with the insides of eighty-year-old men. The pathologists had never seen anything like it. It was this new and hideous phenomenon that subsequently spawned all the pub-lic service announcements coming over the underground FM stations made by people like Grace Slick and Frank Zappa . . . *look, man, smoke all the grass you want, and do acid, if it's Owsley, but for your own good stay away from speed—it'll fry your brains and ruin your liver and, in general, it'll make you about as fucked up as your parents . . . speed kills.*

Amphetamines were first synthesized by L. Edeleano in 1887. It was not until 1920, however, while searching for a synthetic substitute for ephedrine—an herbal central-nervous-system stimulant used in the treatment of asthma—that Gordon Alles discovered that Edeleano's original compound, amphetamine sulfate, and its even more active dextro isomer, dextroamphetamine sulfate, exhibited the properties that make them so popular today—Smith Kline & French, the pharmaceutical house which acquired Alles's patents, wasted no time convincing the American medical establishment that Benzedrine and Dexedrine were modern chemistry's answer to the Crusades. Immediately, things began to look . . . *up.* Reports of attrition—Smith Kline & French never bothered to record the side-effects of the amphetamines—did not start coming in until 1939, but by then speed was an institution, and every doctor's practice depended on it.

The amount of Benzedrine supplied to American soldiers stationed in Britain during the Second World War has been estimated at 180 million pills. Between 1966 and 1969 the American Army consumed more amphetamines than the *combined* British and American armies of World War II. In 1970 over 225,000 pounds—ten billion tablets—of amphetamines and amphetamine substitutes were manufactured legally. In 1971, when production was allegedly being cut back, twelve billion pills—sixty 10mg tablets for every person in the United States—were manufactured. The profits derived by the pharmaceutical companies from amphetamine sales, and the revenues derived by the American Medical Association from advertisements for the drugs in medical journals, account for heavy lobbying by the industry among legislators, FDA officials and the physicians themselves (many of whom make money on every speed prescription they write).

Though amphetamines may be defended as the drug of choice for such rare conditions as narcolepsy, their prescribed use for anything else—other than speeding, of course—is usually no more than an excuse to lay an up on a good customer. A lot of doctors prescribe amphetamines as diet pills—anorexiants, appetite suppressants—but they rarely hand out prescriptions to overweight people. (Speed's anorectic effect is short-term—tolerance is a big problem.) Speed is for people who like to speed, not for people who like to eat. And if you like to speed, far be it from the drug companies or the doctor to stop you . . . *speed is good for America*. Cocaine is to speed what the Bolivian blow gun is to the *Enola Gay*. In the doper's paradise of 427-horsepower freak behavior, speed, not coke, is the real thing.

Speed, the word itself, is America's nickname for the amphetamines—those sympathomimetic amines of the amphetamine group with CNS stimulant activity. The amines are a group of organic compounds of nitrogen that may be considered ammonia (NH_3) derivatives—the word amine is a derivative of the word ammonia just as the word amino (as in amino acid) is a derivative of the word amine—and amphetamine is only one of them. Amphetamine, $C_9H_{13}N$, is *alpha*-methylphenethylamine—or *a(lpha)* m(ethyl) ph(enyl) et(hyl) . . . amine. Sympathomimetic simply refers to its agency as a sympathetic nervous system stimulant. The amphetamines come in many varieties, but they all have one thing in common—they are all called speed.

Smith Kline & French markets Benzedrine and Dexedrine, and it markets another very popular form of speed called Dexamyl, which is a combination of dextroamphetamine sulfate and amobarbital, a barbiturate. Abbot Laboratories markets methamphetamine hydrochloride (the most famous of the grade-one amphetamines, known generically as methedrine, once a brand name) under the trademark Desoxyn. Abbot also markets Desbutal, a combination of methamphetamine hydrochloride and the barbiturate sodium pentobarbital. The famous "Black Beauty," Biphetamine, a resin complex of amphetamine and destroamphetamine sulfate, is marketed by Strasenburgh.

All of the above are marketed in easy-to-pop form. Benzedrine comes in 15mg capsules and in tablets of 5mg and 10mg. Dexedrine comes in 5mg, 10mg and 15mg capsules and in 5mg tablets, and it also comes in the form of an elixir—by the pint. Dexamyl comes in capsules containing 10mg and 15mg and in tablets containing 5mg respectively of dextroamphetamine sulfate. It too is available in the form of an elixir. Desoxyn comes in tablets of 2.5mg (white), 5mg (white), 10 mg (orange) and 15mg (yellow). Desbutal comes in a green capsule containing 5mg and in tablets containing 10mg (orange and blue) and 15mg (yellow and blue) respectively of methamphetamine hydrochloride. Biphetamine is supplied in three strengths, a white capsule containing 3.75mg each, a black and white capsule containing 6.25mg each, and the Black Beauty itself, containing 10mg each of amphetamine and dextroamphetamine sulfate. Biphetamine is also available as Biphetamine-T in two strengths—the T stands for Tuazole, Strasenburgh's brand name for methaqualone.

Commercial speed is available through any physician in the country and through any reputable dope dealer on the street. Illegally manufactured speed, though not as popular as it once was, is still available on the street and comes in many forms. Bathroom variety—as it is called—is very easy to manufacture and was manufactured in quantity in the sixties. Called crystal by those on the spike, illegal methedrine is **what most shooters mainline. The few crazies left**

over from the dope years who still use speed—and of
serious dopers they are very few—usually pop commercial speed when they can. When they cannot, they
generally buy whites, the most popular current variety
of which is called "crossroads." Some MDA (methyl
di-amphetamine) is still available. White is the color
most often attributed to speed today—the most popular word is *ups*. Brain ticklers, browns, cartwheels,
chalk, Christmas trees, coast-to-coasts, dominoes, foot-
balls, greenies, hearts, leapers and truck drivers are
words of the sixties and are out of use now. What is
more important is that speed in any form is pretty
much out of use now by people who paid their dues
in the sixties. Serious dopers know better.

The copy lavished on every amphetamine listed in
the Physician's Desk Reference is preceded by a brief
warning which cautions against prolonged use—"short-
term anorectic effect and rapid development of tolerance" are the token negatives required by the
publisher. What the warning actually points out, then,
but not so clearly that it might be interpreted correctly
by anyone interested, is that as a diet pill speed is
pretty worthless—it might work for a month. (Zachary
Swan had a prescription for diet pills for six years.)
None of the drug companies lists for any of its amphetamines an LD 50, the industry-standard average
lethal dose (that dose measured in milligrams per kilograms of lean body mass which will kill one-half of the
sample of subjects tested), nor do they spend a lot of
time outlining the side-effects of a drug that in many
cases is marketed for no other purpose than as an aid
to dieting (which one has already been warned is not a
very good reason for taking it). The fact is that not
only is tolerance inevitable, but psychological addiction
is guaranteed. The depression that follows speed's use
is deadly. Once you have been up, everything else is
down. And it takes more to get you up every time
you take it. What the drug companies call the
manifestations of overdose are merely the extreme side-

effects of overuse—confusion, assaultiveness, hallucinations and panic; arrhythmias, hypertension and circulatory collapse. With fatal overdose, life terminates in convulsions and coma.

It does not take a cardiologist to figure out that if your heart is pumping twice as fast today as it was yesterday, then today you are one day closer to dead than you would have been under normal circumstances. Think of your body as an automobile with only so many miles on the warranty—speeding puts the mileage on faster than cruising. After all, speed is called speed for a reason. The faster you go, the sooner you are going to get where you are going—the faster you force your body to age, the faster it is going to get old and get where every aging body is headed—dead. And when you speed, whether you are an automobile or a soft machine, the chances of your throwing a connecting rod are always greater. Frank Zappa was right—speed kills. If not today, tomorrow. Sooner than you think. However you cut it, you come up short.

V MARIJUANA ABROAD

Contrary to the prevailing folklore, there is just as much heat smoking dope in Colombia as there is in the United States; more, in fact, given the likelihood that anyone, old or young, who spots you doing it will call the law. As strapped for liberty as U.S. heads claim they are, the fact is that a marijuana charge in the United States is easier to beat than it is anywhere in the world, and that is accounted for more by American justice's emphasis on individual liberty and human rights—manifest, if nowhere else, in its strict rules of evidence—than any liberal marijuana statutes it may engender. Only a failed intellectual with a grudge, a third-rate subversive or a fool would come back from a place like Marrakesh, Istanbul, Port-au-Prince or Rome, or even a place as allegedly enlightened as Am-

sterdam, and try to make a case for its drug laws.
(A zoo like Capetown is so surreal as to defy intelligent consideration; compared to the South Africans,
Indian elephants are an enlightened race. And if the
Iron Curtain countries, such as Czechoslovakia, escape
mention, it is because the issue here is marijuana, and,
so far, as far as anyone has been able to gather anyway, the cops there have never heard of it.) Where
the laws exist, there is heat, and in the whorehouses of
civilized society, like Colombia and the Mediterra-
nean poppy republics, the heat is worse, because high-
level corruption thrives on the corruptibility of the
thug element empowered to enforce those laws. The
image of a young tourist walking the streets of Casablanca or Mazatlán with a joint in his hand is a myth
perpetrated by college-campus travel agents. The only
place you can get away with that is in New York.

VI   A SWAN LEXICON

Zachary Swan's personal undercover lexicon evolved
as an aid to telephone communication; it appeared in
written transmissions where necessary, though in-
stances of such contact were rare, and was almost
never used in up-front conversation. It grew out of
the need for secrecy. There are countless synonyms
for the proper name of every illegal drug, and every
drug dealer's vocabulary is replete with the argot of
his trade, as well as that of the underworld in general
and that of whatever subculture or counterculture to
which he might pay his dues. The glossary which follows is no more than a very particular list of the
words Swan used over the phone to protect himself.

1. *Chanel*—Cocaine; by way of Coco Chanel,
the cosmetic and fashion designer. Cocoa (coco)
and coca were interchangeable in Swan's vocabulary.

2. *Dust*—Cocaine.

3. *A Duster*—The same thing.

4. *Lady* or *Girl*—A specific reference to cocaine; as in "on the girl," or "the girl is fat."

5. *United Parcel Service/U.P.S.*—Amphetamines; ups.

6. *A Johnson*—A pound of marijuana; by way of L.B.J., or Lb./J—a pound of joints.

7. *A Pamphlet*—An ounce.

8. *A Book*—A pound.

9. *Two Books*—A kilo.

Heroin was always smack.

VII COLOMBIA AND BIG BUSINESS

Though it is in fact one of the more inhospitable nations in the world, Colombia, for reasons which are economically understandable, places a premium on tourism. Nor is the government's faith ill-placed—resorts are luxurious, beaches are beautiful, and money goes farther here than it does in any of the major Caribbean resorts. The government's official flag-carrier, Avianca Airlines, the oldest airline in the Western Hemisphere, has promoted Colombia increasingly around the world over the past ten years, spawning an attractive cash flow, and as a growth industry tourism in the country is today unsurpassed. If Avianca's efforts have been undermined in any way, it is by virtue of the fact that the people and the government of Colombia have failed in a corporate way to conceal what manifests itself as an outright hatred for foreigners; but be that as it may, one gets what one pays for, and one can expect that the tourists will continue to converge, like the penny-wise consumers they are, on this bargain basement of the world's black market.

Avianca, of course, sells Bogotá, the capital and

cultural core of the nation, but no Yankee worth his
tan can resist the copy lavished on the country's two
principal seaside resorts, Cartagena and Santa Marta.
(The offshore islands, Providencia and San Andrés,
are slowly achieving similar stature.) Both share the
same attributes—sun, sea and indoor plumbing. Each
has a casino (American-operated) at its leading hotel, and both resorts are long-established enough to
handle in a streamlined fashion what the Colombian
government owes its future to—the acquisition of
American dollars. And if these tourist dollars account
for national stability to any great degree, it must be
said that stability and political longevity, for any
man near the top, rests on the even more streamlined
flow of illegal dollars that float at every level.

When Zachary Swan, in the early 1970s, exploited
Colombia's natural resources, he did so in the company of many other independent businessmen, most of
them younger than he, from North America. Now
however, his and their enterprise has been co-opted by
an organized criminal element with training in the
French heroin markets and influence at the upper
levels of government in South America. Officially con-
demning the drug traffic, South American governments, especially that of Colombia, encourage it
unofficially. The reasons are simple and chiefly economic: cocaine is traded worldwide in American
dollars; whether those dollars come into the country
legally or illegally is of little importance when given
the scope of the trading. And so the independent
smuggler is a thing of the past in Colombia. The low-
level dealer, the college student, and the housewife
from the Texas panhandle, as well as the middle-
level smuggler on the order of Zachary Swan, can
expect to be thrown in jail and make the headlines in
Bogotá while the Corsican heavy and the diplomatic
attaché who pay their dues are encouraged for helping
the balance of payments.

VIII AIRLINE SECURITY

In Colombia, metal detectors notwithstanding, the airline frisk has become a matter of policy. Because of stepped-up airline security checks and the opportunity they afford the Colombian government to conduct a contraband search of every passenger boarding any domestic or international flight, it is effectively impossible today for anyone to get anything like a large white rabbit aboard the cabin of an aircraft without its being at least seen and very likely examined.*

IX DAY OF JUDGMENT

In Peace's own words, he had chosen to "go without a jury, because of the technical, legal deficiencies in the prosecutor's case" and go "forward before a firm but fair judge who could be counted on to give the defendant the benefits of the Law as it applied to this case and to resist pressure from prosecutors and Federal Authorities who would attempt to ensure a jail term for [Swan] regardless of the insufficiency of the evidence. The pressure by Federal authorities," he said, "was impelled more by pique at the failure to induce [Swan] to give up his friends than by what they believed he had done."

Peace said, "The judge rejected the prosecutor's request, refusing to consider what amounted in his mind to innuendos and unconfirmed rumors about [Swan]. Reciting and recalling the minimum of legally proper evidence against [Swan], his clean record and the overwhelming testimonials paid to [Swan] by those who had attested to his good character, the judge

---

* Zachary Swan: "Oh, yeah?"

stated that jail was not a proper sentence." Peace, citing the "character, integrity [and] ability" of the presiding judge in particular, suggesting that "this was one hell of a fair judge who rendered a fair and proper decision despite the obvious pressure upon him," extended his comments to apply to the Suffolk County Court in general.

Author's Note

Work on this book began in the winter of 1974 in New York City and did not end until the finished manuscript was delivered in the spring of 1976. Much of the intervening time was spent in a process of distillation: the separation of the truth from information designed either to cover it up or to glamorize it. The facts, as they emerged, were pieced together en route between New York City, a vegetable farm southwest of there, the Inner Sunset district of San Francisco, the outer reaches of Long Island and the capital and coastal cities of Colombia. The story that evolved owes its internal validity to the author's initial skepticism and to the ultimate faith placed in him by those whose story it is. Because they offered what they offered in confidence, it is impossible for the author to acknowledge many of them, or, for similar reasons, to thank the others who helped him stay alive and out of jail when occasionally taking the assignment to the edge. There are also those whose efforts, if less hazardous, were no less essential to the book as it stands.

For their help in the preparation of the manuscript, or for the research material they provided, the author wishes to thank: *Richard Collier; James Pappas; Walter Peek; Michael Sabbag; Michael Sallette; Gwen M. Vallely; Joseph Vallely; Stephen Wheatly;* and *Oklahoma Nancy Wright.* For their invaluable personal and professional contributions: *James E. Bradof, M.D.,* and *Mary A. Ryan, B.Sc., R.N.* For the faith they demonstrated awaiting the outcome of their professional gamble: *Dorothy L. Pittman* and *Tom Gervasi*. For the use of her diaries and hours of corroborative research: *Alyce Hans*. And for the countless hours of informative conversation, the many recorded hours of audio tape, the firsthand research and the primary-source material, painstakingly secured, without which the book could not have been written; who after everything else and at the risk of his own personal safety unlocked the back doors of Bogotá: *Charles Forsman*.

The author wishes to thank his parents and family for their encouraging and personal support, and to acknowledge the following for their contributions not to the book itself but to its successful writing: *Deborah Meltzer*, who, when the prevailing opinion was that it could never be done, said do it; who more than anyone, in the years of his literary apprenticeship, helped the author pay his dues and finally generated the energy that made writing the book possible. *Carol Doerrer Bradof*, who, lending grace to the simplest of endeavors, took it upon herself to inject humanity into the author's back-street journalism. *Robert L. Billingsley*, a good friend, a great American, ". . . the one fixed point in a changing age," who picked up the bar bill in the hard years. Always there when the going was rough, he never passed the dice when the hard money was on the line. And, with love, *Mary A. Ryan*, whose efforts in behalf of this book are innumerable and whose efforts in its author's behalf are better rewarded elsewhere than in its pages. The last word will always be hers.

New York, May 1976

Index